International Criminal Justice Series

Volume 24

Series Information

The *International Criminal Justice Series* aims to create a platform for publications covering the entire field of international criminal justice. It, therefore, deals with issues relating, among others, to:

- the work of international criminal courts and tribunals;
- transitional justice approaches in different countries;
- international anti-corruption and anti-money laundering initiatives;
- the history of international criminal law.

It is peer-reviewed and seeks to publish high-quality works emanating from excellent scholars.

Editorial Office

Prof. Dr. Gerhard Werle
Humboldt-Universität zu Berlin
Faculty of Law
Unter den Linden 6,
10099 Berlin, Germany
gerhard.werle@rewi.hu-berlin.de
vormbaum@uni-muenster.de

More information about this series at http://www.springer.com/series/13470

Prosper Maguchu

Transitional Justice and Socio-Economic Rights in Zimbabwe

ASSER PRESS

Springer

Prosper Maguchu
Centre for the Politics of Transnational Law
Vrije Universiteit Amsterdam
Amsterdam, The Netherlands

ISSN 2352-6718 ISSN 2352-6726 (electronic)
International Criminal Justice Series
ISBN 978-94-6265-322-1 ISBN 978-94-6265-323-8 (eBook)
https://doi.org/10.1007/978-94-6265-323-8

Published by T.M.C. ASSER PRESS, The Hague, The Netherlands www.asserpress.nl
Produced and distributed for T.M.C. ASSER PRESS by Springer-Verlag Berlin Heidelberg

This T.M.C. ASSER PRESS imprint is published by the registered company Springer-Verlag GmbH, DE part of Springer Nature.
The registered company address is: Heidelberger Platz 3, 14197 Berlin, Germany

Preface

The parameters of transitional justice, as an interdisciplinary field, are expanding. For instance, while it started off conservatively by focusing on judicial and non-judicial measures implemented in order to redress legacies of physical human rights abuses, it has evolved to address socio-economic violations and related issues such as large-scale corruption. Despite this widened remit, which continues to expand, it remains problematic to locate, let alone address, corruption within transitional justice as originally conceived. This is largely due to the lack of a comprehensive framework to unite the fields of anti-corruption and transitional justice. This book therefore seeks to investigate the specific ways in which transitional justice mechanisms should be used to address corruption.

To that end, it examines to what extent cases of corruption in Zimbabwe amount to human rights violations under the transitional justice framework. In doing so, it seeks to identify where crimes of corruption should be situated within theoretical and legal frameworks and to explore ways in which they can be practically addressed at the policy level in the context of Zimbabwe's transition to democracy. Through an analysis of the text of the law and of practice, the book demonstrates how Zimbabwe's official transitional justice processes can engage with socio-economic issues, in particular corruption, and how this has precipitated conflict. It will also examine emerging legal actions and practices by the newly installed government and the ways in which this new regime is attempting to address the issue, and consider whether such efforts are underpinned by a coherent legal position rooted in international law and best practice.

This book will contribute to the ongoing academic inquiry into an appropriate legal framework for addressing corruption in the transitional justice and human rights discourses. It also seeks to undertake an intra- and cross-regional comparative analysis, for example by examining how the 'fourth wave' of democratisation in the Middle East and North Africa (MENA) region has reinvigorated the search for the link between corruption and transitional justice. The book concludes that in cases where corruption has achieved the status of a human rights violation under international law, it can and should be addressed by transitional justice mechanisms and processes.

Amsterdam, The Netherlands Prosper Maguchu

Acknowledgements

I have met a number of people who have greatly assisted me on my journey from the practice of law to academia, and it would be an injustice not to mention them either explicitly or implicitly.

I am indebted to the Catholic Academic Association Service for funding my doctoral studies. My particular gratitude goes to Dr. Hermann Weber, Dr. Marko Kuhn and Simone Saure and the administrative team as well as the national committee in Zimbabwe. I would like to thank Dr. Siegfried Karl of the *Katholische Hochschulgemeinde Gießen* for his spiritual support and Prof. Franz Reimer for his direct and indirect guidance while I was writing this book.

I owe my deepest gratitude to my former supervisor Prof. Thilo Marauhn for his help and guidance. I am also deeply indebted to my mentor Prof. Ben Chigara for sharing his pearls of wisdom with me during the course of this research, and to my friend Prof. Sven Simon, who acted as a *de facto* assistant supervisor and helped to shape the content of this book. He also helped me to develop a good work ethic and his passion for "perfectionism" has had a lasting effect. I would also like to express my deepest gratitude to Ulrike Rein and Susanne Seitz, who were always there for me.

In developing the ideas presented here, I received helpful input from my colleagues at the University of Giessen, Fransiska Asmin, Collins Mbuayang, Kangnikoe Bado, Daniel Behailu, Wisdom Momodu, Joscha Mueller and Eric Che Muma, who were part of the review committee that constantly gave useful feedback on the project. I would also like to thank my former colleagues from the Zimbabwe Human Rights NGO Forum for their support, even if they may not necessarily agree with the interpretations and/or conclusions of my research.

I would also like to express my gratitude to Antony Reeler, Arthur Gwagwa, Arnold Tsunga, Cait Houlbrook, Dr. Godfrey Maringira, Blessing Taona Denhere and Scott Stevens for their editorial assistance and comments on an earlier version of the manuscript, although any errors are my own and should not tarnish the reputations of these esteemed persons.

In addition, a very special thanks to Prof. Moritz Vormbaum for his extensive advice and guidance as I was preparing for the publication of this book. I have greatly benefited from being an alumnus of the South African-German Centre for Transnational Criminal Justice.

I gratefully acknowledge the support and generosity of the Scholars at Risk Network and the Foundation for Refugee Students, who provided funding, insight and expertise that greatly assisted in the later stages of my research and without which the book could not have been published. I have greatly benefited from my hosts in the Department of Transboundary Legal Studies at the University of Groningen, where I was a visiting researcher. The support, encouragement and feedback I received from my colleagues and my supervisor Prof. Marcel Brus were invaluable. I would also like to thank my professional editor Andrew Godfrey, whose services I highly recommend.

Most importantly, I would like to thank my family in the broadest meaning of the word, and especially my wife Esther for her love and support.

Amsterdam, The Netherlands Prosper Maguchu

Contents

Chapter 1
The Linkages Between Corruption and Transitional Justice

If corruption has acquired the status of a grievance even leading to regime change and social conflicts then it should certainly be dealt with in the transition period as part of the post revolution and peacebuilding reforms.

Andrieu Kora (Kora 2012, p. 537)

Contents

Abstract This chapter demystifies the key aspects of addressing corruption within the context of transitional justice. It examines and illustrates how various transitional justice mechanisms have been used to address the violation of socio-economic rights resulting from acts of corruption. It also discusses the possible impediments to the pursuit of accountability for human rights violations attributable to corruption.

Keywords Corruption · transition · justice · accountability mechanisms · socio-economic rights

P. Maguchu, *Transitional Justice and Socio-Economic Rights in Zimbabwe*, International Criminal Justice Series 24,
https://doi.org/10.1007/978-94-6265-323-8_1

1.1 General Introduction and Background

The field of transitional justice traditionally focused exclusively on addressing civil and political rights violations.[1] Its mechanisms were all skewed in favour of addressing these rights while paying scant attention to socio-economic rights. Accordingly, with the intersection of transitional justice and socio-economic rights, it has become imperative to extend its boundaries to closely related socio-economic issues, such as economic policies,[2] structural violence,[3] odious debts[4] and, significantly, economic crimes such as corruption, when they are identified with the root causes of the conflict.[5]

In August 2003 Zimbabwean civil society organisations convened in Johannesburg, South Africa, to discuss options for transitional justice. They recommended creating a special commission to deal with economic crimes such as corruption, asset stripping and debts incurred by previous governments that may be connected to human rights abuses.[6] The symposium was a departure from conventional transitional justice practice and discourse in Zimbabwe, which had mainly focused on civil and political rights violations.

Similarly, the need to forge links between corruption and transitional justice at the international level prompted two leading think tanks on human rights and anti-corruption, Freedom House and Transparency International, to convene a conference in Berlin, Germany, in October 2013.[7] The two-day dialogue brought together human rights lawyers and activists, investigative journalists, anti-corruption and financial experts, economists, members of truth commissions (TCs) and academics, among others. The conference sought to answer the question 'What transitional justice and anti-corruption tools can be used in pre and post-transition settings to build and maintain legitimacy, fight impunity and corruption, provide redress for human rights violations and secure justice?'[8]

The participants of the Berlin conference recommended adopting resolutions such as, designing 'transitional justice processes and anti-corruption initiatives for countries in transition that jointly uncover, link, make accountable, and repair past human rights abuses including socio-economic injustices caused by grand corruption'.[9] Moreover, the Berlin conference report concluded with a discussion of a new possible frontier for transitional justice—addressing corruption. It highlighted the

[1] Mani 2008, pp. 253–264; Miller 2008, p. 266.

[2] Hecht and Michalowski 2012, pp. 3–4.

[3] Laplante 2008. See by way of contrast McGill 2017, pp. 79–101.

[4] Sharp 2014, pp. 47–60, 56.

[5] Cavallaro and Albuja 2008.

[6] Morrell and Pigou 2004.

[7] Pesek 2014, p. 1.

[8] Pesek 2014, p. 2.

[9] Pesek 2014, p. 2.

need for 'a comprehensive and complimentary [*sic*] strategy between transitional justice and anti-corruption fields',[10] and claimed that this alliance will 'improve a transitional country's chances to achieve accountability, truth, repair, reconciliation and non-repetition'.[11]

Such recommendations predate the Berlin conference; scholars and practitioners in the field of transitional justice have long been calling for engagement with corruption, particularly in situations where it had a major impact on a conflict. There is wisdom in the words of Ruben Carranza, who lamented the lack of anti-corruption measures in transitional justice mechanisms in his article 'Plunder and Pain: Should Transitional Justice Engage with Corruption and Economic Crimes?':

> The prevailing assumption seems to be that truth commissions, human rights trials and reparations programs are meant to engage mainly, if not exclusively, with civil and political rights violations that involve either physical integrity or personal freedom, and not with violations of economic and social rights, including such crimes as large-scale corruption and despoliation. To a growing number of transitional justice advocates, particularly those who work in or come from impoverished post-conflict or post-dictatorship countries, this traditional view is inadequate. It ignores the experience of developing countries abused by dictators or warlords who have been both brutal and corrupt. It perpetuates an impunity gap by focusing on a narrow range of human rights violations while leaving accountability for economic crimes to ineffective domestic institutions or to a still evolving international legal system that deals with corruption.[12]

This preliminary study laid the foundation for a nuanced international debate on engagement with corruption within transitional justice even before the Berlin conference.

There have been numerous publications arguing for the need to include corruption within transitional justice, though for reasons of space only a limited number of examples can be given here.[13] Almost every article that has been written on the subject includes a section on how corruption relates to human rights. As noted by Lisa Hecht and Sabine Michalowski, 'acts of massive corruption will translate as an almost inevitable consequence for human rights violations. That is they satisfy the thresholds of human rights violation in themselves; and [...] their investigation is a practical necessity especially in transition processes'.[14] Several authors have questioned the usefulness of such an approach. For instance, Leonard Ghione has argued that if corruption is to be included in the transitional justice debate 'it should be taken out of the "human rights corner"'.[15]

---

[10] Pesek 2014, p. 2.

[11] Pesek 2014, p. 2.

[12] Carranza 2008, p. 310.

[13] See Human Rights Council 2012, p. 15, para 50; see also Seligson 2002; Hayner and Bosire 2003; Cavallaro and Albuja 2008; Sharp 2012.

[14] Hecht and Michalowski 2012, p. 2.

[15] Ghione 2012.

A broader perspective has been adopted by Carranza, albeit inconclusively that:

> Whether the engagement with corruption is founded on the premise that corruption is a human rights violation, or on the theory that economic crimes are part of an indivisible system of crimes committed by the same set of perpetrators or regime, the mechanisms used in transitional justice can in fact be applied.[16]

Together, these studies illustrate the dilemma that practitioners face in trying to make the case that transitional justice should tackle corruption.

What is more, even those scholars who agree that transitional justice should deal with corruption as a human rights violation still face the challenge of showing the connections between the two concepts. Isabel Robinson notes that 'even if the linkages between corruption and human rights are loud and clear, this does not automatically equate with a finding that transitional justice processes should address corruption'.[17] She further adds: 'Indeed the traditional domain of transitional justice has been a focus on human rights violations, not linkages.'[18] In view of what has been mentioned so far, one might suppose that the lack of a theoretical framework would mean that it is still unclear how transitional justice can engage with corruption, which in turn would lead one to expect that this would not yet have been attempted.

But despite the lack of consensus on this question at the level of theory, at the level of practice a few countries have attempted to incorporate corruption into transitional justice structures. Documented cases from a handful of pioneering countries, such as Chad, Sierra Leone and more recently Kenya, Tunisia, Egypt and Morocco, have steadily built up into a growing body of literature.

However, this practice also has a number of serious drawbacks. Attempts to incorporate corruption into transitional justice processes without a sound theoretical framework raise significant questions. The central problematic feature of engagement with corruption within transitional justice is that 'it raises complex questions about the normative foundation of transitional justice: what is it; what was it; what can and should it be?'.[19]

Consequently, in the absence of a strong intellectual basis and universal consensus regarding the inclusion of corruption in transitional justice, the official theory, policy and practice of transitional justice remains, on the whole, restricted to dealing only with violations of civil and political rights. This is clearly illustrated in the transitional justice processes that are currently taking place in Zimbabwe. These exclusively focus on addressing a selection of gross civil and political rights violations, such as torture, enforced disappearances and politically motivated killings,[20] while turning a blind eye to the socio-economic rights violations perpetrated

[16] Carranza 2008, pp. 329–330.
[17] Robinson 2015, p. 6.
[18] Robinson 2015, p. 6.
[19] Robinson 2015, p. 1.
[20] Constitution of Zimbabwe Act Amendment (No. 20) 2013, s252.

through massive corruption, which have crippled the country and eventually led to the end of Robert Mugabe's 37-year rule.

Hence, the purpose of this book is to provide a theoretical and normative framework for how transitional justice should engage with corruption. It follows a case study design, with in-depth analysis of how Zimbabwe should explore ways to mainstream corruption into transitional justice processes. The findings are intended to make an important contribution to the current quest for transitional justice in Zimbabwe and to the understanding of the relationship between corruption, human rights and transitional justice.

1.2 Definition and Discussion of Terms

1.2.1 Transitional Justice

In the literature, 'so far, there is no single theory of transitional justice, and the term does not have a concrete meaning'.[21] It is important to note from the outset that in practice, transitional justice processes can take place in some cases without defining the concept of transitional justice as such. As Clara Sandoval Villalba argues, it is common for states to engage in reparations programmes without acknowledging, or taking legal responsibility for, the human rights abuses or crimes that were committed, and instead act as if they are helping victims to move forward.[22]

This is certainly true in the case of Zimbabwe, where some forms of transitional justice were implemented after the liberation struggle of 1965 to 1979 without any acknowledgment of abuses. Examples such as the granting of amnesties to the members of the Rhodesian security forces and the guerrillas, the demobilisation of the former guerrillas and the payment of compensation to a selected group of victims of human rights violations committed during the struggle for independence may be regarded by some as transitional justice mechanisms.

In the same vein, it can be argued that other late entrants such as the Global Political Agreement (GPA) of 2009 represented yet another transition, though many would instead see this as a peace treaty intended to create a transition. It might also be argued that the Unity Accord of 1987 was also a transition, but again some would argue that this was merely a peace accord leading to a government of national unity of some kind.[23] This is because the 1987 Unity Accord and the 2009 GPA were not victim-driven or victim-focused mechanisms, but rather elite-oriented power-sharing agreements.

Returning to the issue of defining transitional justice: a mapping exercise carried out by the African Transitional Justice Research Network (ATJRN) reported that

---

[21] Arthur 2009, p. 359.

[22] Villalba 2011.

[23] See in general Reeler et al. 2017.

there are challenges associated with the mainstream definitions when it comes to the inclusion of corruption. The ATJRN identified that

> Within Africa, this traditional definition of transitional justice has been challenged by some as being too narrow; for failing to take into consideration adequately a context where mass poverty and socio-economic concerns inform the needs of victims and the object of justice. This criticism has been levelled in particular by organizations in countries such as Nigeria, Kenya and Liberia, all of whom have included issues of corruption as a key crime to be addressed, making the argument that this 'structural violence' has had far wider implications than direct violence, and that it has been and continues to be a fault-line for violent conflict.[24]

This extract echoes addresses the same topic as the present work—the inclusion and exclusion of corruption within the transitional justice framework in Zimbabwe.

It should be noted that, the concept of transitional justice has been constantly and dynamically evolving. No words can better explain this than those of the first UN Special Rapporteur on the promotion of truth, justice, reparation and guarantees of non-recurrence, Pablo De Grief, in his maiden report:

> The measures of truth-seeking, justice initiatives, reparation and guarantees of non-recurrence emerged first as practices and experiences in post-authoritarian settings, such as the Latin American countries of the Southern Cone and, to a lesser extent, those in Central and Eastern Europe and South Africa.
>
> More recently, the measures defined under the mandate have been progressively transferred from their 'place of origin' in post-authoritarian settings, to post-conflict contexts and even to settings in which conflict is ongoing or to those in which there has been no transition to speak of.
>
> Moreover, a common feature of these recent transitions is the prominent role that claims relating to economic rights occupy in these transitions; claims against corruption and in favour of economic opportunities have been raised to a par in the regions with claims for the redress of violations of civil and political rights.[25]

These remarks illuminate the transformative nature of the term 'transitional justice', which has been largely necessitated by the need to address prominent and emerging issues such as corruption.

To fully understand the paradigm shift in the field, we need to first look at its genealogy. The term started to appear in keyword searches in various disciplines 'after its reference in passing' in a *Boston Herald* article about the Charter 77 Foundation's 1992 conference in Salzburg, on the theme 'Justice in Times of Transition'.[26] Before that, there had been the occasional use of the term by scholars such as Ruti Teitel, who later became notable in the field.[27] The term became a global phenomenon following Neil Kritz's publication of his *Transitional Justice* in

---

[24] African Transitional Justice Research Network.

[25] de Greiff 2012, pp. 5–6, paras 15–16.

[26] Paige 2009, p. 329.

[27] Paige 2009, p. 329.

the late 1990s.[28] However, even before this there were a few other notable usages; in 1992 a US-based Argentine sociologist, Juan Corradi, made reference to 'transitional justice', in an essay published in a journal on state terror in Latin America. Prior to Corradi, the philosopher Milton Fisk used the term to describe the transition to socialism.[29] Given, the relative newness of the concept of transitional justice, it is also important to look at the etymology of the term.

1.2.1.1 What Is Transition?

In transitional justice, the noun 'transition' is widely understood to denote the shift from conflict, autocratic rule and civil strife to a state of liberal political democracy, including by the authors who pioneered the concept. For example, Teitel, who is credited with first coining the term 'transitional justice', describes transition as 'the move from less to more democratic regimes'.[30] However, many scholars now challenge this restricted understanding of the term. Dustin Sharp, for example, argues that it is 'simply empirically inaccurate'.[31]

Earlier expositions of the term are now unsatisfactory because transitional justice is increasingly being adopted in situations that do not involve a liberal political transition, for example in Rwanda, Chad, Uganda and Ethiopia, or any political transition at all, such as in Kenya and Colombia, or contexts where there has been a transition 'from one nominally liberal ethno-regime to another', as in the case of Côte d'Ivoire.[32] On the other hand, the term has also been applied in Western countries with established liberal democracies, including Australia, Canada and New Zealand, which in recent times have instituted truth commissions, public apologies, reparations and memorialisation processes.[33]

Moreover, in his very helpful investigation into the theory of restorative justice, Stephen Winter was able to show that the term transition is now largely identified with 'a comprehensive transformation in social and political life' and, furthermore, that transitional justice has taken a 'concurrent interest in social reconciliation and post-traumatic healing'.[34] This corroborates the argument, posited by the majority of scholars advocating the restorative justice theory, that if the 'practice of justice is to be transitional, it needs to transform the daily life of survivors'.[35] It is though that

[28] Kritz 1995 (citation omitted).

[29] Fisk 1989, p. 304.

[30] Teitel 2000, p. 5.

[31] Sharp 2014a, b, p. 7.

[32] Sharp 2014a, b, p. 7.

[33] Sharp 2014a, b, p. 7.

[34] Winter 2013, p. 227.

[35] Winter 2013, p. 227.

this approach places the day-to-day experience of survivors at the centre of the transitional justice practice.[36]

1.2.1.2 What Is Justice?

According to Hans Kelsen, 'no other question has been the object of such intensive thinking by the most illustrious thinkers from Plato to Kant; and yet, this question is today as unanswered as it ever was'.[37] Having said that, Kelsen defines justice as the 'quality of a social order regulating the mutual relationship of men' and goes on to identify the four basic types of justice, namely distributive (also known as economic justice), procedural, retributive and restorative.[38] These different expressions of justice have almost certainly had a significant impact on the modern understanding of transitional justice.

Retributive justice was, arguably, a key factor in the traditional transitional justice discourse. Justice was interpreted in a limited sense as addressing civil and political rights violations, particularly those to do with people's physical integrity, such as murder, rape, torture and forced disappearance.[39] Consequently, to begin with transitional justice did not recognise justice for economic violence such as the plunder of natural resources. Economic and social rights violations, and concepts of economic, social and distributive justice, were trivialised and normalised.[40] Reference to these issues was only made in order to explain and give credence to claims that civil and political rights had been violated.

Therefore, in order to address the unique Zimbabwean history of dealing with a legacy of human rights violations, transitional justice shall be defined here as

> a response to systematic or widespread violations of human rights. It seeks recognition for victims and promotion of possibilities for peace, reconciliation and democracy. Transitional justice is not a special form of justice but justice adapted to societies transforming themselves after a period of pervasive human rights abuse. In some cases, these transformations happen suddenly; in others, they may take place over many decades.[41]

This definition might have its drawbacks; however, one advantage is that it does not limit the understanding of transitional justice to traditional political transitions, which constitute a clean break with the past, as it recognises that the state can still be undergoing a process of transformation. It therefore captures pretransition states such as Zimbabwe.

Before proceeding to discuss the meaning of other key terms for this book, it is important to point out that the field of transitional justice has become

[36] Winter 2013, p. 227.
[37] Kelsen 1957, p. 1.
[38] Kelsen 1957, p. 1.
[39] Sharp 2014a, b, p. 11.
[40] Sharp 2014a, b, p. 11.
[41] ICTJ 2009.

multidisciplinary. In the field of law, its foundation was laid in the landmark decision of the Inter-American Court of Human Rights (IACtHR) in the case of *Velásquez Rodríguez v. Honduras*, which articulated the fundamental obligations of the state to protect and investigate human rights violations.[42] The principles set in this case were later to influence judgments of the European Court of Human Rights (ECtHR), UN treaty bodies such as the Human Rights Committee (HRC) and the creation of the International Criminal Court (ICC) which was created to combat impunity and ensure victims' rights are respected.[43]

1.2.2 Socio-economic Rights

A brief discussion of socio-economic rights is pertinent for the present book, as it helps to identify as clearly as possible the nexus between transitional justice and socio-economic rights violations. In their seminal article, Evelyne Schmid and Aoife Nolan observed that 'an effective debate on the desirability of incorporating ESR into transitional justice processes is only possible where this is based on an accurate understanding of ESR and the obligations they impose'.[44] Once that is clear, this in turn will help us to understand the need to confront corruption using transitional justice mechanisms, with socio-economic rights violations taken as the entry point, which is the main focus of this book.

It has become commonplace to classify human rights into three different categories. This taxonomy was developed by Karel Vasak, a Czech legal expert, who was inspired by the three guiding values of the French Revolution: liberty, equality, fraternity.[45] The first generation of human rights comprises civil and political rights, which are divided into civil and physical security, and liberties and empowerments. The second generation comprises socio-economic rights, such as the provision of goods for social and economic needs. The third-generation rights, collective developmental rights, are further divided into rights of self-determination and special rights. Some commentators are discussing the notion of fourth-generation rights. There is no consensus about what rights are included in this latest generation, save that they tend to relate to the impact of scientific and technological developments, for example communication and information rights.[46]

While a variety of definitions have been suggested for the term 'socio-economic rights', in this book it is used as a paraphrase for economic, social and cultural human rights as enshrined in the UN Universal Declaration of Human Rights

[42] *Velásquez Rodríguez v. Honduras*, 1988, Inter-American Court of Human Rights, Ser. C, No. 4.

[43] ICTJ 2009.

[44] Schmid and Nolan 2014, p. 364.

[45] Vasak 1977.

[46] Rainey et al. 2014.

(UDHR),[47] and elaborated on in the International Covenant on Economic, Social and Cultural Rights (ICESCR).[48] There are now numerous international and regional instruments and declarations which deal with socio-economic rights explicitly or implicitly either in whole or in part.[49] These instruments define socio-economic rights as the rights that give people access to certain basic needs necessary to lead a dignified life. These basic needs include resources, opportunities and services that people need to sustain life.

Notably, the ICESCR specifically guarantees the following eight rights: adequate standard of living for oneself and one's family (including adequate food, clothing and housing); the right to the highest attainable standard of physical and mental health; the right to work, free choice of employment and just and favourable conditions of work; the right to social security; the right to protection and assistance to family; the right to education for everyone; the right to take part in cultural life and to enjoy the benefits of scientific progress; and the right to form and join trade unions.

Another key point to note is that various mechanisms have been provided to measure states' human rights obligations. The most common method is to conceptualise socio-economic rights 'in terms of those which are immediate and those which are progressive; defining the duties imposed by such rights into obligations of conduct and obligations of result'.[50] Another widely accepted framework for structuring states' obligations concerning socio-economic rights is the three-tier typology of respect, protection and fulfilment of these rights.[51] The obligation to respect restrains the state from violating the socio-economic rights of its citizens, the duty to protect imposes an obligation on the state to prevent third parties from violating the socio-economic rights of others and the duty to fulfil imposes a requirement of positive intervention, whereby the state must take action to ensure the attainment of socio-economic rights. Additionally, the '4 As'—accessibility, affordability, availability and adaptability—are used to measure how well states meet their obligations regarding rights.

With regard to the link between socio-economic rights and transitional justice, it has been argued that 'it is often relatively straightforward to assess compliance with the obligations to respect and protect ESR, as well as the obligation of non-discrimination'.[52] Regarding the linkage between socio-economic rights and corruption, by contrast, a ground-breaking study has suggested that the basic obligations that should be taken into account are, firstly, the obligation to take steps

[47] Universal Declaration of Human Rights, 10 December 1948, 217 A (III).

[48] International Covenant on Economic, Social and Cultural Rights, adopted and opened for signature, ratification and accession on 16 December 1966, entry into force on 3 January 1976, United Nations Treaty Series, vol. 993.

[49] Marauhn 2004, p. 316.

[50] Schmid and Nolan 2014, p. 367.

[51] ICJ 1997, guideline number 6.

[52] Schmid and Nolan 2014, p. 368.

to realise these rights progressively; and, secondly, the state's duty to prioritise human rights when allocating resources.[53] Additionally, it recommends applying two analytical tools: the three levels of state obligation discussed above and the principles of availability and accessibility.[54] The present book notes that despite using different frameworks to describe the state's obligations under socio-economic rights in relation to corruption and transitional justice, these frameworks overlap and interact to varying extents.

1.2.3 Corruption

There is no universally accepted definition of corruption. According to Anne Peters, the word 'corruption' is not a term of art; it does not even exist in other criminal codes.[55] That said, there seems to be some consensus among academics and practitioners in the field of anti-corruption that corruption can take many forms. As José Vargas-Hernández has noted, 'corruption is just as multifaceted as there are societies and economic and political systems that embraces from the broad concept of corruption to the narrow concept of bribery'.[56] This exacerbates the challenge to come up with a non-contentious definition of such an elusive concept.

Moreover, corruption is defined differently in different disciplines and institutions. The most often-cited definitions of corruption are probably those given by the World Bank and Transparency International. The World Bank defines corruption as 'the abuse of public power for private benefit'.[57] Transparency International takes a broader approach; they define corruption as 'the misuse of entrusted power for private gain'.[58] These definitions have not gone uncriticised. For instance, according to William De Maria, they represent a narrow section of the interests of the Western business world that does not resemble the realities in Africa.[59]

A comprehensive report issued jointly by the International Council on Human Rights Policy and Transparency International, titled 'Corruption and Human Rights: Making the Connection', asserts that, due to the lack of consensus about how to define corruption,

> In the legal field, the term corruption is usually used to group certain criminal acts, which correspond to the general notion of an *abuse of entrusted power*. International conventions

[53] International Council on Human Rights Policy and Transparency International 2009, p. 45.

[54] International Council on Human Rights Policy and Transparency International 2009, p. 45.

[55] Peters 2015.

[56] Vargas-Hernández 2009.

[57] World Bank 1997, p. 8.

[58] The working definition of Transparency International, found in all their documents.

[59] De Maria 2008, p. 778.

against corruption reflect this, since they do not define and criminalise corruption but instead enumerate criminal acts that amount to corruption.[60]

A probable explanation is that for the same reasons just articulated, Zimbabwean legislation does not have a specific definition of the word corruption, but rather provides a list of offences.[61] They are as follows: giving or receiving a bribe as an inducement or reward, corruptly using a false document, the intentional non-disclosure or concealment of a transaction from [one's] principal in order to deceive, and criminal abuse of power by a public officer. This definition is flawed in that, as we shall see below, it is narrowly restricted in two respects: it punishes only criminal abuse and it is confined to only prosecuting public officials.[62]

In his classic critique of definitions of corruption based on the criminal abuse of power, J. S. H. Gildenhuys observes that 'criminal abuses' only refers to the violation of criminal law. 'If corruption is viewed too narrowly only one fact may be revealed, for example, corruption as a criminal behavior.'[63] What Gildenhuys means by this is that 'in essence, corruption is not only about getting caught with one's fingers in the till, but also about abuse of power or lack of moral integrity in the decision making process'.[64] He explains that corruption has not only been a long-time ally of criminal law but also of non-criminal corruption, including administrative corruption,[65] and adds that 'the fact that some corruptive acts can be classified as non-criminal does not take away its [corruption's] detrimental and sometimes devastating effects on the public'.[66]

Another inherent weakness in the definition of corruption in the Zimbabwean legislation is that it only identifies corruption in the public sector. The act defines a public officer as the president, a vice-president, minister or deputy minister; a judicial officer; a governor appointed in terms of the constitution; a member of a council, board, committee or other authority which is a statutory body or local authority or which is responsible for administering the affairs or business of a statutory body or local authority; or a person holding or acting in a public office.[67] Corruption occurs in both the public and private sector. Needless to say, this creates an impunity gap for people in both the private sector and civil society, which sadly have become associated with allegations of corruption and malpractice.[68]

---

[60] International Council on Human Rights Policy and Transparency International 2009, p. 17. Emphasis mine.

[61] Zimbabwe Anti-Corruption Commission Act 2004, s256.

[62] Maguchu 2018, pp. 354, 361.

[63] Gildenhuys 2004, p. 83.

[64] Gildenhuys 2004, p. 83.

[65] Gildenhuys 2004, p. 83.

[66] Gildenhuys 2004, p. 84.

[67] Zimbabwe Anti-Corruption Commission Act 2004, s1.

[68] *State v. Grace Pfumbidzayi and Another* HH-726-15 (Unreported); two Air Zimbabwe bosses who were arrested, tried and each sentenced to ten years' imprisonment for embezzling US$10

In 2005, some attempts were made to carry out a corruption baseline survey by an independent consultant employed by the government to investigate the nature and incidence of corruption in Zimbabwe.[69] The government of Zimbabwe, through the now defunct Anti-Corruption and Anti-Monopolies Ministry, embarked on this project in order to debunk what it regarded as the myth created by international bodies such as Transparency International.[70] However, the government failed to secure the necessary financial resources.[71] The survey was revived again in 2007 but was stalled for the same reasons. In 2008, after securing US$800,000, another committee was set up.[72] However, it is not known what became of it; there are still a number of unanswered questions.

If we turn now to the question of corruption and human rights, more recent attention has been paid to the precise relationship between the two fields. It has been suggested that addressing corruption using human rights mechanisms can give 'a human face' to both the victims and the perpetrators.[73] Moreover, there are problems with the generalisability of much published research on this issue. For instance, some commentators have argued that all acts of corruption are necessarily linked to human rights because they have a negative impact on the enjoyment of rights. This raises significant questions of causation, which will be discussed in the next chapter.

Overall, there seems to be some evidence that indicates a clear relationship between corruption and human rights violations. Therefore, one of the primary aims of this book is to shine new light on these debates by examining international, regional and national jurisprudence and analysing the text of laws to investigate whether corruption can have more than a negative impact on human rights, and whether in some cases it can be a violation of human rights in and of itself.

Lastly, it is important to note the caveat that although some everyday practices may have a detrimental cumulative effect on human rights and may be regarded as corruption—for example, intentional malfeasance, inefficiencies, errors and differences in judgments and in priorities—legally speaking, none of these acts are classified as corruption under Zimbabwean criminal law. It is for this reason that the present work focuses only on those forms of corruption that are legally defined as violations of criminal law and that should be brought to justice but may not have been. I make the case that these instances of corruption should be dealt with as part of the broader transitional justice programme in order to prevent impunity.

million were later released on the basis that they were wrongly convicted because they are not public officers as defined by the law.

[69] Phiri 2007.

[70] Phiri 2007.

[71] Dube 2005.

[72] Sithole 2008.

[73] Boersma 2012.

1.3 Accountability Mechanisms

There is little consensus about how to define transitional accountability mechanisms. The most comprehensive definition offered in the literature to date appears in the *Encyclopedia of Transitional Justice*:

> Some use the term loosely, as a synonym for transitional justice, but such broad definition lacks analytical clarity, because accountability should focus on the wrongdoers—that is, the persons who, in different ways (through intention, direct action, or support) contributed to wrongful actions. Thus, accountability mechanisms are here understood as institutionalized, procedurally shaped relationships between the wrongdoer and an authoritative domestic governmental or international institution, where the wrongdoer is duty bound to explain his or her actions, while an authoritative institution has the right to pass a judgment and impose sanctions on the wrongdoer.[74]

These mechanisms can be judicial or non-judicial, state-driven or civil-society-driven. The most common methods of accountability include prosecutions, forensic investigations, apologies, reparations, institutional reforms and amnesties.

The field of anti-corruption is also relatively new and its mechanisms still evolving. Some authors have speculated that accountability mechanisms could be used to adequately address corruption in transitional states. The remainder of this section comprises a brief discussion of the minimal mechanisms and processes that underpin the concept of transitional justice and how they can be extended in order to address corruption where it emerges as a grievance on par with human rights violations.

1.3.1 Truth Commissions and Corruption

Before attempting to define a truth commission, it is worth reading Eric Brahm's very instructive words in his seminal article 'What Is a Truth Commission and Why Does It Matter?':

> Why does it matter that the truth commission label is used in different ways? For the average citizen, it matters little whether or not the investigation his or her government creates is formally called a truth commission [...]. The semantics of how the investigation is labeled will matter little to most individuals. As academics, activists, and policymakers, however, we should care about the meaning behind the label. It would be beneficial if a common language was adopted to better facilitate truth commission research and clarify policy discussions.[75]

Unfortunately, however, there is no one universally accepted definition of a truth commission, but rather several competing definitions. One of the first scholars to

[74] Stan and Nedelsky 2013, p. 6.

[75] Brahm 2009, p. 2.

attempt a definition was Priscilla Hayner, who proposed a concise characterisation according to which a truth commission has the following features:

> (1) Truth Commissions focus on the past; (2) they investigate a pattern of abuses over a period of time, rather than a specific event; (3) a Truth Commission is a temporary body, typically in operation for six months to two years, and completing its work with the submission of a report; (4) these Commissions are officially sanctioned, authorized, or empowered by the state.[76]

This definition is the most suitable for present purposes because it is comprehensive enough to include the current commissions in Zimbabwe.

Truth commissions are considered central to transitional justice mechanisms, and to date around forty have been set up to address past human rights violations.[77] It is somewhat surprising that most of these truth commissions 'have failed to include in their mandates economic crimes and corruption—issues only recently embraced by mainstream human rights organisations'.[78] This is despite the fact that truth commissions are widely considered to be the best accountability mechanism capable for addressing issues of corruption.[79]

By their nature, truth commissions are semi-judicial: they can hear testimony from both victims and perpetrators, and although they do not have the authority to sentence or punish the alleged perpetrators, the truth is officially sanctioned.[80] Hence, they are regarded as having 'bark but no bite'. Nevertheless, they offer advantages when it comes to addressing corruption in transitional periods, for a few key reasons:

> Firstly, a truth commission's focus on gathering information would allow it to delve deeply into complex societal issues, exploring the causes and consequences of corruption more fully than in a prosecution scenario. Secondly, granting amnesty can greatly facilitate information gathering and can reduce the amount of time and resources necessary to conduct an investigation. Thirdly, truth commission amnesties have a strong public aspect that contributes to collective justice. Fourthly, and perhaps most important, truth commissions allow for community members to participate in accountability mechanisms by sharing their own stories in a formalized process.[81]

On the other hand, truth commissions also pose challenges for incorporating corruption as a transitional justice issue: firstly, in the absence of a 'transition', something that is at the heart of transitional justice measures, there is little reason to expect sudden and comprehensive change to the status quo even where a truth commission is set up. Secondly, a truth commission's political neutrality can be vulnerable and prone to interference, and can be greatly compromised by politicians. Thirdly, the absence of a logically delineated timeframe for reviewable

---

[76] Hayner 2010, p. 14.

[77] ICTJ and Kofi Annan Foundation 2014, p. 5.

[78] Cavallaro and Albuja 2008, p. 123.

[79] See in general Carranza 2008; Robinson 2015.

[80] Bevernage 2012, p. 9.

[81] Loftus 2015.

misconduct would make any temporal restrictions at best arbitrary and at worst political. Fourthly, truth commissions are based on the premise of voluntary participation, with the granting of amnesty as an inducement factor. However, this incentive is only effective if the threat of detection, prosecution and punishment is credible, which has historically proven to be a difficult proposition in countries with a highly compromised and ineffectual judicial system.[82] Finally, truth commissions are reactive rather than proactive, that is, they lack preventative mechanisms. Therefore, the situation resembles a game of 'catch me if you can' between truth commissions and violators of socio-economic rights.

In spite of the shortcomings noted above, international practice with truth commissions is moving towards an approach that includes economic and social rights abuses. Although still a rare phenomenon, a handful of truth commissions have addressed corruption and economic crimes within their mandates. At a rough count, there have been around ten countries whose truth commissions have included corruption in their mandates or findings. The engagement varies from having corruption as the main and sole mandate, such as the Bangladesh truth commission, to the inclusion of corruption only as part of the wider mandate or as a by-product of the findings that was not initially included in the main mandate of the commission.

1.3.2 Prosecutions and Corruption

These are the most common forms of individual accountability mechanisms for transitional justice. They are also the most controversial, as illustrated in the famous Hart–Fuller debate on the nature of law, which was specifically concerned with the question of the prosecution of Nazi collaborators after the Second World War.[83] The debate centred on the main challenge that post-war German courts found themselves facing, namely whether to accept the reliance on Nazi law as a defence:[84] in other words, 'whether a successor regime could bring a collaborator to justice and, if so, whether that would mean invalidating the predecessor laws in effect at the time the acts were committed'.[85] According to H.L.A. Hart, a fervent advocate of positivism, adhering to the rule of law would include recognising Nazi law as valid, whereas for Fuller, a defender of natural law, the rule of law means denying the validity of Nazi law.[86]

Later studies have revealed that the role and rule of law in transitional times is contingent on 'the states' distinctive political and legal legacies and, in particular,

[82] Loftus 2015.
[83] Fuller 1969.
[84] Fuller 1969, p. 54.
[85] Fuller 1969, p. 54.
[86] Fuller 1969, p. 54.

on the role of law in the predecessor regime'.[87] Consequently, 'in varying contexts, scholars come to disparate conclusions, suggesting that variations in interpretive strategies, whether of positivist or natural law, do not in and of themselves explain the judiciary's role under repressive rule'.[88]

Prosecutions can take place at different levels: domestic trials, at an international level such as the ICC or UN ad hoc tribunals (e.g. the International Criminal Tribunal for the former Yugoslavia or the International Criminal Tribunal for Rwanda), hybrid tribunals (e.g. Sierra Leone, East Timor, Kosovo, Cambodia, Lebanon) or via universal jurisdiction. However, not all cases in transition would require prosecution. Transitional states can decide whether to prosecute or stop proceedings, which perpetrators to charge and what charges to bring.[89] An example is the ICC Statute, Article 55, which allows states to stop prosecutions in the interest of justice.

Prosecutions for corruption in transitional justice scenarios have, in some cases, proved to be effective. A notable example is that of Augusto Pinochet, the former president of Chile, who could not be convicted on the human rights abuses allegedly committed during his years in power. However, he was finally arrested on corruption charges, which unfortunately were brought too late.[90] Similarly, cases such as that of Alberto Fujimori in Peru can further demonstrate how investigations into corruption can pave the way for human rights abuses charges.[91]

Recent controversial corruption prosecutions in the context of transitional justice have been made against ousted leaders. In Tunisia, former president Zine El Abidine Ali Ben Ali was tried in absentia for corruption and then for human rights violations.[92] Hosni Mubarak, the former president of Egypt, and other members of his regime were also tried and convicted of corruption.[93] In Côte d'Ivoire, the first charges against the former president, Laurent Gbagbo, and his associates following their ouster from power were for corruption and pillaging.[94] Prosecutions for grand corruption cases are also taking place in pre-transitional justice processes, for example in Equatorial Guinea, Nigeria and Zimbabwe.[95]

Despite the success story of corruption prosecutions in transitional justice scenarios at a municipal level, it nonetheless still remains to be seen whether there will be international prosecution of corrupt leaders, as 'the possibility for corruption to

---

[87] Teitel 2000, p. 18.

[88] Teitel 2000, p. 18.

[89] Ludwin King 2012, p. 99.

[90] Transparency International 2005.

[91] *In re Fujimori*, judgment of 11 July 2007, Supreme Court of Chile, first instance, no. 5646-05.

[92] United Press International 2011.

[93] Malsin 2015.

[94] Wilsher 2011.

[95] Chapter 5 will show at length how prosecution of corruption charges in transitional states can be different from ordinary criminal prosecutions because of the national interest and the need to stop repetition of the violations.

fall under the mandate of international criminal justice is far more complex'.[96] Moreover, 'international tribunals still heavily rely on an individualistic model of accountability, which neglects structural factors and can therefore hardly be applied to deal with corruption'.[97] As shall be seen below, the possibility of including corruption under the definition of crimes against humanity is still being considered but is not yet accepted under international law.

1.3.3 Amnesties and Corruption

The Office of the United Nations High Commissioner for Human Rights (OHCHR) defines amnesties as follows:

> Legal measures that have the effect of: (a) Prospectively barring criminal prosecution and, in some cases, civil actions against certain individuals or categories of individuals in respect of specified criminal conduct committed before the amnesty's adoption; or (b) Retroactively nullifying legal liability previously established.[98]

This definition is used in this book, in a strict sense, to describe all forms of legal initiatives by which civil and criminal prosecutions are put aside permanently or temporarily. This distinction accommodates the practice in Zimbabwe of using the terms *pardon* and *clemency* interchangeably with the term amnesty. This contrasts with the communication filed by the African Commission on Human and Peoples' Rights (ACmHPR)'s in relation to *Zimbabwe Human Rights NGO Forum v. Zimbabwe*, according to which there is a distinction between the terms, as one may be *pardoned* even before being formally accused or convicted, whereas clemency can only be applied after conviction.[99]

Amnesties are a double-edged sword. On the one hand, they are seen as an act of justice when granted to political prisoners of a repressive regime, releasing them from prison, cancelling the charges brought against them and in some cases annulling their court sentences, for instance the amnesty granted to Nelson Mandela in 1992. On the other hand, amnesties are also used as a means to grant impunity to or pardon perpetrators of human rights abuses under repressive regimes, for example the amnesties granted to key regime members in the final stages of military dictatorships in Latin America. Amnesties are indeed a transitional justice mechanism despite the fact that they can potentially clash with other goals of transitional justice: hence the need to balance the granting of amnesties with other mechanisms in order to mitigate their shortcomings.[100]

---

[96] Kora 2012, p. 538.

[97] Kora 2012, p. 539.

[98] OHCHR 2006, p. 5.

[99] *Zimbabwe Human Rights NGO Forum v. Zimbabwe*, African Commission on Human and Peoples' Rights, communication no. 245/2002, para 196.

[100] Stan and Nedelsky 2013, p. 13.

Despite the settled position of amnesties within the transitional justice toolbox, there is no consensus on whether they can be granted for international criminal acts. One school of thought views amnesties as unsustainable under international law. Ben Chigara, for example, gives four reasons for why amnesties are contrary to international law: firstly, because human rights are inalienable rights vested only in the individual and the state does not have authority to nullify them; secondly, the generally accepted treaty norms and principles of customary international law deny the legality of amnesties offered under national law; thirdly, the idea of national amnesty laws runs counter to the dominant positive human rights law tradition from the perspective of conflicting legal traditions; and fourthly, the emerging state practice of acquiescing with some national amnesty laws, and challenging others, is leading to the development of a new norm of customary international law on the matter.[101]

Other scholars, by contrast, argue that amnesties are not explicitly rejected under international law. William Schabas refers to two international treaties that specifically mention amnesties. The International Covenant of Civil and Political Rights (ICCPR) and Protocol II to the Geneva Conventions both support amnesties.[102] Article 6(4) of the ICCPR states: 'anyone sentenced to death shall have the right to seek pardon or commutation of the sentence. Amnesty, pardon or commutation of the sentence of death may be granted in all cases.' Similarly, Protocol II to the Geneva Conventions, Article 6(5)(5), states:

> At the end of hostilities, the authorities in power shall endeavor to grant the broadest possible amnesty to persons who have participated in the armed conflict, or those deprived of their liberty for reasons related to the armed conflict, whether they are interned or detained.

Schabas concludes that:

> from the standpoint of treaties, which are after all the clearest formulation of legal obligations that states are prepared to assume, it is not only the legality of amnesty but its wisdom, and not the contrary, that emerges. Human societies have been negotiating peace agreements since the beginning of recorded time. Amnesties have often been part of such *transitional justice mechanisms*, which existed, after all, long before the modern term 'transitional justice' had been invented.[103]

As a way out of this quandary, Schabas proposes striking a balance between the encouragement of amnesty in the ICCPR and Protocol II and its condemnation by human rights courts, which have often ruled against amnesties.[104] He argues that amnesties can be partially prohibited and partially tolerated or even encouraged: 'The most common of these intermediate views posits the prohibition of certain types of amnesty. For example, it is often stated that absolute or "blanket

[101] See in general Chigara 2002; Ntoubandi 2007.

[102] Schabas 2012, p. 180.

[103] Schabas 2012, p. 187, emphasis mine.

[104] Schabas 2012, p. 187.

amnesties" are prohibited, whereas amnesties associated with some degree of accountability—as in South Africa or Sierra Leone—may pass muster.'[105]

For example, according to the Belfast Guidelines on Amnesty and Accountability,[106] amnesties fall into two categories. On the one hand, 'illegitimate amnesties are generally unconditional and have the effect of preventing investigations and ensuring impunity for persons responsible for serious crimes';[107] amnesties of this sort are prohibited. However, the guidelines then turn to legitimate amnesties, which are designed primarily 'to create institutional and security conditions for the sustainable protection of human rights and require individual offenders to engage with measures to ensure truth, accountability and reparations'.[108]

There is, therefore, tolerance for amnesties that seek to foster justice and accountability, especially in transitional situations, and even more when the amnesties concerned are linked to the recovery of assets acquired corruptly. Carranza remarks that

> While amnesty-for-truth mechanisms have often immediately (and justifiably) triggered concerns that they encouraging impunity with respect to human rights violations, a similar approach with respect to large-scale corruption and economic crimes may not be as controversial, especially if it results in the recovery of assets amassed through those crimes.[109]

This view is shared by Roman David in his recent study on the efficacy of amnesties in transitional justice and anti-corruption efforts, which argues, 'contrary to the mainstream scholarship', that '(1) measures that lead to clean government differ from measures that contribute to its maintenance; and (2) amnesty may play a crucial role in establishing clean government, if it inspires a change in political culture'.[110]

The practical dilemma of whether to adopt amnesties to address corruption as part of transitional justice is clearly seen in the case of Tunisia. The law that first established transitional justice in Tunisia included amnesty for corruption and the option to suspend judicial and legal proceedings in exchange for reparation and asset recovery.[111] This law was transparent and independently monitored, and was based on public acknowledgment and apology for the crimes committed.

However, in 2015 a new amnesty law[112] was passed that is not based on the idea of truth-telling: it prohibits the use of any information obtained under it for use elsewhere, including any future education or institutional reform based on the findings. The new law further thwarts future vetting of public administration, allowing (former) officials and others who aided, abetted or helped the system of

---

105 Schabas 2012, p. 187.

106 Mallinder and Hadden 2013.

107 Mallinder and Hadden 2013, p. 9.

108 Mallinder and Hadden 2013, p. 10.

109 Carranza 2008, p. 325.

110 David 2010, pp. 391–406.

111 Organic Law on Establishing and Organizing Transitional Justice (Organic Law No. 53/2013).

112 Economic and FinancialReconciliation Law (Draft Organic Law No. 49/2015, Tunisia).

abuse to benefit from a general amnesty without having to tell the truth about what happened or to apologise.[113] Collectively, these laws provide important insights into the application of amnesty in order to address corruption within transitional justice processes.

1.3.4 Reparations and Corruption

International law prescribes the right to a remedy for human rights violations.[114] Generally, the right to reparations is twofold. Firstly, there is the substantive dimension, which translates into 'the duty to provide redress for harm suffered in the form of restitution, compensation, rehabilitation, satisfaction and, as the case may be, guarantees of non-repetition'.[115] Secondly, there is the procedural dimension, which is 'subsumed in the concept of the duty to provide "effective domestic remedies" explicit in most major human rights instruments'.[116]

Reparations are generally classified as material or symbolical, and individual or collective. Material or financial reparations involve the payment of compensation or damages that can be valued in monetary terms, e.g. restitution, whereas symbolic reparations do not involve monetary payments to victims. Examples of the latter include guarantees of the non-recurrence of violence, activities to commemorate victims, and education programmes.[117]

Individual reparations are designed to address the harm suffered by specific persons and involve, for instance, the restoration of liberty and compensation. The main advantage of individual reparations is that they acknowledge victims' suffering and provide them with appropriate recompense. Collective reparations, meanwhile, are directed at addressing the harm to an affected community as a whole. Common examples of community reparations are public apologies, the construction of memorial sites and other initiatives that benefit victims as a group.

As regards the question of addressing corruption using reparations as a transitional justice measure, research has consistently shown that it is a challenging task

---

113 Guellali 2015.

114 Universal Declaration of Human Rights (Article 8), the International Covenant on Civil and Political Rights (Article 2), the International Convention on the Elimination of All Forms of Racial Discrimination (Article 6), the Convention against Torture and other Cruel, Inhuman or Degrading Treatment or Punishment (Article 14) and the Convention on the Rights of the Child (Article 39). International humanitarian law and international criminal law are also relevant in this regard, in particular the Hague Convention respecting the Laws and Customs of War on Land (Article 3), the Protocol Additional to the Geneva Conventions relating to the Protection of Victims of International Armed Conflicts (Article 91) and the Rome Statute of the International Criminal Court (Articles 68 and 75).

115 OHCHR 2008, p. 6.

116 OHCHR 2008, p. 6.

117 Walker 2013, p. 211.

to award individual reparations to victims of corruption in situations where there is a multitude of victims. Moreover, as the present book will show, it is difficult to identify direct victims of grand corruption. Corruption has long been regarded as a victimless crime because it is the community or a group of people that suffers. Although this is where collective or community reparations could play a role further research on identifying victims of grand corruption would be worthwhile.

Because of the enormous challenges of reparations in general and connecting reparations to corruption cases, there are very few examples of countries that have adopted reparations to address corruption within transitional justice processes. However scholars have identified possible advantages of reparations for addressing corruption. Naomi Roht-Arriaza has argued that 'expanding the focus of ESC rights violations to include the scope of economic crimes like corruption could also provide funds for reparations programs'.[118] This mostly occurs in the context of collective reparations: for example, the Philippines passed a law giving compensation and other forms of reparations to victims of the Marcos dictatorship, funded with the US$680 million recovered from the Marcos family.[119] Other salient examples include Nigeria and the DRC.

1.3.5 Institutional Reforms and Corruption

Institutional reform includes measures such as:

> Vetting: examining personnel backgrounds during restructuring or recruitment; Structural reform: restructuring institutions; Oversight bodies: creating publicly visible oversight bodies within state institutions; Transforming legal frameworks: reforming or creating new legal frameworks; Disarmament, demobilization, and reintegration: disbanding armed actors; Education: training programs for public officials and employees on applicable human rights and international humanitarian law standards.[120]

As elements of transitional justice were expanded, institutional reforms became a key instrument following prosecutions or truth-finding. The converse is now the case: it is now common for security sector reform (police, army and the judiciary) to be a precondition for the implementation and success of all the other transitional justice mechanisms discussed above.

There has been speculation about the use of certain institutional reform mechanisms to deal with corrupt regimes in transitional justice processes, such as vetting and purges of corrupt elements from new government positions, structural reform to ensure transparency and accountability in institutions, and legal reform in which constitutional amendments or international anti-corruption treaties are adopted. It is

---

118 Roht-Arriaza 2014, p. 4.

119 Republic Act 10368, also known as the Human Rights Victims' Reparation and Recognition Act 2013 (Philippines).

120 ICTJ 2019.

thought that vetting and purges can bolster the fight against corruption, structural reforms can help to promote integrity and legitimacy, and legal reforms can eliminate or sanction corrupt officials in public service, ensure accountability to civilian governance through establishing anti-corruption watchdogs/commissions, and establish codes of ethics for public officials.

There has been no in-depth examination of the question of institutional reforms in their various forms and how they may address corruption in post-conflict situations. The only published longitudinal study focuses solely on how lustration may increase corruption by reducing bureaucratic expertise. The preliminary results of this study, which analyses original panel data from thirty post-communist states from 1996 to 2011, show that lustration is effective at lowering corruption. The findings suggest that lustration disrupts the political, economic and administrative malpractice of the preceding regimes by limiting former communist elites' opportunities for corruption, citing the case of Estonia to illuminate the causal mechanism.[121] A few selected examples in which lustrations and other institutional reforms have been used to deal with corruption are further discussed in the comparative analysis in Chap. 6.

Questions have been raised about the suitability of adopting institutional reforms as a mechanism of transitional justice for addressing corruption. For example, a critical article by Luca Uberti casts doubt on the effectiveness of institutional reforms in curbing corruption on the basis that corruption is not a result of dysfunctional institutions, as the proponents of using institutional reforms suggest; hence, a wholesale importation of institutional reforms cannot curb or reduce corruption.[122] According to Uberti, corruption is 'imbedded in socio-cultural structures that are endemic to the process of transition'.[123]

1.4 Conclusion

Transitional justice as a field is growing; it has gradually shifted from its comfort zone of focusing exclusively on civil and political rights in post-autocratic states to being applied in states in pretransition periods where conflict is ongoing, to states with minimal democratic reforms and even to stable democracies. Moreover, it has grown in terms of its remit to encompass all forms of injustices and socio-economic rights. Recent events and peculiar demands have called for a broader and deeper justice, which seeks to uncover the violations that are caused by corruption. It is both logical and possible to map the linkages between transitional justice and corruption, as this book seeks to do in the following chapters.

---

[121] Rožič and Nisnevich 2016, p. 257.

[122] Uberti 2016, p. 317.

[123] Uberti 2016, p. 334.

References

Arthur P (2009) How "Transitions" Reshaped Human Rights: A Conceptual History of Transitional Justice. Human Rights Quarterly 31: 321–367

Bevernage B (2012) History, Memory, and State-Sponsored Violence: Time and Justice. Routledge, Abingdon

Boersma M (2012) Corruption: A Violation of Human Rights and a Crime under International Law? Intersentia, Cambridge

Brahm E (2009) What is a Truth Commission and Why Does it Matter? Peace and Conflict Review 3: 1–14

Carranza R (2008) Plunder and Pain: Should Transitional Justice Engage with Corruption and Economic Crimes. International Journal of Transitional Justice 2: 310–330

Cavallaro JL and Albuja S (2008) The Lost Agenda: Economic Crimes and Truth Commissions in Latin America and Beyond. In: McEvoy K and McGregor L (eds) Transitional Justice from Below: Grassroots Activism and the Struggle for Change (Human Rights Law in Perspective). Hart, Oxford, pp. 121–141

Chigara B (2002) Amnesty in International Law: The Legality under International Law of National Amnesty Laws. Longman, London

David R (2010) Transitions to Clean Government: Amnesty as an Anticorruption Measure. Australian Journal of Political Science 45: 391–406

de Greiff P (2012) Report of the Special Rapporteur on the Promotion of Truth, Justice, Reparation and Guarantees of Non-Recurrence. Accessed at http://www.ohchr.org/Documents/HRBodies/HRCouncil/RegularSession/Session21/A-HRC-21-46_en.pdf

De Maria W (2008) Measurements and Markets: Deconstructing the Corruption Perception Index. International Journal of Public Sector Management 27: 777–797

Dube L (2005) Govt fails to raise $300b for Corruption Survey. Zimbabwe Independent. Available at https://www.theindependent.co.zw/2005/01/28/govt-fails-to-raise-300b-for-corruption-survey/ Last accessed on 23 June 2019

Fisk M (1989) The State and Justice: An Essay in Political Theory. Cambridge University Press, New York

Fuller LL (1969) The Morality of Law Yale. University Press, New Haven

Ghione L (2012) Justice in Transition and Corruption–Changing the Agenda. Available at http://www.righttononviolence.org/rn-seminar-constitutionalism-justice-in-transition/

Gildenhuys JSH (2004) Ethics and Professionalism: The Battle Against Corruption. Stellenbosch University Press, Stellenbosch

Guellali A (2015) Tunisia: Transitional Justice in the Crosshairs. Open Democracy. Available at https://www.opendemocracy.net/arab-awakening/amna-guellali/tunisia-transitional-justice-in-crosshairs

Hayner PB (2010) Unspeakable Truths: Transitional Justice and the Challenge of Truth Commissions, 2nd edn. Routledge, New York

Hayner PB and Bosire L (2003) Should Truth Commissions Address Economic Crimes? Considering the Case of Kenya. ICTJ. Available at http://www.tikenya.org/documents/TruthComm.doc

Hecht L and Michalowski S (2012) The Economic and Social Dimensions of Transitional Justice. Essex Transitional Justice Network Concept Paper. Available at https://www.essex.ac.uk/tjn/documents/TheeconomicandsocialdimensionsofTJ.pdf

ICTJ (2009) What is Transitional Justice? ICTJ Fact Sheet. Available at https://www.ictj.org/sites/default/files/ICTJ-Global-Transitional-Justice-2009-English.pdf

ICTJ (2019) Institutional Reforms, ICTJ Website. Available at https://www.ictj.org/our-work/transitional-justice-issues/institutional-reform Last accessed on 23 June 2019

ICTJ and Koffi Annan Foundation (2014) Challenging the Conventional: Can Truth Commissions Strengthen Peace Processes? ICTJ https://www.ictj.org/publication/challenging-conventional-can-truth-commissions-strengthen-peace-processes Last accessed on 23 June 2019

International Council on Human Rights Policy and Transparency International (2009) Corruption and Human Rights: Making the Connection. International Council on Human Rights Policy, Geneva
Kelsen H (1957) What is Justice? Justice Law and Politics in the Mirror of Science. University of California Press, Berkeley
Kora A (2012) Dealing With a 'New' Grievance: Should Anticorruption be Part of the Transitional Justice Agenda? Journal of Human Rights 11: 537–557
Kritz NJ (1995) Transitional Justice: How Emerging Democracies Reckon with Former Regimes Vol 2. US Institute of Peace Press, Washington DC
Laplante L (2008) Transitional Justice and Peace Building: Diagnosing and Addressing the Socioeconomic Roots of Violence through a Human Rights Framework. International Journal of Transitional Justice 2: 331–355
Loftus L (2015) Anticorruption Truth Commissions? Lessons to be Learned from Human Rights and Transitional Justice. The Global AntiCorruption Blog. Available at https://globalanticorruptionblog.com/2015/08/17/anticorruption-truth-commissions-lessons-to-be-learned-from-human-rights-and-transitional-justice/ Last accessed on 23 June 2019
Ludwin King EB (2012) Does Justice Always Require Prosecution? The International Criminal Court and Transitional Justice Measures. George Washington International Law Review 45: 85–120
Maguchu PS (2018) The Law is Just the Law: Analysing the Definition of Corruption in Zimbabwe. Journal of Financial Crime 25: 354–361
Mallinder L and Hadden T (2013) Belfast Guidelines on Amnesty and Accountability: With Explanatory Guidance. Transitional Justice Institute, Belfast
Malsin J (2015) Egypt: Hosni Mubarak Sentenced to Three Years in Prison. The Guardian. Available at https://www.theguardian.com/world/2015/may/09/egypt-hosni-mubarak-sentenced-to-three-years-in-prison Last accessed on 17 July 2019
Mani R (2008) Editorial Dilemmas of Expanding Transitional Justice, or Forging the Nexus between Transitional Justice and Development. International Journal of Transitional Justice 2: 253–264
Marauhn T (2004) Social Rights Beyond the Traditional Welfare State: International Instruments and the Concept of Individual Entitlements. In: Benvenisti E and Nolte G (eds) The Welfare State Globalization and International Law. Springer Verlag, Berlin, Heidelberg, pp. 275–319
McGill D (2017) Different Violence, Different Justice? Taking Structural Violence Seriously in Post-Conflict and Transitional Justice Processes. State Crime Journal 6: 79–101
Miller Z (2008) Effects of Invisibility: In Search of the 'Economic' in Transitional Justice. International Journal of Transitional Justice 2: 266–291
Morrell P and Pigou P (eds) (2004) Civil Society and Justice in Zimbabwe, Proceedings of a symposium held in Johannesburg, 11–13 August 2003. Themba Lesizwe on behalf of the Southern African Trauma Coalition, Johannesburg
Ntoubandi FZ (2007) Amnesty for Crimes Against Humanity Under International Law. Martinus Nijhoff Publishers, Leiden
OHCHR (2006) Rule-of-Law Tools for Post Conflict States: Truth Commissions. United Nations, New York and Geneva
OHCHR (2008) Rule-of-Law Tools for Post-Conflict States: Reparations Programmes. United Nations, New York and Geneva
Paige A (2009) How "Transitions" Reshaped Human Rights: A Conceptual History of Transitional Justice. Human Rights Quarterly 31: 321–367
Pesek S (2014) Combating Impunity: Transitional Justice and Anti-Corruption Conclusions from Practitioners' Dialogues on Transitional Justice. Freedom House, Washington DC
Peters A (2015) Corruption and Human Rights' Basel Institute of Governance Working Paper 20. Available at http://www.mpil.de/files/pdf4/Peters_Corruption_and_Human_Rights20151.pdf
Phiri G (2007) Zanu to study corruption. The Zimbabwean. Available at https://www.thezimbabwean.co/2007/02/zanu-to-study-corruption-22-02-07/ Last accessed on 23 June 2019

Rainey B et al (2014) White and Ovey: The European Convention on Human Rights, 6th edn. Oxford University Press, Oxford

Reeler T, Tarisayi E, and Maguchu P (2017) Transitional Justice in Pre-Transitional Times: Are there any Lessons for Zimbabwe? Sable Press, Harare

Robinson I (2015) Truth Commissions and Corruption: Towards a Complementary Framework. International Journal of Transitional Justice 9: 31–50

Roht-Arriaza N (2014) Reparations and Economic, Social, and Cultural Rights. In: Sharp D (ed) Justice and Economic Violence in Transition. Springer, New York, pp. 109–138

Rožič P and Nisnevich YA (2016) Lustration Matters: A Radical Approach to the Problem of Corruption. St Comp Int Dev 51: 257–285

Schabas W (2012) Unimaginable Atrocities: Justice, Politics, and Rights at the War Crimes Tribunals. Oxford University Press, Oxford

Schmid E and Nolan A (2014) Do No Harm? Exploring the Scope of Economic and Social Rights in Transitional Justice. International Journal of Transitional Justice 8: 362–382

Seligson MA (2002) The Impact of Corruption on Regime Legitimacy: A Comparative Study of Four Latin American Countries. Journal of Politics 64: 408–433

Sharp D (2012) Addressing Economic Violence in Times of Transition: Toward a Positive-Peace Paradigm for Transitional Justice. Fordham International Law Journal 35: 780–814

Sharp D (2014a) Emancipating Transitional Justice from the Bonds of the Paradigmatic Transition. International Journal of Transitional Justice 1: 150–169

Sharp D (2014b) The Significance of Human Rights for the Debt of Countries in Transition. In: Bohoslavsky JP and Cernic JL (eds) Making Sovereign Financing and Human Rights Work. Hart, Oxford, pp. 47–60

Sithole J (2008) Corruption a Way of Life in Zimbabwe, Institute for War and Peace Reporting. Available at https://iwpr.net/global-voices/corruption-way-life-zimbabwe

Stan L and Nedelsky N (eds) (2013) Encyclopedia of Transitional Justice, Vol. 1. Cambridge University Press, New York

Teitel RG (2000) Transitional Justice Oxford. University Press, New York

Transparency International (2005) Chile Sets Precedent For Holding Dictators Accountable For Corruption. Available at https://www.transparency.org/news/pressrelease/chile_sets_precedent_for_holding_dictators_accountable_for_corruption Last accessed on 23 June 2019

Uberti LJ (2016) Can Institutional Reforms Reduce Corruption? Economic Theory and Patron–Client Politics in Developing Countries. Development and Change 47: 317–345

United Press International (2011) Ousted Ben Ali sentenced in absentia. World News. Available at https://www.upi.com/Top_News/World-News/2011/07/05/Ousted-Ben-Ali-sentenced-in-absentia/50181309870197/ Last accessed on 6 July 2019

Vargas-Hernández JG (2009) The Multiple Faces of Corruption: Typology, Forms and Levels. Available at http://ssrn.com/abstract=1413976

Vasak K (1977) Human Rights: A Thirty-Year Struggle: the Sustained Efforts to give Force of Law to the Universal Declaration of Human Rights UNESCO Courier 30:11, United Nations Educational, Scientific, and Cultural Organization, Paris

Villalba CS (2011) Transitional Justice: Key Concepts, Processes and Challenges. Institute for Democracy & Conflict Resolution. Briefing Paper. Available at www.idcr.org.uk/wp-content/uploads/2010/09/07_11.pdf

Walker MU (2013) The Expressive Burden of Reparations: Putting Meaning into Money, Words and Things. In: MacLachlan A and Speight A (eds) Justice, Responsibility and Reconciliation in the Wake of Conflict. Springer, Dordrecht, pp. 205–226

Wilsher K (2011) Ousted president Laurent Gbagbo charged in Ivory Coast, The Guardian. Available at https://www.theguardian.com/world/2011/aug/19/ivory-coast-charges-laurent-gbagbo Last accessed on 23 June 2019

Winter S (2013) Towards a Unified Theory of Transitional Justice. International Journal of Transitional Justice 7: 224–244

World Bank (1997) Helping Countries Combat Corruption: The Role of the World Bank. World Bank, Washington DC

Chapter 2
Understanding Corruption and Human Rights

Thus, it is unsurprising that justice for corruption is emerging as a priority in the 'window of opportunity' presented by a transition from conflict to peace and/or from a repressive regime to democracy. Given the complexities of this broad phenomenon, however, it is also unsurprising that crafting an appropriate response to corruption in transitioning societies poses serious challenges.

Isabel Robinson (Robinson 2015, p. 1)

Contents

P. Maguchu, *Transitional Justice and Socio-Economic Rights in Zimbabwe*,
International Criminal Justice Series 24,
https://doi.org/10.1007/978-94-6265-323-8_2

Abstract Central to the entire discourse of linkages between corruption and transitional justice is the relationship between the former and human rights. This chapter deconstructs the connections between corruption and human rights. In the first part, it unravels some of the mysteries surrounding this debate. It then gives an overview of various theories on the linkages, focusing on the relationship between corruption and specific socio-economic rights. Part of the aim of this chapter is to suggest a framework that integrates the two fields.

Keywords Freedom from corruption · corruption and the right to health · socio-economic rights and issues · corruption–human rights framework

2.1 Introduction

There is nothing more difficult than trying to link two or more distinct fields that are based on different legal and normative frameworks. Hence, making the connection between anti-corruption and transitional justice is a very daunting task, as the extract above elucidates. Furthermore, as explained in Chap. 1, the task is made more challenging because there is not yet any consensus among scholars about the direct link between corruption and transitional justice.

However, corruption is becoming an increasingly important area in transitional justice practice and discourse. In mainstream scholarship, the core foundation of transitional justice is undergoing critical review, with growing demands for a more extensive theory of justice that incorporates 'economic violence', including corruption and the plunder of natural resources.[1] Recent events in the Middle East and North Africa have given rise to calls for the option of incorporating corruption into the transitional justice agenda to be brought to the fore.

Nevertheless, some scholars remain sceptical of the alliance, suggesting instead that 'if transitional justice processes respond to corruption, it is unclear whether justice is possible, and if so, what form such justice should take'.[2] There are doubts over the efficacy of transitional justice mechanisms to handle corruption. Arguing about the suggested alternative forms is beyond the scope of this book.[3] Instead, the focus here is on empirical studies which suggest that transitional justice mechanisms and processes can and should address corruption.

This chapter will explore the literature in order to design a framework for incorporating corruption into the transitional justice agenda. A natural progression would be to analyse the link between corruption and human rights violations. Accordingly, this chapter will discuss in detail the link between transitional justice and corruption, viewed from the perspective that corruption is connected to, and in

---

[1] Robinson 2015, pp. 1–19; Arbour 2007, pp. 1–27; Muvingi 2009, pp. 163–182.

[2] Robinson 2015, p. 1.

[3] See Gready et al. 2010. See also Gready and Robin 2014, pp. 339–361.

some cases can meet the threshold for, human rights violations. By deductive reasoning it will prove that those acts of corruption that can be classified as human rights violations and others that are linked to the violation of human rights qualify to be addressed under transitional justice. It will analyse different suggestions and provide a viable and legally tenable method for including corruption within the mandate of transitional justice mechanisms and processes.

2.2 Preliminary Considerations

It is necessary to deal briefly with a few preliminary issues before delving into the link between corruption and transitional justice, in order to have a clear understanding of the main arguments raised in this book. Although these issues deserve more detailed attention, this would go beyond the purposes of the present investigation.

2.2.1 Is Freedom from Corruption a Human Right?

Is freedom from corruption a human right *de lege lata* (in the law as it exists)? A minority of scholars have argued that it is. For instance, Ndiva Kofele-Kale has boldly claimed that 'the right to a corruption-free environment can be viewed as a freestanding, autonomous right, if you will, a right in its own right'.[4] Likewise, Matthew Murray and Andrew Spalding have argued that corruption should be treated as a 'fundamental and inalienable human right',[5] basing their argument on John Locke's theory of fundamental rights, Chinese Confucianism theories and Islamic jurisprudence, which they say supports the view that freedom from corruption is a fundamental human right.[6]

This chapter does not seek to advance the argument that freedom from corruption is a human right; that is not the aim of this book, and this idea is not necessary for the argument that corruption is a violation of human rights already recognised under international human rights law. Instead it takes the view that corruption is not a freestanding right: major international anti-corruption conventions, such as those of the AU and UN, do not frame corruption as a rights violation. Nor do human rights instruments such as the UN Universal Declaration of Human Rights or the two International Covenants include corruption among their lists of internationally recognised rights. With this in mind, it is not correct to call corruption a freestanding human right either *de lege lata* or even *de lege feranda* (with a view to the future law).

[4] Kofele-Kale 2000, p. 152.

[5] See Spalding 2014; Murray and Spalding 2015; Kofele-Kale 2000; Spalding 2014. For a contrasting perspective, see Rothstein and Varraich 2017.

[6] Spalding 2014. See also Murray and Spalding 2015.

2.2.2 *Is Corruption a Human Rights Violation?*

There is a large body of published literature investigating the question of whether corruption is a human rights violation. For instance, it has been reported that 'in Africa, massive human rights violations and large-scale corruption not only intersect but also overlap across various political transitions'.[7] However, most of the literature identified by this book fails to explain the exact relationship between the two social evils.[8]

However the literature offers contradictory findings concerning what international human rights and anti-corruption treaties say about corruption and human rights violations. One study by Spalding, which examined the trend in corruption and human rights violations, found that 'contemporary anticorruption writings have not yet embraced the principle that corruption is an inherent rights violation, asserting instead that corruption is merely the means of violating rights'.[9]

In the same vein, Morag Goodwin and Sarah Kathleen Rose-Sender have observed that 'arguments in support of a connection between human rights and corruption focus overwhelmingly upon the impact that corruption has upon the actualization of rights'.[10] In other words, this is not the same as saying acts of corruption lead to a violation of human rights in a strict judicial sense. The meaning of the term 'negative impact on human rights' is much broader than 'violation of human rights'.[11]

Anne Peters goes a step further and draws attention to international law instruments such as the United Nations Convention against Corruption (UNCAC), which she argues has some provisions that establish corruption as a human rights violation:

> From the perspective of general international law, these are obligations to prevent. Because the formulation of the UNCAC obligations is rather soft, it is hardly possible to hold a State party internationally responsible if it fails to fulfil its obligations or does so only poorly. But if we interpret them in conformity with human rights law (Article 31(3)(c) of the Vienna Convention on the Law of Treaties), it becomes apparent that the measures mentioned here must in fact be taken in an effective way in order to fulfil the obligations to protect and to fulfil (including to prevent) grounded in human rights law. Moreover, accordingly, the procedural obligations under UNCAC, especially the disclosure and publication requirements, which can be an effective way to curtail corruption, are equally grounded in human rights. Viewed in that light, failure to satisfy these obligations simultaneously constitutes a violation of the relevant human rights.[12]

---

7 Carranza 2008, p. 312.

8 Carranza 2008, pp. 329–330 (emphasis added).

9 Spalding 2014, p. 1365.

10 Goodwin and Rose-Sender 2010.

11 Human Rights Council 2015a, p. 8, para 21.

12 Peters 2015.

Therefore, this chapter seeks to investigate whether corruption is synonymous with human rights violations.[13] Consequently, this book will show that corruption can figure in transitional justice both as a contributory factor to human rights violations and as a human rights violation in and of itself.

2.2.3 *What Links Corruption to Transitional Justice?*

So far this chapter has managed to establish that in the literature corruption has been associated with the violation of human rights. This finding has important implications for establishing linkages between corruption and transitional justice. It suggests that corruption is linked to transitional justice because it is thought to be a violation or to cause a violation of human rights.

Much of the recent literature on transitional justice pays particular attention to the violation of socio-economic rights. It has been argued that socio-economic rights more clearly show the linkages between corruption and human rights than the violation of civil and political rights. The implication of this is that, in practice, countries are now investigating corruption as a violation of socio-economic crimes, as exemplified by the Kenya truth commission.

What we know about the inclusion of corruption within transitional justice processes is largely based on studies that focus only on grand corruption. However, far less attention has been paid to petty corruption as both a contributing factor and a violation of socio-economic rights in itself.

To give an illustration of what this means, in Chap. 6 we will look in detail at several examples of countries that have engaged with corruption in their transitional justice processes not as part of broader socio-economic issues, but as an independent contributor or as a violation of such rights on its own. The next section will address the question of socio-economic rights in detail.

[13] Human rights violations are defined here according to the Maastricht Guidelines on Violations of Economic and Social Rights, para 9; Committee on Economic, Social and Cultural Rights, General Comment No. 3, 5th Sess., 1990, UN Doc. E/1991/23, Annex III, para 10. 'Violations of the Covenant occur when a State fails to satisfy what the Committee on Economic, Social and Cultural Rights has referred to as "a minimum core obligation to ensure the satisfaction of, at the very least, minimum essential levels of each of the rights [...]. Thus, for example, a State party in which any significant number of individuals is deprived of essential foodstuffs, of essential primary health care, of basic shelter and housing, or of the most basic forms of education is, prima facie, violating the Covenant."'

2.2.4 What Is the Distinction Between Socio-economic Rights and Issues?

The engagement with socio-economic rights and issues within the sphere of transitional justice is sometimes misunderstood. As Evelyne Schmid and Aoife Nolan note, in the discourse 'on the desirability and feasibility of including a socio-economic dimension to transitional justice, the distinction between ESR and broader socio-economic issues often gets lost, with problematic implications for both opponents and proponents'.[14] It is therefore important at this juncture to distinguish between socio-economic rights and the broader socio-economic issues within the context of transitional justice.

The term socio-economic rights is used in this study as a shorthand for economic, social and cultural human rights as enshrined in the International Bill of Rights and numerous other international and regional human rights instruments and declarations.[15] These instruments define socio-economic rights as those privileges that grant people access to certain basic needs that are necessary to lead a decent and dignified life. These basic needs include resources, opportunities and services that people need in order to sustain a humane and decent life, such as food, shelter, land and access to education, clean water and work.

While the definition of socio-economic *rights* is settled in law, scholars are still struggling to pin down a common definition of socio-economic *issues*. It is widely recognised that socio-economic issues are broader than rights. As the former UN Special Rapporteur (on the enjoyment of economic, social and cultural rights and the promotion of the right to drinking water supply and sanitation for the United Nations Sub-Commission on the Promotion and Protection of Human Rights) El Hadji Guissé explains, 'practices and procedures which are sources of violations of the economic rights of individuals or groups in all societies cannot be exhaustively listed because of their commonplace nature'.[16]

If the above suggestion is correct, then it is impossible and perhaps unnecessary to try to come up with a definition of socio-economic issues. In the field of transitional justice, Lisa Hecht and Sabine Michalowski have identified a number of factors that can be regarded as socio-economic issues, including economic crimes, corruption, economic policies, odious debts, structural violence and human developmental issues.[17]

Having mapped the general distinction between socio-economic rights and issues, it is important to mention that the main difference between the two is that socio-economic rights are binding on states, whereas socio-economic issues are not. Therefore, if corruption is linked to transitional justice on the basis that it is linked

[14] Schmid and Nolan 2014, p. 364.

[15] Marauhn 2004, p. 316.

[16] UN Sub-Commission on the Promotion of and Protection of Human Rights 1997.

[17] Hecht and Michalowski 2012.

to, if not a violation of, socio-economic rights, there must be a clearly established framework that makes it possible.

The first systematic study of the linkages was carried out in a publication by the International Council on Human Rights Policy (ICHRP) and Transparency International (TI), *Corruption and Human Rights: Making the Connection*. The study provides a more sophisticated framework for analysing this issue. It cautions that although 'all forms of corrupt practice may in the long-run have an impact on human rights, it cannot be concluded mechanically that a given act of corruption violates a human right'.[18] Thus, there is a need to make reference to a framework that underscores with 'precise terms what the links are between acts of corruption and violations of human rights'.[19] The next section will give an overview of various proposed theories on the link between corruption and human rights.

2.3 Overview of Corruption and Human Rights Methodologies

The relationship between corruption and human rights is a two-way street: 'human rights can be used in support of or against corruption'.[20] There are several other scenarios in which corruption interacts with human rights: (a) Corruption and human rights violations often flourish in the same environment in the sense that they go hand in glove with each other. Consequently, a government that is corrupt is less likely to respect human rights; similarly, a state with a poor human rights record is more likely to be corrupt. (b) Thus, human rights are key in the fight against corruption and act as a double-edged sword for both the perpetrators and victims of corruption.[21] (c) On the other hand, anti-corruption laws should respect the human rights of the accused, such as the right to privacy and the right to a fair trial. (d) Anti-corruption laws should also pay due attention to the human rights of vulnerable groups. Measures taken by states to address corruption should also focus on improving the situation of the poor, and not solely on improving the position of (foreign) investors. (e) Some corruption practices may violate human rights.

A full discussion of all these factors lies beyond the scope of this book, which focuses only on the nexus between corruption and human rights violations. Research in this area can be classified into three different categories according to the methodologies used to explain the linkages. It should be emphasised that these theories only seek to highlight the links between corruption and human rights; they

[18] International Council on Human Rights Policy and Transparency International 2009, p. 24.

[19] International Council on Human Rights Policy and Transparency International 2009, p. 23.

[20] Gathii 2010, p. 125.

[21] The importance of the right to freedom of expression, including the right to seek, receive and impart information (Article 19(2) ICCPR), the right of peaceful assembly (Article 21 ICCPR) and the right to freedom of association (Article 22 ICCPR).

do not argue for an overhaul of the human rights system to be corruption-focused, as wrongly assumed by many who are against the notion that corruption and human rights are linked. The next sections highlight how the link has been approached using doctrinal, empirical and normative methodologies.

2.3.1 Doctrinal-Research-Based Studies

Doctrinal-research-based studies analyse anti-corruption law and human rights law to map the relationship between the two fields. To this end, they examine legal instruments and policy documents relating to corruption and human rights to bring out the connections. The majority of the studies focus on the preambles to international and regional human rights and corruption instruments, which are increasingly acknowledging the relationship between human rights violations and corruption, as well as declarations produced by prominent organisations that have been driving the anti-corruption agenda.[22]

The core focus of doctrinal-research-based studies is the effect of corruption on established and recognised human rights. The most nuanced doctrinal research on the link between corruption and human rights is the aforementioned comprehensive work done by TI and ICHRP.[23] It prescribes a twofold process to determine whether a particular corrupt practice violates a human right: firstly it is necessary to establish the scope and content of the human right obligation in question and secondly to determine whether this obligation derives from domestic law, international treaty, custom or general principles of law.[24]

The present book argues that where there is an established legal obligation to uphold a human right, any form of corruption that leads to a state's failure to conform to that legal obligation in one of the three ways briefly discussed below is a violation of human rights.

2.3.1.1 Direct Violations

Corruption can directly lead to a human rights violation in the following cases. Firstly, when an act of corruption has been used intentionally as a means to violate a right.[25] Secondly, direct violations can be inferred where there is no deliberate act from a public official but he or she fails to act with reasonable diligence when a human right is at risk of being violated.[26] Thirdly, direct violations may also occur

---

22 Global Organization for Parliamentarians Against Corruption 2013.

23 International Council on Human Rights Policy and Transparency International 2009.

24 International Council on Human Rights Policy and Transparency International 2009, p. 24.

25 International Council on Human Rights Policy and Transparency International 2009, p. 27.

26 International Council on Human Rights Policy and Transparency International 2009, p. 27.

when a state official or an individual acting in an official capacity 'acts or fails to act in a way that prevents' other individuals from having access to fundamental rights.[27]

2.3.1.2 Indirect Violations

These occur when corruption acts as a 'necessary condition' that triggers events that lead to human rights violations.[28] What must be shown here is that 'without corruption the violation would not have occurred'.[29] In other words, corruption is 'an essential factor contributing to a chain of events that eventually lead to violation of a right'.[30] Similarly, indirect violations may also occur when corrupt state authorities are complicit in obstructing the exposure and prosecution of corruption cases.[31]

2.3.1.3 Remote Violations

The link between corruption and human rights is not always clear. In some cases corruption cannot be directly connected to human rights abuses, nor can it be causally linked through a single direct chain of events, even as a secondary cause. However, corruption can still be responsible for the human rights violations, albeit only as a remote factor among many others in the violation of a particular right. Remote violations pertain to the situation 'where corruption is one factor among others' that lead to the violation.[32]

These findings have faced criticism from other scholars. Isabel Robinson rejects the distinction between direct and indirect violations as merely academic, and claims that it is simply an alternative way of explaining the effect of corruption on human rights.[33] She further argues that the framework does not correspond to international human rights law: in short, indirect and remote violations cannot lead to the violation of rights.[34] However, she concedes that *direct violations* might be classified as human rights violations in certain scenarios.[35]

---

27 International Council on Human Rights Policy and Transparency International 2009, p. 27.

28 International Council on Human Rights Policy and Transparency International 2009, p. 27.

29 International Council on Human Rights Policy and Transparency International 2009, p. 27.

30 International Council on Human Rights Policy and Transparency International 2009, p. 27.

31 International Council on Human Rights Policy and Transparency International 2009, p. 27.

32 International Council on Human Rights Policy and Transparency International 2009, p. 27.

33 Robinson 2015, p. 10.

34 Robinson 2015, p. 10.

35 Robinson 2015, p. 10.

The present book notes that, although indirect violations can also be classified in terms of human rights,[36] when dealing with corruption it is prudent to limit oneself to cases that involve a clear direct violation of human rights. At the time of writing, it is still difficult to make cases based on indirect and remote violations.

This is exemplified in one of the few cases to be brought on the subject under discussion here: in *SERAP v. Nigeria*, the Economic Community of West African States (ECOWAS) Community Court of Justice made the key finding that

> Admittedly, embezzling stealing or even mismanagement of funds meant for the education sector will have a negative impact on education since it reduces the amount of money made available to provide education to the people. Yet it does not amount to a denial of the right to education, without more. The reason is not far to seek. [...] There must be a clear linkage between the acts of corruption and a denial of the right to education.[37]

This case has shown that the relationship between corruption and human rights depends on the factors of each case. Where corruption is directly linked to human rights violations, it is synonymous with the violation. However, in some other cases, it is linked to the violation indirectly and remotely; in these cases, it is independent of the violation of human rights and may only have a negative impact.

2.3.2 *Empirical-Research-Based Studies*

Empirical research methodologies focus on the correlation between corruption and human rights violations, that is, how the two flourish in the same environment. Proponents of these methodologies, such as Lucy Koechlin and Magdalena Carmona, argue, for instance, that corrupt regimes are also the worst human rights violators, and that corruption and human rights violations reinforce each other.[38]

More strongly empirically based studies aim to give corruption a human face—a social aspect, so to speak. Such studies highlight how corruption has evolved: while it started off as an administrative and political issue, its effect on the costs of goods and services made it an economic issue, and because of the massive suffering it can cause to people it is now acquiring a social or human face. Empirical theories emphasise the effect of corruption on individuals' enjoyment of human rights, rather than its impact on state institutions, which may then be linked to some human rights violations. This helps us to develop a general analysis of the role of state

[36] For instance, indirect discrimination is regarded as a violation of human rights where it is proved.

[37] *Socio-Economic Rights and Accountability Project v. Federal Republic of Nigeria and Universal Basic Education Commission*, judgment of 30 November 2010, ECW/CCJ/JUD/07/10 ECOWAS, para 19.

[38] Koechlin and Carmona 2009.

institutions in corruption and focus more on the role of the state in providing human rights and protecting them from corruption.[39]

Julio Bacio-Terracino has examined how corruption can lead to human rights violations through direct and indirect means, as explained above.[40] However, his three-pronged approach to the link between corruption and human rights offers a more empirical analysis of the nexus between the two discourses. It focuses, firstly, on the corrupt practice; secondly, on how the harm to the victims affects their human rights; and, thirdly, on evaluating whether the corrupt practice constitutes a violation of a human right.[41]

Bacio-Terracino concludes that 'it is important to distinguish cases where corruption is at the origin of subsequent violations of human rights from cases where corruption is itself part of the violation or a means to achieve a violation'.[42] He presents a strong case for incorporating corruption into the transitional justice agenda, which has its roots firmly established in the human rights discourse. The main advantage of empirical theories is that they make a clear distinction between direct and indirect causes of corruption in relation to human rights violations, which is not clear under the doctrinal theories.

2.3.3 *Normative-Research-Based Studies*

Recently, normative methodologies have been developed to explain the links between corruption and human rights. At the centre of these theories is the argument that the normative development of the two concepts originates in religious teachings. They also argue that both started as private issues before developing into collective societal issues—in other words, they went from being political issues to real social ones. There are also notable differences between anti-corruption measures and human rights: for instance, human rights moved from the international to the national level, whereas anti-corruption measures were promoted from national to international. Furthermore, human rights are accused of having a top-down approach, by contrast with the bottom-up anti-corruption approach.[43]

Notable normative-research-based theories include Balakrishnan Rajagopal's early attempt to develop a theory of *state legitimacy*, which sought to prove that corruption flourishes where there are human rights violations.[44] A nuanced normative approach has been provided only recently by Bo Rothstein and Aiysha Varraich. This theory builds on some of the points that have already been presented:

---

39 Gathii 2010, p. 197.

40 Bacio-Terracino 2008.

41 Bacio-Terracino 2008, p. 11.

42 Bacio-Terracino 2008.

43 Rothstein and Varraich 2017, pp. 64–67.

44 Rajagopal and Balakrishnan 1999, pp. 1–19.

for example, the authors identify the emphasis on corruption or human rights in the preambles of legal documents and instruments, as well as the correlation between corruption and human rights.[45] Further, they note that corruption and human rights place restrictions on state authority.

More importantly, these theorists note that anti-corruption measures and human rights are both opposed to discrimination. Whereas human rights discourse is concerned with the violation of private rights by public power, the anti-corruption discourse focuses on the abuse of public office for private gain.[46] The authors critically examine the key terms that connect different corruption–human rights nexuses across methodologies, such as discrimination, justice and morality. The normative basis linking both human rights and anti-corruption efforts are most clearly expressed in the legal tools developed. Both human rights and anti-corruption codes focus on the right to non-discrimination. They argue that corruption involves different forms of discrimination, and human rights concern people's right to remain free of discrimination.

2.4 Corruption and Specific Human Rights vis-à-vis the Right to Health

Recent human rights studies have shown that it is plausible to directly connect corruption and specific socio-economic rights violations. Nonetheless, while there have been numerous studies on the link between corruption and human rights in general, the nexus between corruption and specific socio-economic rights remains relatively under-researched.[47] There are a handful of reports from organisations such as the UN Human Rights Council (UNHCR),[48] as well as an earlier report by the UN Special Rapporteur investigating corruption and its impact on the full enjoyment of human rights, in particular economic, social and cultural rights.[49] The most recent is a report by the UN Special Rapporteur on health on 'Corruption and the Right to Health'.[50] Building on this literature, the following sections will highlight how certain forms of corruption can, under very specific conditions, violate human rights, in particular socio-economic rights, taking the right to health as an example.

---

[45] Rothstein and Varraich 2017.

[46] Rothstein and Varraich 2017, p. 67.

[47] International Council on Human Rights Policy and Transparency International 2009 and 2010; Bacio-Terracino 2010; Gathii 2010, pp. 125–202; De Beco 2011, pp. 1107–1124.

[48] Human Rights Council 2015b.

[49] Resolution 2003/2 of the former Sub-Commission on the Promotion and Protection of Human Rights. Its mandate ended in 2006 when it was replaced by the Advisory Committee.

[50] Human Rights Council 2015c.

2.4.1 Background

Corruption is a serious challenge in healthcare systems globally. For example, according to the European Healthcare Fraud & Corruption Network (EHFCN), every year €180 billion is lost globally to corruption.[51] It has been reported that corruption is so pervasive within healthcare that it has become normalised. From the politician to the patient, corruption is part of doing business in the healthcare sector all over the world.[52]

In order to understand how corruption can be a violation of the right to health, we need first to understand its causes. The UN Special Rapporteur on health has identified that corruption in the health sector is attributable to three main factors:

> (a) power asymmetries or an imbalance of information, inter alia, between health-care provider and patient and between government, the private sector and rights holders; (b) uncertainty inherent in selecting, monitoring, measuring and delivering health-care services; and (c) the complexity of health systems: the large number of parties involved makes it more difficult to generate and analyse information in a transparent manner.[53]

The main areas affected by corruption in the health sector include the management of financial resources, such as budget allocation; distribution of medical supplies; and the point where health workers interact with patients.[54] Similarly, it has been observed that the health sector is pervaded by virtually all types of corruption activities, including 'petty bribery, nepotism, informal payments and mismanagement of resources, absenteeism and state capture'.[55]

2.4.2 Normative Content

The right to health, which is also known technically as the right to the highest attainable standard of physical and mental health, is defined as the 'right to the enjoyment of a variety of facilities, goods, services and conditions necessary for the realisation of the highest attainable standard of health'.[56] This right does not mean the right to be healthy; however, it does guarantee certain minimum standards that the state should meet to ensure people are adequately healthy, such as providing food, water, health-related education, a safe working environment and housing, all of which are distinct rights in themselves and also vulnerable to corruption.[57]

---

[51] Gee and Button 2014.

[52] Petkov 2016, p. 1.

[53] Transparency International 2006, p. xvii; Savedoff and Hussmann 2006.

[54] Benjamin 2012, p. 31.

[55] Nawaz and Chêne 2009.

[56] UN Committee on Economic, Social and Cultural Rights 2000, Article 12, para 9.

[57] OHCHR 2008.

This chapter will focus on the right to health in order to illuminate how corruption can be a violation of human rights under international law, because this right provides the most suitable normative framework, constituting a legally binding imperative to analyse and address how corruption affects socio-economic rights. The framework of the right to health encompasses tenets of good governance, transparency, accountability and participation, which are relevant in the anti-corruption discourse. For instance, popular debate and common wisdom have it that adhering to notions of good governance, transparency, accountability and various forms of participation can be an antidote for corruption; the world's biggest anti-corruption NGO is even called Transparency International.

2.4.3 State Obligations and Violations

2.4.3.1 Article 2(1) of the ICESCR

Four obligations can be derived from a literal reading of Article 2(1) ICESCR, which states that:

> Each State Party to the present Covenant undertakes *to take steps*, individually and through international assistance and cooperation, especially economic and technical, *to the maximum of its available resources, with a view to achieving progressively the full realization of the rights recognized in the present Covenant* by *all appropriate means*, including particularly the adoption of legislative measures.[58]

These obligations are 'to take steps'; and to do so 'to the maximum of its available resources'; 'with a view to achieving progressively the full realization of the rights recognized in the present Covenant'; and 'by all appropriate means'. Each of these obligations may become difficult or impossible to fulfil in the circumstances of grand or petty corruption, as explained *in seriatim* below.

The first element, which is also regarded as the core obligation, is that states need 'to take steps'. According to the ICESCR, these steps must be 'deliberate, concrete and targeted'.[59] Needless to say, the steps which a state chooses to adopt must eliminate any obstacles to the realisation of socio-economic rights. As corruption can be a hindrance, the ICESCR requires states to take anti-corruption measures.[60] For example, the Inter-American Commission on Human Rights (IACmHR)[61] considers ratification of the Inter-American Convention against

[58] CRC, Article 4; Convention on the Rights of Persons with Disabilities, adopted 24 January 2007, A/RES/61/106, Article 4(2). Emphasis mine.

[59] UN Committee on Economic, Social and Cultural Rights 1990, Article 2(1), para 2.

[60] Boersma 2012, pp. 229–230.

[61] Statute of the Inter-American Commission on Human Rights, 1 October 1979, entered into force 30 days after its approval, O.A.S. Off. Rec. OEA/Ser.P/IX.0.2/80.

Corruption (IACAC)[62] and the existence, powers and budget of a domestic anti-corruption authority to be structural indicators for national progress reports.[63]

The second component of the obligation set out in Article 2(1) of the ICESCR is to take steps 'with a view to achieving progressively the full realization of the rights recognized in the present Covenant'. Under this obligation, states do not have unfettered discretion regarding the allocation of resources but must give priority to the attainment of human rights.[64] Therefore, misallocation of 'public funds at the highest level violates this obligation, because in such cases the financing of the standard of living of high-level public officials is given priority over the realization of social human rights'.[65] The most compelling argument is presented by Christopher Albin-Lackey, who argues that grand corruption is a sign of situations 'where it is the easiest to perceive a clear state violation of the obligation to progressively realise ESC rights'.[66]

Third, the state has an obligation to exhaust all possibilities it has at its disposal 'to the maximum of its available resources'.[67] It is the responsibility of the state to determine which resources are available and 'what the maximum is'.[68] It follows that states are prohibited from diverting resources that should be used for the enjoyment of socio-economic rights.[69] Many states' human rights mechanisms make reference to this obligation to point out the link between corruption and human rights violations.[70]

Finally, Article 2(1) of the ICESCR imposes an obligation on states to employ 'all appropriate means' to ensure the provision of socio-economic rights. Thus, a state should employ effective means to curb corruption, which is linked to, or can be an obstacle to the attainment of, socio-economic rights. A state experiencing rampant corruption will be in violation of its fundamental obligation arising from the ICESCR if it pursues a manifestly deficient anti-corruption policy.[71]

2.4.3.2 Tripartite Typology

The former UN Special Rapporteur Asbjørn Eide popularised the tripartite typology of a state's obligations to respect, protect and fulfil human rights in his 1987 report

[62] Inter-American Convention against Corruption, adopted on 29 March 1996, entry into force on 6 March 1997.

[63] Peters 2015, p. 17.

[64] UN Committee on Economic, Social and Cultural Rights 1999, Article 11(12), para 17.

[65] Peters 2015, p. 17.

[66] Albin-Lackey 2014, p. 147.

[67] Peters 2015, p. 17.

[68] Saul et al. 2014, p. 143.

[69] See in general Carmona and Baci-Terracino 2010.

[70] Peters 2015, p. 17.

[71] Peters 2015, p. 18.

to the UN Sub-Commission on Prevention of Discrimination and Protection of Minorities.[72] However, the tripartite terminology can be traced as far back as 1980, when Henry Shue introduced the obligations 'to avoid depriving', 'to protect from deprivation' and 'to aid the deprived'.[73]

The obligation to respect requires members to refrain from interfering with the enjoyment of human rights; the obligation to protect requires members to prevent violations of such rights by third parties; and the obligation to fulfil requires members to take appropriate measures (legislative, budgetary, judicial) to guarantee the full realisation of such rights.[74]

The CESCR (Committee on Economic, Social and Cultural Rights) in turn divides the obligation to fulfil into the three subcategories of facilitating, providing and promoting.[75] This typology is the most common approach used to classify human rights.[76] It was initially adopted into the right to food before being applied to other socio-economic rights,[77] and has been described as 'perhaps the most striking example of this cross-fertilization' of the application of the concept of obligations across different categories of rights.[78]

In order to determine how corruption can violate the tripartite typology, it is imperative to distinguish the specific corrupt conduct of an individual official that is attributed to the state vicariously due to the official's status and the general anti-corruption policy of the state as an international legal person.[79]

First, an act of corruption by a public official may, 'depending on the context and the human right in question, potentially violate each of these dimensions' of the tripartite obligation.[80]As with all human rights, the right to health imposes three types or levels of obligations on states parties: the obligations to respect, protect and fulfil.[81] The tripartite typology, strictly speaking, is a practical guide used to understand human rights treaty obligations.[82] It has been argued that the absence of opposition within the interpretative community provides evidence of the strong supportive structure necessary to justify its use as a tool by which to classify the types of *other measures* required to secure the effective implementation of the right to health.

Second, when it comes to government anti-corruption policies, the analysis should consider acts of omission where the state has failed to adopt, apply and

---

72 UN Commission on Human Rights, UN Doc, E/CN.4/RES/1988/29

73 Shue 1996, p. 52.

74 See, for example, Van Boven et al. 2008.

75 Peters 2015, p. 13.

76 Schmid and Nolan 2014, p. 367.

77 De Schutter 2013, p. 5.

78 Rosga and Satterthwaie 2009, p. 265, n. 43.

79 Peters 2015, p. 13.

80 Peters 2015, p. 13.

81 UN Committee on Economic, Social and Cultural Rights 2000, Article 12, para 33.

82 Maastricht Guidelines on Violations of Economic and Social Rights, para 6.

enforce robust anti-corruption mechanisms.[83] This is because having an effective anti-corruption regime is regarded as a means of complying with 'one of the three facets of the positive obligation to fulfil, namely; facilitate, provide, promote'.[84] If it is a cliché that rampant corruption poses serious challenges to the enjoyment of numerous human rights, by corollary scenarios where the state is not taking action to curb corruption or is manifestly inefficient in implementing and enforcing the anti-corruption structures, it is in any event responsible under international law for its failure to fulfil its human rights obligations to prevent and protect.[85]

2.4.3.3 The '4 As' Typology

The standards of availability, accessibility, acceptability and adaptability, colloquially known as the '4 As', are generally used to assess the delivery of public services such as healthcare.[86] The 4 As were first introduced to the socio-economic rights regime in 1999 by the UN Special Rapporteur on the right to education, Katarina Tomasevski.[87] They are also partly attributable to the CESCR General Comment on the Right to Adequate Housing.[88]

The '4 As' typology has been applied to 'clarify the content' of states' obligations regarding other socio-economic rights.

> The '4-As' scheme can be combined with [...] differentiation within the obligations of the State to respect, protect and fulfill human rights. Indeed, the '4-As' *describe the characteristics of the good or service* that the individual right holder has a right to; the respect/protect/fulfil framework describes the different obligations of the State either not to interfere with the enjoyment of that good or service, or to regulate private actors, or to facilitate access to that good or service by market mechanisms, or in certain cases to provide it.[89]

In assessing the linkage between corruption and socio-economic rights, only two principles need to be taken into account: namely, availability and accessibility.[90] In terms of availability, states should ensure that health facilities, goods and services are available in sufficient quantity and with continuous supply. Corruption can negatively impact on this availability. For instance, when money that has been

[83] Peters 2015, p. 13.

[84] Peters 2015, p. 13.

[85] Peters 2015, p. 13; *Hugh Glenister v. President of the Republic of South Africa and Others*, judgment of 17 March, CCT 48/10 ZACCTA \s "Hugh Glenister v President of the Republic of South Africa and others, 17 March 2011, (CCT 48/10) [2011] ZACC 6, para 177: 'The state's obligation to "respect, protect, promote and fulfil" the rights in the Bill of Rights thus inevitably, in the modern state, creates a duty to create efficient anti-corruption mechanisms.' In the literature, see Carmona and Bacio-Terracino 2010, p. 27.

[86] International Council on Human Rights Policy and Transparency International 2009, p. 48.

[87] Commission on Human Rights Resolution 1999, pp. 42–74.

[88] UN Committee on Economic, Social and Cultural Rights 1991, Article 11(1).

[89] De Schutter 2013, p. 294 (emphasis added).

[90] International Council on Human Rights Policy and Transparency International 2009, p. 45.

allocated to import medicine is embezzled, the availability of these goods is affected. With regards to accessibility, health facilities, goods and services must be accessible to everyone physically and economically/financially. Corruption can distort prices, making goods and services more expensive and less accessible to those who need them most.

2.4.3.4 Non-Discrimination

An overarching principle that cuts across states' human rights obligations is the responsibility to guarantee that rights be exercised without discrimination of any kind. This principle is central to any system of human rights protection. It is explicitly stated in the ICCPR as follows:

> The States Parties to the present Covenant undertake to guarantee that the rights enunciated in the present Covenant will be exercised without discrimination of any kind as to race, colour, sex, language, religion, political or other opinion, national or social origin, property, birth or other status.[91]

The specific grounds mentioned above are not exhaustive. The ECOSOC Committee explains that the nature of discrimination varies according to context and evolves over time, and recommends 'a flexible approach to the ground of "other status"', which needs to take account of other forms of discrimination.[92] Therefore, any discrimination in access to healthcare, as well as in means and entitlements to achieving this access, which has the intention or effect of impairing the equal enjoyment or exercise of the right to health is prohibited on the basis of the aforementioned grounds or *other status*.

The right to health should, like any other human right, be enjoyed on the basis of equality and without discrimination. Corruption violates the principle of non-discrimination because it is an inherently discriminatory practice.[93] For instance, according to Peters, corruption can be regarded as discrimination in the context of Article 2(2) ICESCR on the basis of a suspect classification which might be considered an 'other status' if a person is unable or unwilling to pay a bribe and this results in unequal treatment.[94] The same view is shared by the aforementioned CESCR General Comment on non-discrimination, which states that individuals and groups must not be 'arbitrarily treated on account of belonging to a certain economic or social group'.[95] Strictly speaking, therefore, the inability of a person to

---

[91] Article 2(2).

[92] The UN Committee on Economic, Social and Cultural Rights, General Comment No. 20 on Non-Discrimination in Economic, Social and Cultural Rights, adopted on 22 May 2009.

[93] CESCR General Comment on Corruption and Human Rights: A Draft Proposal, para 7, available as Boersma 2012, annexure 2, p. 407. See also Rothstein and Varraich 2017.

[94] Peters 2015, p. 23.

[95] The UN Committee on Economic, Social and Cultural Rights, General Comment No. 20 on Non-Discrimination in Economic, Social and Cultural Rights, adopted on 22 May 2009, para 35.

pay a bribe is a criterion worthy of protection.[96] Other forms of corruption that are widespread in the health sector also have serious consequences for the enjoyment of the right to health on the basis of equality and non-discrimination.[97]

2.4.3.5 Accountability and Participation

Two additional principles should be considered when measuring a state's obligations in relation to the right of health—accountability and participation.[98]

First, the principle of accountability requires states to ensure that their duty-bearers are answerable for the observance of human rights and to have mechanisms in place to assist in the accountability of human rights abuses. Such mechanisms typically include courts, ombudsmen or public protectors and anti-corruption or human rights commissions, which can investigate cases of human rights abuses and corruption. In cases of institutional corruption, these mechanisms are unavailable or ineffective; the theory is that the state is then in violation of the principle of accountability.

Second, the principle of participation in relation to the right to health requires all states to ensure that relevant stakeholders, including non-state actors, should be consulted about health programmes.[99] Moreover, it is required that participation should go beyond consultation and include explicit strategies to empower citizens, especially the most marginalised, so that their expectations are recognised by the state.

Participation and accountability provide the necessary checks and balances, which prevent arbitrary and unilateral exercise power.

2.4.3.6 Indicators and Benchmarks

Human rights indicators are defined as 'specific information on the state of an event, activity or outcome related to human rights norms and standards which are used to assess and monitor the promotion and protection of human rights'.[100] They are normally expressed quantitatively in percentages and numbers. Once indicators have been identified, states are required to 'set appropriate national benchmarks in

---

[96] Peters 2015, p. 23.

[97] Report of the Special Rapporteur on the Right of Everyone to the Enjoyment of the Highest Attainable Standard of Physical and Mental Health (Report on Health), UN Doc. GA 72/137, 14 July 2017.

[98] See ICCPR, Article 25; American Convention on Human Rights, adopted on 22 November 1969, entry into force on 18 July 1978, Article 23(2); African Convention on Human and Peoples' Rights ('Banjul Charter'), 27 June 1981, entry into force on 21 October 1986, CAB/LEG/67/3 rev. 5, 21 I.L.M. 58, Article 13(1).

[99] Hallo De Wolf and Toebes 2016, p. 89.

[100] Bantekas and Oette 2013, p. 386.

relation to each indicator'.[101] Bantekas and Oette indicated that 'these benchmarks will vary from country to country on the basis of availability of resources and technical capacity and will serve to commit each country to the particular performance standard agreed'.[102] Tools and professional practices initially developed for the purposes of monitoring the implementation of civil and political rights have in some cases proved insufficient for monitoring the implementation of socio-economic rights.[103] Ilias Bantekas and Lutz Oette found that 'one of the shortcomings associated with the monitoring of states' obligations to respect, protect and fulfil human rights is the lack of verifiable quantitative criteria through which to measure with some degree of accuracy success and failure'.[104]

Socio-economic rights are difficult to measure because of the inherent and obvious limitations associated with the vague and ambiguous language of 'progressive realisation' and 'availability of resources' at the cornerstone of their implementation. Measuring socio-economic rights using tools originally designed for civil and political rights may be misleading. For example: 'on the eve of the Arab Spring, there were still reports about the remarkable economic and social progress and general improvements in governance and the rule of law that some countries in the region were achieving.'[105]

Socio-economic scholars and practitioners have been working hard to come up with customised tools. They turned to the use of indicators 'since they seemed to promise a way to monitor whether the State's conduct resulted in the fulfilment of individual and group rights'.[106] The former UN Special Rapporteur on the realisation of economic, social and cultural rights, Danilo Türk, mooted the idea of using indicators to measure socio-economic rights.[107] Similarly, the CESCR, concerned about the vagueness of the 'maximum available resources' clause, argues that states should adopt indicators for monitoring progress in their implementation of socio-economic rights.[108] The CESCR continues to use indicators and benchmarks for monitoring, to name and shame countries that perform poorly on these measures and to praise those that perform well, although 'their use has not been systematic'.[109] UN Special Rapporteur Paul Hunt has recommended systematically adopting indicators and benchmarks.[110]

[101] Rosga and Satterthwaie 2009, p. 277.

[102] Bantekas and Oette 2013, p. 388.

[103] See Rosga and Satterthwaie 2009, p. 263.

[104] Bantekas and Oette 2013, p. 386.

[105] OHCHR 2012.

[106] Rosga and Satterthwaie 2009, p. 266.

[107] United Nations Commission on Human Rights 1990.

[108] UN Committee on Economic, Social and Cultural Rights 1990, Article 2(1).

[109] OHCHR 2012, p. 2.

[110] Human Rights Council 2015a.

2.5 Towards a Framework

The traditional framework that has been used to assess the linkage between corruption and socio-economic rights proposes that one should start with the basic obligations under Article 2(1) of the ICESCR, supplemented by the tripartite typology and the principles of availability and accessibility.[111] The present work, however, takes a different approach: following Peters, it proposes a simple framework for analysing violations of socio-economic rights as a result of corruption.

Before setting out a framework for determining how corruption can be a violation of human rights, it is important to establish why such a framework is needed. The violation of the obligations and principles discussed immediately above will only be a violation of the obligations, but does not necessarily prove a violation of the rights.

This study acknowledges that there is no easy solution to the problem of how to frame the violation of human rights as a result of corruption. The framework set out below leaves open a grey area where a reasonable person may disagree about what constitutes a violation and what corresponding steps a government must take. But hopefully it clarifies that, in some cases, it is fairly simple to show whether a government is violating socio-economic rights due to corruption.

In the previous sections, reference was made to the research done by Peters on the link between corruption and human rights. The next section will borrow heavily from this work. Peters' seminal article not only helps us to understand the linkages between corruption and human rights but may also guide us towards a framework categorising these linkages.

2.5.1 *Step One: Analyse the Situation*

Corruption is a violation of human rights under very specific condition: that is to say, only in extreme conditions where corruption is rampant and systemic does it amount to a human rights violation. These are conditions where there is no effective remedy to address corruption, even when it is obvious or detected, and human rights provision is poor. Where there is an egregious human rights record and perceived (or actual) high levels of corruption.

It is also important to note that there should be a crime of corruption under domestic laws and that the state should be a member state to anti-corruption instruments. Many reports seem to suggest that only grand corruption can lead to a violation of human rights or be linked to transitional justice.

[111] International Council on Human Rights Policy and Transparency International 2009, p. 45.

2.5.2 *Step Two: Identify the Human Rights Obligations Being Violated*

It is necessary to look carefully at the obligations placed on the state by the normative content of the human right in question. This should be followed by an analysis of how an act or omission of corruption violates the obligations and principles discussed above. Taking into account that human rights are interconnected and indivisible, the precise human rights that are being violated must be identified.

2.5.3 *Step Three: Determine the Causal Link*

One practical impediment to determining how corruption can lead to a human rights violation is the difficulty of showing the causal link between either an omission by the state or acts of corruption by individual public officials. Courts confronted with the question of whether corruption is a violation of human rights have insisted on a 'clear linkage between the acts of corruption and a denial of the right' without explaining how this can be established.[112]

The determination of legal causation is based on the principles of the law of state responsibility regarding violations of human rights.[113] As Peters has shown, state practice depends on the causal link between the legal breach and the damage in human rights violations.[114] It has been argued that causation either as a *conditio sine qua non* or 'necessity', or in terms of a '"but for" test' must be supplemented by an element of legal contemplation which cuts off chains of causation that are excessively long.[115]

There must be 'proximity' between the legal breach and the damage. To determine 'proximity', scholars and practitioners use the objective criterion of 'natural and normal consequence'[116] and the subjective criterion of 'foreseeability'.[117] Similar criteria are used in the case of corruption, these criteria are used to determine the causal link between a corrupt state action and the legal breach—for the acts (or omissions) of corruption to cause human rights violations in the legal sense, the violation must be foreseeable and not too far removed from the corrupt public officials or omission of the state.[118]

---

[112] *SERAC v. Nigeria* ECW/CCJ/APP/12/07; ECW/CCJ/JUD/07/10.
[113] International Law Commission 2001, Articles 33(2) and 55.
[114] Peters 2015, p. 19.
[115] Peters 2015, p. 20.
[116] Peters 2015, p. 20.
[117] Peters 2015, p. 20.
[118] Peters 2015, p. 20.

However, in some situations the human rights violation has several causes, only one of which is corruption, and has only been brought about by all the various causes in combination ('cumulative causation'). This is a case of 'concurrent', 'dual', 'competing' or 'alternative' causality. In this situation, if any of the factors, taken by themselves, would have sufficed to bring about the effect, then none of them was a 'necessary condition', because the violation would have occurred anyway. However, causality in the legal sense should nevertheless be affirmed based on the principle of 'competing' or 'concurring'.[119] The fact that there were other causes in addition to corruption does not mean that corruption may not be considered to be the legal cause of a human rights violation.[120]

This leads us to the conclusion that when their use has become systematic, human rights indicators can be a useful tool for measuring omissions by states to meet their human rights obligations. Statistical correlation of corruption indicators and human rights non-compliance indicators could plausibly be used to show a violation of human rights through the omission of anti-corruption efforts by the state, similarly to how statistical evidence is commonly used to show indirect discrimination.

2.5.4 Step Four: Attribution

The final step is to resolve the question of attribution—or, to put it another way, to determine who is responsible for the corruption that has led to the human rights violation. According to the ILC Articles on State Responsibility, the conduct of any state organ is attributable to the state itself.[121] This is unproblematic in regard to the omissions discussed above, which violate obligations of prevention and protection under human rights law. Such omissions are committed by the legislative, executive and judicial organs of the state that fail to fulfil the obligations addressed directly to them.

By contrast, cases of individual acts by public officials, especially in the area of petty corruption, are difficult to attribute to the state as a whole such that they trigger state responsibility for the resulting human rights violations. It is clear that corrupt public officials are acting *ultra vires* their formal authority. Under the norms of state responsibility, however, *ultra vires* acts are in principle also attributable to the state.[122] The condition is that an organ of the state or a person empowered to

---

119 Peters 2015, p. 20.
120 Peters 2015, p. 20.
121 Article 4.
122 Peters 2015, p. 21.

exercise governmental authority is acting 'in that capacity'.[123] According to the ILC commentary, what matters is whether the corrupt person was purportedly acting in an official capacity and with 'apparent authority'.[124]

2.6 Conclusion

This chapter has illustrated the strong links between corruption and the violation of socio-economic rights. Different theories help us to understand the underlying linkages between the anti-corruption and human rights fields. For transitional justice practitioners and commentators, the framework of the TI and ICHRP serves as the starting point for engaging with corruption within the transitional justice agenda.[125] It cannot be emphasised enough that not all cases of corruption lead to violations of human rights, and it is only in specific situations where corruption is the grievance that warrants the attention of transitional justice. Both advocacy and practice are needed for corruption to be dealt with through the transitional justice mechanisms and processes. As simple as the idea may be, the route to engaging with the subject of corruption within the field of transitional justice is sometimes convoluted and winding. However, as more countries have ventured into this previously uncharted territory of economic justice, it has led to an innovative approach to mapping the way forward. The link between corruption and transitional justice has been extended beyond the margins of the traditional link with human rights violations to include the promotion of a bottom-up approach and the establishment of long-lasting peace.[126]

References

Albin-Lackey C (2014) Corruption, Human Rights and Activism: Useful Connections and their Limits. In: Sharp D (ed) Justice and Economic Violence in Transition. Springer, New York, pp. 139–163

Arbour L (2007) Economic and Social Justice for Societies in Transition. International Law and Politics 40: 1–27

Bacio-Terracino J (2008) Corruption as a Violation of Human Rights. International Council on Human Rights Policy. Available at http://ssrn.com/abstract=1107918

Bantekas I and Oette L (2013) International Human Rights Law and Practice. Cambridge University Press, New York

Benjamin J (2012) Corruption: Violation of Human Rights. In: Vishwanathan VN (ed) Corruption and Human Rights. Allied Publisher, New Delhi, pp. 23–32

---

[123] International Law Commission 2001, Article 7.

[124] Peters 2015, p. 21.

[125] International Council on Human Rights Policy and Transparency International 2009 and 2010.

[126] See Robinson 2015, pp. 1–19.

Boersma M (2012) Corruption: A Violation of Human Rights and a Crime Under International Law. Intersentia, Cambridge

Carmona MS and Bacio-Terracino J (2010) Corruption and Human Rights: Making the Connection. In Boersma M and Nelen H (eds) Corruption and Human Rights: Interdisciplinary Perspectives. Intersentia, Antwerp, pp. 25–50

Carranza R (2008) Plunder and Pain: Should Transitional Justice Engage with Corruption and Economic Crimes? International Journal of Transitional Justice 2: 310–330

De Beco G (2011) Monitoring Corruption from a Human Rights Perspective. International Journal of Human Rights 15: 1107–1124

De Schutter O (2013) Economic, Social and Cultural Rights as Human Rights: An Introduction. CRIDHO Working Paper 2013/2. Available at https://cridho.uclouvain.be/documents/Working.Papers/CRIDHO-WP2013-2-ODeSchutterESCRights.pdf

Economic and Social Council (1990) The New International Economic Order and the Promotion of Human Rights. E/CN.4/Sub.2/1990/19

Gathii JT (2010) Defining the Relationship Between Human Rights and Corruption. University of Pennsylvania Journal of International Law 31: 125–202

Gee J and Button M (2014) European Healthcare Fraud & Corruption Network. Financial Cost of Healthcare Fraud Report. University of Portsmouth-Centre for Counter Fraud Studies. Available at http://www2.port.ac.uk/media/contacts-and-departments/icjs/ccfs/The-Financial-Cost-of-Healthcare-Fraud-Report-2015.pdf

Global Organization for Parliamentarians Against Corruption (2013) GOPAC Declares Grand Corruption a Crime Against Humanity. Available at http://www.gopacnetwork.org/Docs/NewsReleases/2013/NR_FoPDeclaration_Nov28103_EN.pdf Last accessed on 23 June 2019

Gready P and Robin S (2014) From Transitional Justice to Transformative Justice: A New Agenda for Practice. International Journal of Transitional Justice 8: 339–361

Gready P et al (2010) Transformative Justice: A Concept Note. Transformative Justice Workshop. Centre for Applied Human Rights, University of York

Hallo de Wolf A and Toebes B (2016) Assessing Private Sector Involvement in Health Care and Universal Health Coverage in Light of the Right to Health. Health and Human Rights 18: 79–92

Hecht LK and Michalowski S (2012) The Economic and Social Dimensions of Transitional Justice. Available at http://www.essex.ac.uk/tjn/documents/TheeconomicandsocialdimensionsofTJ.pdf

Human Rights Council (2015a) Final report of the Human Rights Council Advisory Committee on the issue of the negative impact of corruption on the enjoyment of human rights. A/HRC/28/73

Human Rights Council (2015b) The negative impact of corruption on the enjoyment of human rights Resolution adopted by the Human Rights Council on 2 July 2015 A.HCR.RES.29.11

Human Rights Council (2015c) Report of the Special Rapporteur on the right of everyone to the enjoyment of the highest attainable standard of physical and mental health A.72.137. Human Rights Council resolutions 6/29 and 24/6

International Council on Human Rights Policy and Transparency International (2009) Corruption and Human Rights: Making the Connection. International Council on Human Rights Policy, Geneva

International Council on Human Rights Policy and Transparency International (2010) Integrating Human Rights into the Anti-Corruption Agenda: Challenges, Possibilities and Opportunities. International Council on Human Rights Policy, Versoix

International Law Commission (2001) Responsibility of States for Internationally Wrongful Acts Resolution 56/83 of 12 December 2001. Available at http://legal.un.org/ilc/texts/instruments/english/draft_articles/9_6_2001.pdf Last accessed on 23 June 2019

Koechlin L and Carmona M (2009) Corruption and Human Rights: Exploring the Connection. In: Rotberg RI (ed) Corruption, Global Security, and World Order. Brookings Institution, Washington DC, pp. 310–340

Kofele-Kale N (2000) The Right to a Corruption-Free Society as an Individual and Collective Human Right: Elevating Official Corruption to a Crime under International Law. The International Lawyer 34: 149–178

Marauhn T (2004) Social Rights Beyond the Traditional Welfare State: International Instruments and the Concept of Individual Entitlements. In: Benvenisti E and Nolte G (eds), The Welfare State Globalization and International Law. Springer Verlag, Berlin, Heidelberg, pp. 275–319

Murray M and Spalding A (2015) Freedom from Official Corruption as a Human Right. Governance Studies at Brookings, Washington DC

Muvingi I (2009) Sitting on Powder Kegs: Socioeconomic Rights in Transitional Societies. International Journal of Transitional Justice 3: 163–182.

Nawaz F and Chêne M (2009) Gender, Corruption and Health. U4 Helpdesk, Transparency International. Available at http://www.u4.no/publications/gender-corruption-and-health/

OHCHR (2008) The Human Rights Case Against Corruption. Available at https://www.ohchr.org/Documents/Issues/Development/GoodGovernance/Corruption/HRCaseAgainstCorruption.pdf Last accessed on 23 June 2019

OHCHR (2012) Human Rights Indicators: A Guide to Measurement and Implementation. United Nations, New York and Geneva

Peters A (2015) Corruption and Human Rights. Basel Institute on Governance, Working Paper Series 20. Available at http://www.mpil.de/files/pdf4/Peters_Corruption_and_Human_Rights 20151.pdf

Petkov M (2016) Diagnosing Corruption in Healthcare. Transparency International, London

Rajagopal B (1999) Corruption, Legitimacy and Human Rights: The Dialectic of the Relationship. Connecticut Journal of International Law 14: 1–19

Robinson I (2015) Truth Commissions and Corruption: Towards a Complementary Framework. International Journal of Transitional Justice 9: 33–50

Rose-Sender K and Godwin M (2010) Linking Anticorruption and Human Rights: A Dangerous Addition to the Development Discourse. In: Boersma M and Nelen H (eds) Corruption and Human Rights: Interdisciplinary Perspectives. Intersentia, Antwerp, pp. 221–239

Rosga A and Satterthwaie ML (2009) The Trust in Indicators: Measuring Human Rights. Berkeley Journal of International Law 27: 253–315

Rothstein B and Varraich A (2017) Making Sense of Corruption. Cambridge University Press, New York

Saul B et al (2014) The International Covenant on Economic, Social and Cultural Rights: Commentary, Cases, and Materials. Oxford University Press, Oxford

Savedoff W and Hussmann K (2006) Why are Health Systems so Prone to Corruption? In: Transparency International (ed) Global Corruption Report, Special Focus – Corruption and Health. Pluto Press, London, pp. 4–16

Schmid E and Nolan A (2014) Do No Harm? Exploring the Scope of Economic and Social Rights. International Transitional Justice Journal 8: 362–382

Shue H (1996) Basic Rights: Subsistence, Affluence and US Foreign Policy 2nd edn. Princeton University Press, Princeton

Spalding A (2014) Corruption, Corporations, and the New Human Right. Washington University Law Review 91: 1365–1428

Türk D (1990) The New International Economic Order and the Promotion of Human Rights, Realization of Economic, Social and Cultural Rights, Progress Report, U.N. Doc. E/CN.4/Sub.2/1990/19

United Nations Commission on Human Rights (1990) Realization of economic, social and cultural rights: Progress Report prepared by Danilo Türk, Special Rapporteur. E/CN.4/Sub.2/1990/19

Van Boven Th et al (eds) (2008) The Maastricht Guidelines on Violations of Economic, Social and Cultural Rights. SIM Special No. 20. Netherlands Institute of Human Rights

Chapter 3
The Phenomenon of Corruption and Socio-economic Rights in Zimbabwe

Contents

Abstract No previous study has investigated the role of corruption in human rights violations in Zimbabwe. This chapter will give an account of corruption and human rights challenges in Zimbabwe and examines laws and practices in relation to both crimes of corruption and human rights violations. Finally, it discusses a specific case which illustrates the interrelatedness of major corruption scandals and the violation of socio-cconomic rights in Zimbabwe.

Keywords Corruption typologies · socio-economic rights · Corruption · Perceptions Index · politicisation · cronyism · prebendalism · rent seeking · patrimonialism

P. Maguchu, *Transitional Justice and Socio-Economic Rights in Zimbabwe*, International Criminal Justice Series 24,
https://doi.org/10.1007/978-94-6265-323-8_3

3.1 Introduction

Corruption is a global phenomenon. However, actual and perceived levels of corruption differ between states.[1] In the worst cases, corruption has spiralled out of control, leading to a vicious circle in which the state has been 'captured' and is unable to free itself.[2] This is the situation in Zimbabwe, which has been hit especially hard by the scourge of corruption. Corruption in Zimbabwe is augmented by its presence at all levels of government, from the point of decision-making to the point of implementation. Not surprisingly, therefore, corruption has in some circumstances led to the violation of human rights.

This chapter will give an overview of corruption in Zimbabwe, focusing mainly on cases of grand corruption. It will critically analyse the legal, policy and judicial frameworks that have been employed in Zimbabwe over the years to address corruption and uphold socio-economic rights. Finally, it will explore how some high-profile cases of corruption have led to socio-economic rights abuses that should be investigated as part of the broader transitional justice accountability processes.

3.2 Corruption

3.2.1 Typology

In order to analyse corruption trends, we need first to understand that 'classifications and typologies can provide useful points of departure and much-needed orientation in a field that seems prone to get grounded in juicy stories and anecdotes'.[3] At this stage, it is therefore important to distinguish different types of corruption. According to José Vargas-Hernández, 'corruption is just as multifaceted concept [*sic*] as there are societies and economic and political systems that embraces from the broad concept of corruption to the narrow legal concept of bribery'.[4]

Vargas-Hernández identifies three major types of corruption: political corruption, economic corruption and corruption in public administration.[5] He also critically examines the popular characterisation that differentiates between subcategories of business corruption and individual/political corruption.[6] He claims

---

1 De Maria 2008, pp. 777–797.

2 Hellman and Kaufman 2001.

3 Anders and Nuijten 2009, p. 26.

4 Vargas-Hernández 2009.

5 Vargas-Hernández 2009.

6 Vargas-Hernández 2009.

that the magnitude of corruption varies from grand to petty,[7] while the depth of corruption varies from being perpetrated by an individual to systemic corruption.[8]

3.2.1.1 Sporadic Versus Systemic Corruption

Sporadic corruption refers to acts of corruption which occur irregularly and do not pose a threat to the mechanisms of governance or the economy as such. However, it can still undermine morale and deny the economy much-needed resources. Systemic corruption, on the other hand, is an integrated part of the economic, social and political system of a country. In a state experiencing systemic corruption, all institutions and processes are characteristically dominated and used by corrupt individuals and groups, and most people are left with no alternatives to dealing with corrupt officials.

In Zimbabwe, corruption started as sporadic. However, because of impunity it has grown to become more systemic.[9] It started off with a few cases that were immediately condemned and investigated, though no sanctions were taken against perpetrators. It is perhaps because of this impunity that corruption went from being sporadic to becoming systemic and embedded in the socio-political domain. Consequently, Zimbabwe is said to have joined the ranks of the many other countries that have entrenched corruption, such as Nigeria and Kenya.

It is interesting to note that both of these contemporary examples of highly corrupt countries have established truth commissions to address systemic corruption in the government as a violation of rights. This is covered in Chap. 6, which offers a comparative analysis. When analysing the link between corruption and human rights, the classification 'systemic corruption' serves no purpose, since an isolated case of corruption may also lead to human rights violations if all the conditions are met. However, when dealing with transitional justice, it is practical to address systemic rights abuses rather than isolated incidents.

3.2.1.2 Petty Versus Grand Corruption

The UNCAC preamble states that grand corruption is 'about cases of corruption that involve vast quantities of assets, which may constitute a substantial proportion of the resources of States, and that threaten the political stability and sustainable development of those States'.[10] In the literature, the term 'grand corruption' is used to describe acts of corruption which pervade the highest levels of government,

[7] Vargas-Hernández 2009.

[8] Vargas-Hernández 2009.

[9] Yamamoto 2014.

[10] UNCAC, preamble.

engendering major abuses of power.[11] Grand corruption is also referred to as 'state capture', which is where 'external interests illegally distort the highest levels of a political system to private ends'.[12]

Petty or administrative corruption, on the other hand, involves the exchange of very small amounts of money and the granting of small favours.[13] These acts of corruption may still cause considerable public losses. The essential difference between grand and petty corruption is that the former involves the distortion of central functions of government by senior public officials whereas the latter develops within the context of functioning governance and social frameworks.[14]

An important aspect of the transitional justice and anti-corruption discourse is that the literature tends to focus on grand corruption. Most academics and practitioners suggest that only systemic and grand corruption should be included in transitional justice frameworks. For instance, Isabel Robinson argues that 'at the level of grand corruption, embezzlement diverts resources away from the provision of state services, undermining a state's ability to respect, protect and fulfil human rights'.[15] Michael Johnston recommends institutional reform to address systemic corruption in transitional states.[16]

As far as petty corruption is concerned, one may assume that because of its nature it can be left out of the transitional justice matrix. However, the present book acknowledges that petty corruption affects a lot of people, and its effect on human rights should not be overlooked. Whereas grand corruption impacts a country by taking large sums of money away from the public purse, petty corruption has a direct impact on individuals, especially the poor and marginalised, by contrast with the bigger corruption cases which create scandals and grab the headlines.[17]

Furthermore, the issue of discrimination, including the indirect institutional discrimination that occurs as a consequence of petty corruption, inevitably touches on the connection between corruption and some fundamental human rights. My findings reveal that petty corruption can lead to discrimination against people with poor economic or social status, which in turn may lead to a violation of the principles of equality and non-discrimination, the fundamental principles of human rights affirmed in all the main human rights treaties.[18]

---

[11] Rose-Ackerman 2002.

[12] Pesic 2007.

[13] COSP 2015, p. 2.

[14] UN 2004.

[15] Robinson 2015, p. 3.

[16] Johnston 1998, pp. 85–104.

[17] Jackson and Köbis 2018.

[18] Adžanela 2012, p. 8.

3.2.1.3 Public Corruption Versus Private Corruption

Public corruption relates to the function of the person carrying out corruption. It can also be called abuse of function. According to the UNCAC,

> Each State Party shall consider adopting such legislative and other measures as may be necessary to establish as a criminal offence, when committed intentionally, the abuse of functions or position, that is, the performance of or failure to perform an act, in violation of laws, by a public official in the discharge of his or her functions, for the purpose of obtaining an undue advantage for himself or herself or for another person or entity.[19]

Under Zimbabwe's penal law, public corruption is recognised as the offence of criminal abuse of public office.[20]

Public corruption is linked to the concept of transitional justice because of the direct involvement of the state and its impact on democracy and the rule of law,[21] things that transitional justice aims to restore. However, it is also worth noting that 'the decisive role of the state is also reflected in most definitions of corruption'.[22] Suffice it to say that 'almost every definition (or rather conceptualisation) of corruption has a principal focus on the state and politics ("the corrupted"), and a "demand-oriented" perspective'.[23] In her thoroughly researched book, Martine Boersma also states that 'corruption, especially in the public sector, can have a severe negative impact upon both civil and political rights, as well as upon economic, social and cultural rights'.[24] The next section will give an overview of corruption in Zimbabwe.

3.2.2 *Legislative Framework*

This section identifies and analyses the main legal framework and institutions that have a bearing on anti-corruption efforts, focusing mainly on identifying the legal and institutional weaknesses that need to be addressed. The aim is not to denigrate these efforts but to identify areas that need remedying through transitional justice mechanisms. As observed in a Freedom House report, 'a comprehensive and complimentary [*sic*] strategy between TJ and anti-corruption fields is needed to address civil and political rights violations and socio-economic injustices to improve a transitional country's chances to achieve accountability, truth, repair,

---

[19] UNCAC, Article 19.

[20] Criminal Codification and Reform Act Criminal Law (Codification and Reform) Act 23, 2004 s174.

[21] See in general Warren 2004, pp. 328–343.

[22] Amundsen 1999, p. 7.

[23] Amundsen 1999, p. 7.

[24] Boersma 2012.

reconciliation and non-repetition'.[25] Hence, the observations made at this juncture will form part of the final recommendations, in the subsequent chapters, concerning what Zimbabwe should do to address past corruption linked to socio-economic rights violations.

3.2.2.1 International Legislation

Zimbabwe has ratified five international and regional instruments: UNCAC (ratified 8 March 2007); United Nations Convention against Transnational Organized Crime (ratified 12 December 2007); United Nations Convention against Illicit Traffic in Narcotic Drugs and Psychotropic Substances (acceded 20 July 1993); African Union Convention on Preventing and Combating Corruption (ratified 17 December 2006); and Southern African Development Community (SADC) Protocol against Corruption (ratified 8 October 2004).

3.2.2.2 Primary Domestic Legislation

Constitution

In terms of domestic legislation, Zimbabwe has passed the following legal enactments to address corruption: Prevention of Corruption Act 1983, Serious Offences (Confiscation of Profits) Act 1990, Public Service Act 1995, Procurement Act 2001, Anti-Corruption Commission Act 2004, Criminal Law (Codification and Reform) Act 2004, Bank Use Promotion and Suppression of Money Laundering Act 2004, Criminal Procedure and Evidence Amendment Act 2004, Public Finance Management Act 2010 and Money Laundering and Proceeds of Crime Act 2013.

In spite of having a broad spectrum of laws, fighting corruption in Zimbabwe has been fraught with many challenges. At the domestic level: the legal environment is not conducive and there is a general belief that there is selective application of the law, targeting political opponents. Some of the legislation also requires amendment to keep up to date with changes in forms of corruption. There is also a lack of harmonisation within the anti-corruption legislation.

Regarding international treaties, there is no full domestication of the UNCAC and some violations are not criminalised in Zimbabwe.[26] One suggestion would be to criminalise illicit enrichment, which would make it easier to fight political corruption in the situation the country is facing.[27] Moreover, assuming that it is fully implemented, the international legal regime to combat corruption is still evolving,

[25] Pesek 2014, p. 1.

[26] COSP 2017.

[27] See Muzila et al. 2002.

and thus Zimbabwe cannot be expected to curb corruption using international and regional instruments that are still relatively new.[28]

3.2.2.3 Subsidiary Domestic Legislation

a. Commissions of Inquiry Act

The government of Zimbabwe has a special 'weapon of choice' to fight corruption, namely the ad hoc commissions of inquiry established by the Commissions of Inquiry Act.[29] Fighting corruption is not the primary aim of commissions of inquiry; however, the law allows the president to appoint an independent investigation on any matter of public interest. The law in question reads:

> The President may, when he considers it advisable, by proclamation, appoint a commission of inquiry consisting of one or more commissioners and may authorize the commissioner or commissioners or any quorum of them specified in the proclamation to inquire into the conduct of any officer in the Public Service, the conduct of any chief [...] the conduct or management of any department of the Public Service or of any public or local institution, or into any matter in which any inquiry would, in the opinion of the President, be for the public welfare.[30]

Commissions of inquiry have been used in other parts of the world to investigate corruption.[31]

Since independence, Zimbabwe has appointed commissions of inquiry into major corruption scandals, such as the Sandura Commission of Inquiry into the Mazda Willowvale scandal in 1988 and the War Veteran Compensation Commission of Inquiry into the scandal of war victims' compensation money in 1997. At the time of writing, there is a commission investigating corrupt land deals in the public administration of Bulawayo, the largest city in Zimbabwe. Commissions have not been entirely successful in their mission; however, every time there is a scandal many Zimbabweans call for commissions of inquiry. In reality, commissions of inquiry into corruption in Zimbabwe have only enabled the government to prove its governance credentials, especially at a time when it was being discredited for its reluctance to fight corruption.[32]

The question is whether commissions of inquiry are effective at combating and monitoring corruption. J. S. H. Gildenhuys argues that the findings of a commission are, unlike a court judgment, not binding and are based on a balance of probability,

---

[28] See Carranza 2008, p. 310.

[29] Commissions of Inquiry Act 1991.

[30] Commissions of Inquiry Act 1991, Section 2(1).

[31] For example, the Fitzgerald Inquiry into corruption in Scotland, the Turks and Caicos Islands Commission of Inquiry 2008–2009, the commission of inquiry into allegations of fraud, corruption, impropriety and irregularity in the Strategic Defence Procurement Packages (SDPP) in South Africa.

[32] See Kirya 2011.

and if a criminal prosecution takes place the facts will have to be proved all over again. However, commissions help to bring to the fore information which regular police methods are incapable of proving.[33] They need to be efficiently conducted and their findings must be acted on. Generally, the effectiveness of a commission of inquiry depends on how the state president responds to the report. Commissions are a double-edged sword; they can be used to 'find solutions for problems, or for postponing problems the government does not want to tackle, which would be a deed of corruption in itself'.[34]

b. National Code of Ethics and Governance

It is now globally acknowledged that a lack of integrity and a lack of ethics can result in corruption. The African Union Convention on Preventing and Combating Corruption urges member states to 'create an internal committee or a similar body mandated to establish a code of conduct and to monitor its implementation, and sensitize and train public officials on matters of ethics'.[35] The SADC Protocol against Corruption similarly calls for 'standards of conduct for the correct, honourable and proper fulfilment of public functions as well as mechanisms to enforce those standards'.[36] The UNCAC also stresses the importance of having codes of ethics as an essential element in corruption prevention.[37]

Recently, Zimbabwe adopted a national code of ethics, which provides the framework for corporate conduct in both the public and private sector.[38] When the document was published, then vice president of Zimbabwe Emmerson Mnangagwa, explained the background to how the code was developed:

> Several years ago the economy witnessed moral bankruptcy, unethical behaviour and absence of executive accountability experienced by some organisations. The result of all this was business failure and the eventual collapse of a number of corporations resulting in significant economic and social costs to the country as a significant number of people lost their jobs. Rampant corruption designed to cripple the economy and diminish the condition of livelihood of the Zimbabwean people was experienced. Harsh economic difficulties brought about immense suffering to a vast number of Zimbabwean families.[39]

Thus, one of the key aims of the code is to address the issue of corruption in the public and private sectors. The national code is still relatively new and its effect in fighting corruption remains to be seen.

---

[33] Gildenhuys 2004, p. 200.

[34] Gildenhuys 2004, p. 200.

[35] African Union Convention on Preventing and Combating Corruption, Article 7(2).

[36] SADC Protocol against Corruption, Article 4(1)(a).

[37] UNCAC, Article 8.

[38] The most notable such codes include the Cadbury Committee Report (UK, 1992), the King Committee Reports (SA, 1994, 2002 and 2009), the UK Combined Codes (2002 and 2006), the OECD Principles of Corporate Governance (1999, 2003), the CACG Principles of Corporate Governance in the Commonwealth (1999) and the Corporate and Auditing Accountability and Responsibility Act 2002 (USA).

[39] The Herald 2015.

3.2.3 *Policy Framework*

3.2.3.1 Ministry of State Enterprises, Anti-Corruption and Anti-Monopolies

This ministry was created in 2005 in the wake of a new election under the terms of the old constitution of Zimbabwe and the Anti-Corruption Commission Act.[40] Its agenda was set out as follows:

> The government of Zimbabwe has demonstrated its resolve and political will to effectively combat corruption through the creation of the ministry of State Enterprises, Anti-Corruption & Anti-Monopolies. The Ministry is dedicated to fight corruption through systems of integrity that ensure transparency and fairness both in the private and public sectors.[41]

The timing of the ministry's founding was seen as a government strategy to win votes by making people believe it was finally doing something about corruption. It was alleged that those running the ministry were using it to protect their interests and not to ensure accountability. The ministry made no significant results and, as a result, was abolished in 2010 with the implementation of the transitional government.

3.2.3.2 Zimbabwe Anti-Corruption Commission

The Zimbabwe Anti-Corruption Commission (ZACC) was created under the old constitution and the Anti-Corruption Act of 2004 at the same time as the Anti-Corruption Ministry. The constitution gave the ZACC the mandate to combat corruption through public education, prevention and punishment/prosecution of offenders after thorough investigation.[42] However, it should not be mistaken for a body with prosecutorial powers, as it still relies on the police and prosecutor general for investigations and case prosecutions. In line with its constitutional mandate, ZACC comprises a secretariat with three operating arms: Corruption Prevention and Corporate Governance; Investigation and Prosecution; Publicity and Education.

ZACC commissioners are handpicked from the circle of loyalists of the ruling party, excluding other parties and civil society. According to analysts, the commission is highly inefficient and 'has very little authority to take steps aimed at stopping corruption in Zimbabwe'.[43] For instance, out of 147 corruption cases reviewed by the ZACC in 2006, only four were completed.[44] During the Mugabe

[40] Zimbabwe Anti-Corruption Commission Act 2004.

[41] Ministry of State Enterprises, Anti-Corruption and Anti-Monopolies (website no longer available).

[42] Constitution of Zimbabwe Amendment (20) Act 2013, s256.

[43] Global Integrity 2012.

[44] Global Integrity 2012.

administration, the ZACC did not successfully deal with any serious cases of corruption involving senior politicians. It was accused of being a partisan organisation and filled with sympathisers of the ruling party. It lacks independence from political interference. In five years, it only submitted a single report to parliament, which moreover contained scant information. As a result of the inefficiency, the ZACC became a point of discussion in the transition talks. Following the formation of the Government of National Unity (GNU) in September 2009, the ZACC was relaunched in August 2011 as part of the new government's socio-economic development plan.

Paradoxically, the new ZACC is itself not immune to corruption. One of its senior officers was jailed in 2015 over allegations of embezzling around US $480,000 from the embattled organisation, which he then proceeded to use for the purchase of personal property.[45] This was after he had also registered the property of the ZACC under the name of a shell company that he and his subordinates owned.[46] According to the auditor-general's report, the ZACC also has other irregularities.[47] It continues to use a headquarters registered in the name of individuals, and has no work contracts or proper bookkeeping system to account for finances. Between 2013 and 2016, the ZACC again spent three years without commissioners. It was sued in the courts for failing to successfully carry out its work.[48]

3.2.3.3 Auditor-General

The auditor-general's primary role in Zimbabwe is to curb abuse of government revenues by public departments. The auditor-general also has a role in fighting corruption derived from Section 7 of the Audit Office Act.[49] This provision authorises the auditor-general to ensure that:

(a) All reasonable precautions have been taken to safeguard the collection of public moneys and that all provisions of the regulations, directions and instructions have been followed;
(b) All payments of public moneys have been made with proper authority, is [*sic*] properly charged and is supported with appropriate proof;

[45] Chitemba 2016.

[46] *S v. Gumbo*, ZLR judgment of 2013 citation not available.

[47] Auditor-General's Report.

[48] *Kereke v. Zimbabwe Anti-Corruption Commission and Others* (citation not available). A former advisor of the Reserve Bank of Zimbabwe, Munyaradzi Kereke, sued the Zimbabwe Anti-Corruption Commission, arguing that the commission was acting unconstitutionally by failing to investigate allegations of abuse of office, corruption and theft against the former Reserve Bank of Zimbabwe governor Gideon Gono.

[49] Audit Office Act 12 2009.

(c) All appropriation expenditure incurred has been applied for the intended purposes and that it is in conformity with the proper authority;
(d) That reasonable precautions have been taken to safeguard and control state property.

Therefore, the auditor-general can be regarded as one of the mechanisms for fighting financial corruption in government departments.

The office of the auditor-general is using its narrow mandate to fight corruption in an unprecedented way. It has revealed some gross mismanagement in government transactions in its annual reports. The audit reports from the past five years have exposed damning corruption in government ministries and state enterprises. However, their recommendations have never been followed up with investigations or prosecutions. There is a lack of coordination between anti-corruption agencies, such as the ZACC and the Prosecution Authority, to follow up on investigations.

Though the auditor-general is showing some prudence in tackling serious corruption, there are deep institutional and legal irregularities in the office.[50] The constitution and enabling legislation do not give the office authority to compel ministries, departments and other public bodies to comply with the Treasury's instructions.[51] Moreover, the appointment procedures, termination procedures, tenure of office, financial autonomy and ability retain staff have a negative impact on the independence of the auditor-general.[52] Additionally, the system of producing reports leaves much to be desired, with some reports delayed for years owing to financial and human resources and budgetary constraints—allowing corruption to flourish in the meantime.[53]

3.2.3.4 The Public Protector (Ombudsman)

The Zimbabwean ombudsman featured in the statute books of the Zimbabwe–Rhodesia constitution but was never implemented. The office was reinstated in the 1979 Lancaster House constitution, but it was not until the 1982 Ombudsman Act that it was actually implemented in practice. It was a transitional mechanism from the oppressive Rhodesian state, as the minister of justice remarked in the House of Assembly during the presentation of the bill:

> this country has never had an ombudsman before, as in the colonial days people had to 'suffer in silence' when aggrieved by the often heavy handed actions of government officials. It is the present government's policy that the Public Service should be the servant and not the master of the people, and it is in accordance with this policy that I am pleased to present this Bill to Parliament.[54]

[50] Zinyama 2013, pp. 267–282.
[51] The Constitution of Zimbabwe Amendment (20) Act 2013, s256.
[52] The Constitution of Zimbabwe Amendment (20) Act 2013, s256.
[53] Zinyama 2013, pp. 267–282.
[54] Zimbabwe Parliament Debates, 17 June 1982, col. 59, quoted in Hatchard 1986, pp. 267.

In 2007, the name of the office was changed from ombudsman to public protector; however, the role remained the same: to investigate any complaints from members of the public against government departments and statutory corporations.[55]

The office of ombudsman has a peculiar advantage when it comes to curbing corruption, especially where it is related to human rights violations, because it can operate with a broader definition of 'corruption' that is not restricted by criminal law. The ombudsman's competence to investigate goes much further than merely investigating complaints that could be classified as criminal acts. There is a large grey area between criminal behaviour and acceptable behaviour, and that is where the ombudsman can play a role, by investigating behaviour in this grey area and recommending corrective action or procedures.[56] For example, they could investigate matters that fall into the frequently grey and ill-defined area of ethics, where a law may not have been transgressed but where the community's sense of right and wrong is offended.[57] Because of this characteristic, the institution is able to operate as an early warning system, with the responsibility to monitor, inter alia, deviations from the standards of ethical conduct that fall short of the narrow definition of criminal corruption.[58]

Surprisingly, the defunct office of ombudsman never played a significant role in curbing corruption in Zimbabwe.[59] Most of the ombudsmen in Zimbabwe were political appointments, with a vested interest in not investigating their party colleagues. The office did not respond to cases with urgency and as a result had a huge backlog, taking an unnecessarily long time to action cases.[60] Furthermore, it was not publicised and only a few potential complainants knew of its existence. In principle, it was supposed to issue publicly available reports; in reality, it took five years to publish a single annual report.

Another practical constraint was that the ombudsman was barred from investigating government departments such as the office and personal staff of the president, the Cabinet Office, judicial officers, the attorney-general, the secretary to the ministry and the government's legal advisors.[61] This was anti-progressive in a country where political corruption is a major challenge among senior politicians and government officials.

The new constitution has abolished the office of the public protector, and transferred all of its functions to the Zimbabwe Human Rights Commission (ZHRC).[62] The main argument for the abolition was that in other countries, such as

---

[55] Sixth Schedule, para 16. Amendment 18 of 2007 to the constitution.

[56] Pienaar 2000, p. 4.

[57] Pienaar 2000, p. 4.

[58] Pienaar 2000, p. 4.

[59] SOAS 1997, p. 247.

[60] Phiri 2006.

[61] Phiri 2006.

[62] Chiduza 2015, p. 19.

Namibia and Ghana, the offices of the ombudsman and the human rights commission perform similar functions. The ZHRC does not currently address corruption, but has only focused on human rights. Further research should be carried out to investigate whether the ZHRC can or should address cases of corruption.

3.2.4 Judicial Framework

3.2.4.1 Ordinary Courts

Although corruption is prosecuted in ordinary criminal courts, a special courtroom and a few selected judicial officers and prosecutors have dealt with corruption cases in Zimbabwe as a matter of practice. The results have been far from satisfactory; some cases may be complicated for the prosecutors and the presiding officers.

3.2.4.2 Specialised Economic Crimes Courts

Since 2008, Zimbabwe has had legislation providing for the establishment of specialised economic crimes courts (SECCs). However, these courts never saw the light of day during Mugabe's presidency. Following the military intervention, the new administration has accelerated efforts to establish economic crimes courts in all provinces in order to speed up trials for corruption cases, which has culminated in SECCs finally being created.

The SECCs are essentially a division of the magistrates' courts, which have original jurisdiction to hear cases involving economic crimes such as corruption but do not have any separate rules of procedure. The courts are presided over by a handful of selected magistrates, and prosecutors have received specialised training on handling complicated corruption cases.

3.2.5 Compliance and Ranking

Zimbabwe is regarded as one of the most corrupt countries not just in Sub-Saharan Africa but in the world. In TI's Corruption Perceptions Index (CPI), Zimbabwe is ranked 156th out of 176 countries, with a score of just 20 out of 100.[63] The CPI measures perceptions of corruption in the public sectors of states around the globe.[64] After Zimbabwe was first included in the index in 1998, it went into freefall, with corruption perceived to be on the increase: a reflection of the evidence

[63] Transparency International 2017.

[64] Transparency International 2017.

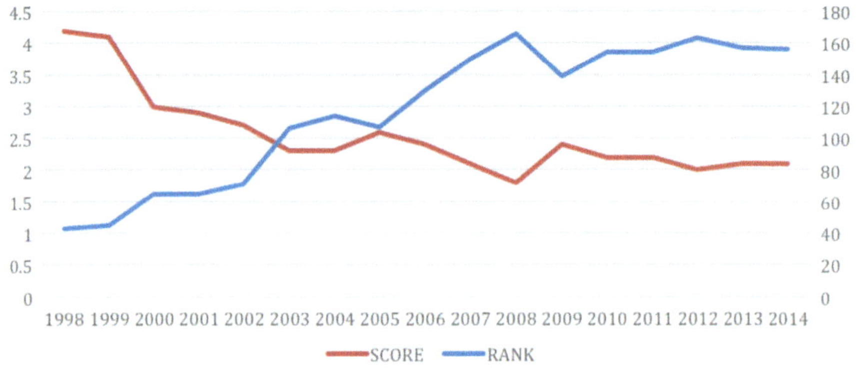

Fig. 3.1 Zimbabwe Corruption Perceptions: International Ranking [*Source* Transparency International]

on the ground. Its lowest ranking was in 2008, when it came 166th. Unsurprisingly, this coincides with the escalating human rights crisis in 2008. This serves to illustrate the inter-relationship between corruption and human rights violations in the country. Further evidence of this relationship was found by Human Rights Watch (HRW), which specifically draws attention to the role of corruption in the violation of socio-economic rights in the country, such as the rights to water, sanitation, education and health.[65] The graph below shows the CPI index of Zimbabwe over a period of seventeen years (see Fig. 3.1).

To understand this worrying fact, it is necessary to trace the origins and causes of corruption in the country. According to Stephen Moyo, the current status of corruption in Zimbabwe cannot be understood without looking at the historical context.[66] More significantly, the postcolonial period, which witnessed a new independent state with a constitution, ushered in an era where a powerful economic elite wielded enormous power to control political and economic matters[67] The state's autocratic behaviour ensured a stranglehold on state-controlled enterprises, with the aim of furthering the ruling party's policies and ideologies, and turning the enterprises into organs for patronage and clientelism.[68] 'This allowed the state to become more oppressive, tyrannical and devoid of transparency, and accountability as corruption manifested itself in every state institution and the private sector.'[69]

TI came to similar findings in an unpublished 2003 National Integrity System (NIS) report, where it attributes grand corruption in Zimbabwe to the political

[65] Human Rights Watch 2017, p. 631.

[66] Moyo 2014, p. 311.

[67] Moyo 2014, p. 311.

[68] Moyo 2014, p. 311.

[69] Moyo 2014, p. 311.

concentration of power through a 1987 constitutional amendment.[70] This is also clearly supported by empirical evidence which shows that before the amendment 'the State enjoyed a relatively high level of integrity', with 'the few incidences of grand corruption' coming from politicians, who received condemnation from the highest authorities.[71] The prevalence of corruption in Zimbabwe has increased over the last decade. It is no coincidence that this was the same period in which human rights were worsening. Thus, corruption cannot be separated from the sum total of transitional justice in Zimbabwe.

3.3 Socio-economic Rights

3.3.1 Typology

Zimbabwe guarantees all three categories of human rights to its citizens. With regards to socio-economic rights, its constitution expressly provides for access to food, water, housing, healthcare, education and social security (albeit only for selected categories of citizens), recognising them as enforceable individual entitlements.

3.3.2 Legislative Framework

3.3.2.1 International Legislation

The constitution of Zimbabwe respects international human rights treaties when they have been domesticated.[72] Additionally, customary international law may be adopted by Zimbabwe if it is consistent with the constitution.[73] Although Zimbabwe is considered a dualist system in terms of the application of international

[70] The 2003 NIS report on Zimbabwe (by a necessarily anonymous author, who sensibly left the country before finishing it) is rich in detail, names and events. As a result, T.I has been reluctant to release it on the grounds that it is journalistic, lurid and potentially libellous.

[71] Shana 2006.

[72] Section 327(2) states that 'an international treaty which has been concluded or executed by the President or under the President's authority—

(a) does not bind Zimbabwe until it has been approved by Parliament; and

(b) does not form part of the law of Zimbabwe unless it has been incorporated into the law through an Act of Parliament'.

[73] Section 326 of the Constitution stipulates that 'customary international law is part of the law of Zimbabwe, unless it is inconsistent with this Constitution or an Act of Parliament. When interpreting legislation, every court and tribunal must adopt any reasonable interpretation of the legislation that is consistent with customary international law applicable in Zimbabwe, in preference to an alternative interpretation inconsistent with that law'.

law, it exhibits some monist qualities by requiring its judiciary to keep abreast of and apply international law.[74]

Zimbabwe is a party to several core international instruments on socio-economic rights, namely the UDHR,[75] the International Covenant on Economic, Social and Cultural Rights (ICESCR)[76] and the African Charter on Human and Peoples' Rights (ACHPR).[77] Zimbabwe is also party to a number of individual treaties that recognise individual socio-economic rights.[78]

3.3.2.2 Domestic Primary Legislation

Constitution

As mentioned above, the constitution of Zimbabwe guarantees the right to education;[79] healthcare services;[80] sufficient food and safe, clean and potable water;[81] a healthy environment;[82] and social security for women,[83] children,[84] the elderly,[85] people with disabilities[86] and veterans of the liberation struggle.[87]

Furthermore, the Zimbabwean constitution provides for the horizontal application of the Bill of Rights where applicable. The provision in question states that 'the

---

[74] Section 165(7) of the constitution stipulates that 'members of the judiciary must take reasonable steps to maintain and enhance their professional knowledge, skills and personal qualities, and in particular must keep themselves abreast of developments in domestic and international law'.

[75] Universal Declaration of Human Rights, adopted on 10 December 1948, G.A. Res. 217A(III), UN Doc. A/180 at 71 (1948).

[76] International Covenant on Economic, Social and Cultural Rights, adopted on 16 December 1966, entry into force on 3 January 1976, acceded to by Zimbabwe on 13 August 1991, G.A. Res. 2200A(XXI), 21 UN GAOR Supp. (No. 16) at 49, UN Doc. A/6316 (1966), 993 U.N.T.S. 3.

[77] African [Banjul] Charter on Human and Peoples' Rights, adopted on 27 June 1981, entry into force on 21 October 1986, ratified by Zimbabwe on 30 May 1986, OAU Doc. CAB/LEG/67/3 rev. 5, 21 I.L.M. 58 (1982).

[78] Zimbabwe itself is a party to the ICESCR, ICCPR and ACHPR, as well as the Convention on the Elimination of All Forms of Discrimination against Women (acceded 12 June 1991), the Convention on the Rights of the Child (acceded 11 October 1990), the International Convention on the Elimination of Racial Discrimination (acceded 12 June 1991), the African Charter on the Rights and Welfare of the Child (ratified 19 January 1995) and the Protocol to the African Charter on Human and Peoples' Rights on the Rights of Women in Africa (ratified 5 September 2008).

[79] Constitution of Zimbabwe Amendment (No. 20) Act, 2013, s. 75.

[80] Constitution of Zimbabwe Amendment (No. 20) Act, 2013, s. 76.

[81] Constitution of Zimbabwe Amendment (No. 20) Act, 2013, s. 77.

[82] Constitution of Zimbabwe Amendment (No. 20) Act, 2013, s. 73.

[83] Constitution of Zimbabwe Amendment (No. 20) Act, 2013, s. 80.

[84] Constitution of Zimbabwe Amendment (No. 20) Act, 2013, s. 81.

[85] Constitution of Zimbabwe Amendment (No. 20) Act, 2013, s. 82.

[86] Constitution of Zimbabwe Amendment (No. 20) Act, 2013, s. 83.

[87] Constitution of Zimbabwe Amendment (No. 20) Act, 2013, s. 84.

State and every person, including juristic persons, and every institution and agency of the government at every level must respect, protect, promote and fulfil the rights and freedoms set out in this Chapter'.[88] Moreover, this provision 'binds natural and juristic persons to the extent that it is applicable to them, taking into account the nature of the right or freedom concerned and any duty imposed by it'.[89] Thus, Zimbabwe allows individuals to sue other private parties for violations of socio-economic rights.

Administration of Justice Act

In Zimbabwe, administrative law is governed by the Administrative Justice Act.[90] Administrative law can also be used to protect human rights entitlements since it constrains the exercise of public power in areas of public policy, focusing on the fairness of procedures and the effectiveness of remedies. In his seminal book on administrative law in Zimbabwe, Geoffrey Feltoe writes that 'administrative Law is the law relating to the administration of the State. Administration of the State is the detailed and practical implementation of the policies of the central government aimed at the running of the State'.[91] Feltoe notes that one of the primary functions of administrative law is to 'exert reasonable legal control over the way in which administrative authorities exercise their functions in order to ensure that these authorities do not exceed or abuse their powers'.[92]

3.3.3 *Policy Framework*

3.3.3.1 Zimbabwe Human Rights Commission

The ZHRC has a mandate to 'promote the development of human rights and freedoms' and 'to monitor and assess the observance of human rights in Zimbabwe'.[93] Additionally, the ZACC has taken over the former office of the ombudsman, which in theory gives it enormous powers to investigate human rights violations, including corruption cases against civil servants which may be linked to human rights violations.

---

[88] Constitution of Zimbabwe Amendment (No. 20) Act, 2013, ss. 44 and 45.

[89] Constitution of Zimbabwe Amendment (No. 20) Act, 2013, s. 45.

[90] Act 12, 2004.

[91] Feltoe 2012, p. 2.

[92] Feltoe 2012, p. 2.

[93] Constitution of Zimbabwe Amendment (No. 20) Act, 2013, s. 243 1 b and c respectively.

3.3.3.2 Other Independent Commissions and Authorities

Several other independent commissions are constitutionally mandated to focus on specific rights, such as the Gender Commission (which focuses on gender rights), the Land Commission (which focuses on the right to land), the Zimbabwe National Social Security Authority (which focuses on the right to social security) and the National Peace and Reconciliation Commission (NPRC) (which focuses on past human rights abuses). I will discuss how the NPRC can be ideal for addressing corruption-related abuses in detail in the next chapter, which looks at transitional justice mechanisms.

3.3.4 Judicial Framework

3.3.4.1 Ordinary Courts

The constitutional court hears cases arising from the Bill of Rights, and adjudicates any constitutional applications.[94] As stated above, the constitution of Zimbabwe allows courts to use international law when interpreting socio-economic rights. The constitution also allows Zimbabwean judges to review foreign law when considering rights protections. The former chief justice of Zimbabwe Anthony Gubbay once remarked that

> whether ratified or not, all these international and regional instruments embody human rights norms which are broadly accepted by the entire international community. They should and must be incorporated into domestic jurisprudence by judicial interpretation.[95]

3.3.4.2 Administrative Courts

An administrative court specialises in administrative law issues such as disputes concerning the exercise of public authority, and determines whether or not officials have acted within the confines of the law. In Zimbabwe, administrative courts are established in terms of the constitution.[96] They have jurisdiction over specific administrative matters as conferred to them by statute, but generally act as a court of appeal for a wide range of administrative tribunals.

Moreover, the Administrative Court Act and the constitution make it clear which court a defendant should appear before when faced with a human rights violation: for vertical applications, the constitutional court; for horizontal applications by a public official, the administrative court.

---

[94] Constitution of Zimbabwe Amendment (No. 20) Act, 2013, s. 167 1 b.

[95] Gubbay 1997, p. 233.

[96] Constitution of Zimbabwe Amendment (No. 20) Act, 2013, s. 173.

Contrary to expectations, human rights lawyers have not yet taken it upon themselves to launch more human rights cases in the administrative courts to force the state to publicly accept responsibility for other abuses carried out by its agents. A recent judgment made it clear that the administrative court has jurisdiction over human rights matters and a legal mandate to advance the protection of these rights: 'The concept of administrative justice is now embedded in our Constitution. It provides the skeletal infrastructure within which official power of all sorts affecting individuals must be exercised.'[97] This is a positive development.

3.3.5 *Compliance and Ranking*

In contrast to measurements of corruption, which rank countries according to compliance, the human rights field avoids the use of rankings, which in some cases may be viewed as confrontational. For instance, *Human Rights Indicators: A Guide to Measurement and Implementation* does not rank countries according to their human rights performance. However, international and local civil society organisations have identified Zimbabwe's compliance with human rights as very poor. This poor human rights record is documented by various human rights indices, such as the Cato Institute's Human Freedom Index, which measures a broad range of personal, civil and economic rights when Zimbabwe was ranked 146th out of 159 countries.

The question, therefore, is what this says about the recent development of incorporating socio-economic rights into the Bill of Rights. With the aid of empirical studies it is possible to obtain a true picture of current and future trends in respect for socio-economic rights in Zimbabwe. Empirical legal theorists have found evidence to support the view that some regimes only make constitutional amendments to bills of rights for the sake of cosmetic appearances.[98] The Bill of Rights does not have any effect on the enjoyment of rights and might even be followed by worse human rights violations (a decoupling effect).[99]

3.4 Corruption and Socio-economic Rights Violations: The Cholera Outbreak

In 2008, Zimbabwe experienced a cholera epidemic, which resulted in 98,585 reported cases of illness and 4,287 reported deaths.[100] The epidemic attracted investigations from various human rights groups. Most of these investigations

[97] *Telecel Zimbabwe (Private) Limited v. Postal and Telecommunications Regulatory Authority of Zimbabwe and Others*, HH/446/15.

[98] Keith 2010, p. 370.

[99] Howard 1991; Epp 1998. Cited in Keith 2010, p. 370.

[100] Human Rights Watch 2013.

revealed that corruption was at the centre of the outbreak, and could immediately and for the purposes of human rights be identified as a violation of the right to health. Below, I examine findings by major human rights organisations on the precise role corruption played in the outbreak.

The aim of this section is to show that some cases of corruption, both grand and petty, may constitute human rights violations as defined in law. Although this may seem to stretch the definition of human rights law, this can provide the roadmap for transitional justice to engage with corruption. No case has yet been brought before Zimbabwean courts to test whether provisions from anti-corruption law can be used in defence of human rights. However, Zimbabwe has numerous cases that touch on corruption and human rights violations, such as the National Railways housing scandal (1986), the war victims compensation scandal (1994), the GMB grain scandal (1995), the VIP housing scandal (1996), the Boka banking scandal (1998), the Harare city council refuse tender scandal (1998), the housing loan scandal (1999), the GMB scandal (1999) and the pillaging of the central bank which has left many Zimbabweans without their life savings. These are some of the numerous cases that could be included in transitional justice anti-corruption efforts.

So far, however, there has been little discussion about the scandals referred to above and their effects on the enjoyment of human rights, particularly socio-economic rights. However, few writers have been able to draw on systematic research into corruption and human rights using the 2008 cholera outbreak.[101] The situation may change as the amount of scholarly work that draws links between corruption law and human rights law increases; lawyers and prosecutors will certainly test particular theories of human rights. In the following sections, I present hypothetical scenarios to illustrate how corruption leads to human rights violations, using the framework for the right to health developed in Chap. 2.

3.4.1 Hypothesis One: Politicisation

3.4.1.1 Facts

A US-based NGO that uses medicine and science to document violations of human rights, Physicians for Human Rights (PHR), investigated the country's health infrastructure for possible connections between the cholera outbreak and corruption. Its investigations revealed that the cholera epidemic was exacerbated by a series of human rights abuses, including the politicisation of water, healthcare, aid and information. PHR revealed that ZANU-PF's loss at the municipal elections in 2005 led party officials in the government to refuse to fund municipal budgets for cities where it had been defeated. These retaliatory cuts led to water purification being suspended, eventually resulting in raw human sewage being redirected into

[101] Youde 2010, pp. 687–704; Ncayiyana 2009, p. 7; Ahmed et al. 2011, pp. 541–546.

the main reservoirs. According to PHR, the politicisation of public health, in an effort to punish supporters of an opposition party, directly contributed to the spread of the cholera bacteria.[102]

3.4.1.2 Law

The UN Committee on ESCR specifies that the minimum core obligations of the right to health include duties to ensure the right of access to health facilities, goods and services on a non-discriminatory basis, and to ensure equitable distribution of all health facilities, goods and services.[103] These duties are violated by the government's refusal to fund municipal budgets from the central government budget as a way of punishing those perceived as opposition party supporters.

States have an internationally recognised duty to fulfil socio-economic human rights obligations by providing necessary resources: in this case, providing monetary resources to enable the provision of clean water, which the Zimbabwean government neglected to do.[104] Another case in which this duty was recognised is *Free Legal Aid Assistance Group and Others v. Zaire*, where the African Commission on Human and Peoples' Rights (ACmHPR) ruled that the failure of the government to provide basic services such as safe drinking water, electricity and medicine constituted a violation of the right to enjoy the best state of physical and mental health (Article 16).[105]

3.4.2 Hypothesis Two: Cronyism

3.4.2.1 Facts

An alternative explanation for the cholera and corruption linkages in Zimbabwe was given by Chris Beyrer, a professor of epidemiology at the Johns Hopkins Bloomberg School of Public Health. Beyrer investigated the healthcare system in Zimbabwe on behalf of PHR.[106] He argues that the reasons for the epidemic and its high mortality rate stem from the corruption of former president Robert Mugabe's administration, which enriched itself at the public's expense.[107] For political reasons, the government handed over public water supply contracts to cronies who did

---

[102] Price-Smith 2009.
[103] UN Committee on ESCR, The Right to the Highest Attainable Standard of Health, para 43.
[104] UNCESCR, Article 2(1).
[105] *Free Legal Assistance Group and Others v. Zaire*, Comm. No. 25/89, 47/90, 56/91, 100/93.
[106] Beyrer 2002.
[107] Beyrer 2002.

not have the capacity to purify water, and as a result untreated sewage flowed into reservoirs of drinking water.[108]

3.4.2.2 Law

In terms of international human rights law, embezzlement in this case meant fewer resources to clean and purify water. This point is illustrated by a joint communication submitted by four NGOs against Zaire (now: the DRC). The claimants alleged that grave and massive violations of human rights occurred as a result of gross mismanagement of public finances by the government, leading to degrading conditions, including shortages of basic services, education and medicine, which the government had failed to provide. The ACmHPR ruled that the DRC's 'failure to provide basic services such as safe drinking water and electricity and the shortage of medicine' constituted a violation of the right to health.[109] Importantly, although not explicitly, the ACmHPR seems to have shown its willingness to address mismanagement of resources by a country by considering the state's failure to provide basic necessities *in casu* as serious, massive human rights violations.

Furthermore, the awarding of contracts to cronies resulted in poor service provision, such as improper disposal of untreated sewage that flowed into drinking water reservoirs (a violation in its own right). The OHCHR cites the contamination of water as a quintessential socio-economic rights violation.[110]

3.4.3 Hypothesis Three: Prebendalism

3.4.3.1 Facts

Similarly, HRW has observed numerous corrupt activities in the water sector, which severely hamper efforts to improve water and sewage service delivery.[111] For instance, budget guidelines for city councils stipulate that only 30 percent of the budget is to be spent on salaries; the rest is to be allocated to capital development, such as improvements to the water delivery system.[112] Investigations by HRW showed that funds were poorly accounted for and unlawfully allocated to paying the salaries and benefits of city council members.[113] Likewise, investigations into city of Harare salaries by a local NGO revealed that senior employees were reportedly

---

[108] Beyrer 2002.

[109] *Free Legal Assistance Group and Others v. Zaire*, Comm. No. 25/89, 47/90, 56/91, 100/93.

[110] Office of the United Nations High Commissioner for Human Rights Fact Sheet 33.

[111] Human Rights Watch 2013.

[112] Human Rights Watch 2013, p. 5.

[113] Human Rights Watch 2013, p. 5.

earning up to US$21,000 in monthly salaries and allowances for vehicles, housing, mobile phones and attending workshops, alongside other grotesque fringe benefits.

3.4.3.2 Law

In terms of international human rights law, there is a breach of the human rights principle of allocating all available resources to services; the city council was spending available resources on luxuries at the expense of service delivery. As a result, residents experienced a cut in water supply, as the Zimbabwe National Water Authority (ZINWA) had stopped pumping water from its main treatment plant due to a lack of funds to purchase chemicals it had been using to treat the water.

In the inter-state communication concerning *Democratic Republic of Congo v. Burundi, Rwanda and Uganda*, the ACmHPR stated that:

> the looting, killing, mass and indiscriminate transfers of civilian population, the besiege and damage of the hydro-dam, stopping of essential services in the hospital, leading to deaths of patients and the general disruption of life and state of war that took place while the forces of the Respondent States were occupying and in control of the eastern provinces of the complainant State are in violation of article 16 of the African Charter, which provide for the right to health.[114]

3.4.4 *Hypothesis Four: Rent Seeking*

3.4.4.1 Facts

HRW investigations also revealed another dynamic between corruption and the cholera outbreak. It was found that water was the main source of revenue for the city council and was used for rent seeking. Consequently, weeks after parliamentary elections in which the MDC won significantly in urban areas, ZANU-PF issued a national directive to overturn the 1976 Water Act and bring municipal water authorities across the country under the ZINWA, a government body that it controlled. The ostensible reason for this was to relieve Zimbabweans' 'persistent water woes'. Instead, the ZINWA raised water rates for residents while simultaneously neglecting infrastructure and diverting revenue to military and security forces. This led to widespread service disruptions, discontent among residents and the spread of water-borne diseases, particularly in and around Harare.

Moreover, the decision to usurp municipal authority over water, which had been under the control of the MDC in many areas of opposition support, provided the cash-strapped ZANU-PF regime with a major new stream of revenue, since residents were in some instances charged as much as US$3,000 per month, which they

[114] *Democratic Republic of Congo v. Burundi, Rwanda, Uganda*, 227/99, para 88.

were unable to pay, resulting in disconnections from the public water supply.[115] Most residents with municipal debts and disconnected water resorted to the use of water from unprotected water sources, which in turn led to the cholera outbreak.

3.4.4.2 Law

Exorbitant water bills impeded accessibility, making water very expensive and resulting in residents resorting to the use of unpurified water. The problem was compounded by the suspension of refuse collections and other unhygienic conditions. The government failed to protect residents from local councils unfairly increasing water rates and imposing restrictions on those who could not pay. Clean water became expensive and inaccessible for the majority of Zimbabweans.

Moreover, according to General Comment No. 15 on the right to water,

> The right to water contains both freedoms and entitlements. The freedoms include the right to maintain access to existing water supplies necessary for the right to water, and the right to be free from interference, such as the right to be free from arbitrary disconnections or contamination of water supplies. By contrast, the entitlements include the right to a system of water supply and management that provides equality of opportunity for people to enjoy the right to water.[116]

Thus, according to the OHCHR, arbitrary and illegal disconnection of water for personal or domestic use is considered a violation of the right to water.[117]

However, unlike with the first, second and third hypotheses, where acts of corruption that are punishable under Zimbabwean law were identified, in the present case it is difficult to ascribe corruption as a factor in the violation of the right to water and therefore as the main cause of the cholera outbreak, because the relevant acts (such as rent seeking) are not classified as corruption in Zimbabwe.

3.4.5 Hypothesis Five: Patrimonialism

3.4.5.1 Facts

HRW also noted that service delivery in general and the right to water in particular were used as a tool to buy votes. For instance, a week before the national elections, the minister responsible for water purification announced that all debts that residents owed municipal authorities in urban areas throughout the country would be cancelled.[118] While cancelling the debts provided relief for residents who were

[115] Human Rights Watch 2013, p. 5.

[116] General Comment No. 15, para 10.

[117] Office of the United Nations High Commissioner for Human Rights Fact Sheet 33.

[118] Human Rights Watch 2013, p. 5.

struggling to pay bills, this gesture also bankrupted the city council and Harare Water, the department of the council responsible for providing clean water to residents. Not only does cancelling debts affect past money owed, but it may also affect the willingness of people who have been paying consistently to continue to pay future bills.[119]

3.4.5.2 Law

In this case, the decision to cancel the water bills was purely driven by the intention to favour the political party of the officials concerned, which counts as abuse of public authority and is therefore an act of corruption. Although there is a clear link between the aforementioned act of corruption and the violations of human rights, in that what the corrupt act of debt cancellation and the resultant drop-off in willingness to pay bills (since residents now had reason to hope they might be cancelled in the future), there is no causal link; there is a break in the chain of events.

3.5 Conclusion

At the very least, Zimbabwe has missed out on billions of dollars due to corruption. This money could have been used to fund education, healthcare, water, job creation and other essential services. The days when large-scale corruption was treated as a mere violation of national criminal norms are largely consigned to history. The major scandals discussed above are clear examples of a close relationship between corruption and human rights abuses.

To be complete and effective, transitional justice in Zimbabwe must include a serious and thorough investigation that brings to light the actual sources of the violations of socio-economic rights in the form of corruption and identifies the perpetrators and the victims, so that the former can be punished and the damage done to the latter appropriately remedied. One international anti-corruption specialist, Alan Doig, has given a reasoned argument on the need to include corruption in transitional strategies that focus on establishing democracy in the post-Mugabe era:

> For the past twenty years, government ministers, civil servants and officials in law enforcement and state security, armed forces and the judiciary have increasingly been ZANU PF members, or personally appointed by Mugabe, or now own an expropriated farm (or in a significant number of instances at senior level, all three). Some have been involved in illicit, sometimes criminal conduct. Not only have many of them been largely responsible for the mess the country is in, but many have personally benefited from it. Unless donors

[119] Human Rights Watch 2013, p. 5.

demand complete change, they will be working with people with dirty hands, potentially in those institutions to whom donors will look to promote the rule of law, public integrity and the rights of the public.[120]

If Zimbabwe does not include corruption during the transitional phase it will risk falling into the same trap that other transitional states have entered. A trap where corrupt elements from the old regime find their way into the nascent democratic politics and hijack the new agenda, destabilising the goals of transitional justice.

References

Adžanela A (2012) Petty Corruption and Human Rights Implications –The Case of Bosnia and Herzegovina. Available at http://www.humiliationstudies.org/documents/AdzanelaPetty-CorruptionBosniaandHerzegovina.pdf

Ahmed S et al (2011) The 2008 cholera epidemic in Zimbabwe: Experience of the ICDDR, B Team in the Field. Journal of Health Population, and Nutrition 29: 541–546

Amundsen I (1999) Political Corruption: An Introduction to the Issues. Chr. Michelsen Institute Development Studies and Human Rights Working Paper 19991. Available at https://www.cmi.no/publications/file/1040-political-corruption.pdf

Anders G and Nuijten M (eds) (2009) Corruption and the Secret of Law: A Legal Anthropological Perspective. Ashgate, Aldershot

Beyrer C (2002) Zimbabwe Cholera Outbreak Has Roots in Corruption. Yale Medical Journal. Available at http://ymm.yale.edu/spring2009/dialogue/oncampus/52597#

Boersma M (2012) Corruption: A Violation of Human Rights and a Crime Under International Law? Intersentia, Cambridge

Carranza R (2008) Plunder and Pain: Should Transitional Justice Engage with Corruption and Economic Crimes? International Journal of Transitional Justice 2: 310–330

Chiduza L (2015) The Zimbabwe Human Rights Commission: Prospects and Challenges for the Protection of Human Rights. Law Democracy and Development. Available at http://www.scielo.org.za/scielo.php?script=sci_arttext&pid=S2077-49072015000100008

COSP (2015) Countering Grand Corruption. Available at https://www.unodc.org/documents/treaties/UNCAC/COSP/session6/V1507721e.pdf Last accessed on 23 June 2019

COSP (2017) State of Implementation of the United Nations Convention against Corruption: Criminalization, Law Enforcement and International Cooperation. Available at https://www.unodc.org/unodc/en/corruption/COSP/session7-documents.html Last accessed on 23 June 2019

de Maria W (2008) Measurements and Markets: Deconstructing the Corruption Perception Index. International Journal of Public Sector Management 21: 777–797

Doig A (2006) Dirty Hands and the Donors: Dealing with Corruption in a Post Mugabe Zimbabwe. Political Quarterly 77: 71–78

Epp CR (1998) The Rights Revolution Lawyers, Activists and Supreme Courts in Comparative Perspective. Chicago University Press, Chicago

Feltoe G (2012) A Guide to Administrative Law and Local Government Law in Zimbabwe. Legal Resources Foundation, Harare

Gildenhuys JSH (2004) Ethics and Professionalism: The Battle Against Public Corruption. Stellenbosch University Press, Stellenbosch

[120] Doig 2006, p. 71.

Gubbay AR (1997) The Protection and Enforcement of Fundamental Human Rights: The Zimbabwean Experience. Human Rights Quarterly 19: 227–254

Hatchard J (1986) The Institution of the Ombudsman in Africa with Special Reference to Zimbabwe. International and Comparative Law Quarterly 35: 255–270

Hellman J and Kaufmann D (2001) Confronting the Challenge of State Capture in Transition Economies. Finance and Development 38: 31–35

Howard AED (1991) The Essence of Constitutionalism. In: Thompson KW and Ludwikowski RT (eds) Constitutionalism and Human Rights in America, Poland, and France. Lanham, New York, pp. 3–41

Human Rights Watch (2013) Zimbabwe: Water and Sanitation Crisis - Government Mismanagement, Corruption Risks Lives of Millions. Available at https://www.hrw.org/news/2013/11/19/zimbabwe-water-and-sanitation-crisis Last accessed on 23 June 2019

Human Rights Watch (2017) World Report 2015. Available at https://www.hrw.org/world-report/2015/country-chapters/zimbabwe Last accessed on 23 June 2019

Jackson D and Köbis N (2018) Anti-corruption Through a Social Norms Lens, U4. U4 Anti-Corruption Resource Centre, Chr. Michelsen Institute. Available at https://www.u4.no/publications/anti-corruption-through-a-social-norms-lens Last accessed on 23 June 2019

Johnston M (1998) Fighting Systematic Corruption: Social Foundations for Institutional Reform. European Journal of Development Research 10: 85–104

Keith LC (2010) Human Rights Instruments. In: Cane P and Kritzer H (eds) The Oxford Handbook of Empirical Legal Research. Oxford University Press, New York, pp. 353–375

Kirya T (2011) Performing "Good Governance": Commissions of Inquiry and the Fight against Corruption in Uganda. (Unpublished PhD Thesis) University of Warwick

Moyo S (2014) Corruption in Zimbabwe: An Examination of the Roles of the State and Civil Society in Combating Corruption. (Unpublished PhD Thesis) University of Central Lancashire

Muzila L et al (2002) On the Take: Criminalizing Illicit Enrichment to Fight Corruption. Washington, DC: World Bank. Available at https://openknowledge.worldbank.org/handle/10986/13090

Ncayiyana DJ (2009) The Zimbabwe Mayhem—How Many People Must Die for the Neighbours to Act? South African Medical Journal 99:7

Pesek S (2014) Combating Impunity: Transitional Justice and Anti-Corruption. Freedom House, Washington DC

Pesic V (2007) State Capture and Widespread Corruption in Serbia. CEPS Working Document no. 262. Available at https://www.ceps.eu/publications/state-capture-and-widespread-corruption-serbia

Phiri G (2006) Ombudsman's Office a Shambles. Zimbabwe Independent. Available at https://www.theindependent.co.zw/2006/04/21/ombudsmans-office-a-shambles/ Last accessed on 23 June 2019

Pienaar G (2000) The Role of the Public Protector in Fighting Corruption. African Security Review 9: 52–66

Price-Smith A (2009) Cholera and the Collapse of Governance in Zimbabwe. Harvard International Review. Available at http://hir.harvard.edu/article/?a=1819

Robinson I (2015) Truth Commissions and Corruption: Towards a Complementary Framework. International Journal of Transitional Justice 9: 31–50

Rose-Ackerman S (2002) Grand Corruption and the Ethics of Global Business. Journal of Banking and Finance 26:1889–1918

Shana G (2006) The State of Corruption in Zimbabwe. Mass Public Opinion Institute Seminar, Harare

SOAS (1997) Expanding the Role of the Ombudsman in Zimbabwe. Journal of African Law 41: 247–247

Transparency International (2017) Corruption Perception Index 2016, released 25 January 2017, https://www.transparency.org/news/feature/corruption_perceptions_index_2016 Last accessed on 23 June 2019

UN (2004) The United Nations Anti-Corruption Toolkit, 3rd edn. Vienna, UNODC. Available at https://www.un.org/ruleoflaw/files/UN_Anti%20Corruption_Toolkit.pdf Last accessed on 23 June 2019

Vargas-Hernández J G (2009) The Multiple Faces of Corruption: Typology, Forms and levels. Available at https://papers.ssrn.com/sol3/papers.cfm?abstract_id=1413976

Warren ME (2004) What Does Corruption Mean in a Democracy? American Journal of Political Science 48: 328–343

Yamamoto K (2014) Mugabe Fighting Corruption Forget It. New Zimbabwean. Available at https://allafrica.com/stories/201404100145.html Last accessed on 23 June 2019

Youde J (2010) Don't Drink the Water: Politics and Cholera in Zimbabwe. International Journal 65: 687–704

Zinyama T (2013) Efficiency and Effectiveness in Public Sector Auditing: An Evaluation of the Comptroller and Auditor General's Performance in Zimbabwe from 1999 to 2012. International Journal of Humanities and Social Science 3: 267–282

Chapter 4
Revisiting Methods of Addressing Past Corruption and Human Rights Violations in Zimbabwe

Contents

Abstract Corruption is at the heart of understanding human rights violations in Zimbabwe. This chapter discusses and evaluates accountability mechanisms adopted over the past four decades, analysing their link to socio-economic rights and corruption. The surprising results uncovered in this chapter provide further support for the view that corruption needs to be investigated in transitional justice processes, and help us understand what needs to be done.

Keywords Unilateral declaration of independence · post-Mugabeism · Gukurahundi · anti-dissident

P. Maguchu, *Transitional Justice and Socio-Economic Rights in Zimbabwe*, International Criminal Justice Series 24, https://doi.org/10.1007/978-94-6265-323-8_4

4.1 Introduction

It is important to note that Zimbabwe has had multiple transitional mechanisms, resulting in uncertainty over where the country is now and where it is going. This chapter traces the history of accountability mechanisms for past human rights abuses/corruption scandals in Zimbabwe. The results show that some attempts have been made to address cases of corruption linked to various human rights abuses using accountability mechanisms.

The long history of gross human rights violations in Zimbabwe is well documented elsewhere. It suffices to say that the country has been intermittently engulfed by periods of violence at decisive political stages.[1] During these periods, gross civil and political rights violations were committed against the citizens. But it was not only these rights that were violated; socio-economic rights were violated too, largely as a result of massive corruption. The aim of this chapter is to shed new light on this well-trodden issue by examining how anti-corruption could have been investigated.

This chapter examines the history as far back as the colonial era, when the settlers' administration embarked on measures similar to the conventional components of transitional justice (amnesties, prosecutions and reparation policies), through to measures undertaken by the current government. It will highlight the government's mandate and the rights that were investigated to examine how issues of corruption were dealt with, and seek to establish why, in spite of having all these measures, the popular demands for transitional justice in Zimbabwe remain unfulfilled.

There is, however, a caveat, since the history of transitional justice in Zimbabwe is long and complex, especially if one is not limited by the conventional definitions of the concept. In order to avoid arbitrary starting points, the genealogy of transitional justice in this chapter will be structured in juxtaposition to the periods of human rights violations mentioned above. While these mechanisms appear independent from each other and are sometimes associated with different actors, from a historical perspective they are interconnected events that can illustrate the measures Zimbabwe has taken in reviewing its past.

4.2 First Phase: The Post UDI Period (1965–1979)

4.2.1 Background

The 1960s are regarded as the golden age of decolonisation. It was in this decade that British Prime Minister Harold Macmillan made his famous remark that a 'wind of change' was blowing through the African continent. 'Whether we like it or not',

[1] Other scholars have also noted these periods: see for instance Reeler 2009; Redress 2004 and Chikwanha 2009.

he continued, 'this growth of national consciousness is a political fact'.[2] In the case of Zimbabwe, new evidence shows that there still remains controversy about whether or not the British foreign secretary Rab Butler, who was in charge of decolonisation, promised the Rhodesian delegation independence under minority governance at the Victoria Falls conference of 1963.[3] The white minority party made a unilateral declaration of independence (UDI) on 11 November 1965, declaring Rhodesia independent from Britain.[4]

The UDI only brought independence to the white settlers, and intensified denial of basic human rights to the African Rhodesians, who continued to be disenfranchised: in particular, they were barred from owning land and active participation in politics. These restrictions were enforced through a racial segregation system similar to that in apartheid South Africa.[5] Shortly after the UDI was made, the two major African political parties, the Zimbabwe African National Union (ZANU) and the Zimbabwe African Peoples' Union (ZAPU), launched an armed struggle against the colonial government in the form of guerrilla warfare. They carried this out through their military wings, known respectively as the Zimbabwe African National Liberation Army (ZANLA) and the Zimbabwe People's Revolutionary Army (ZIPRA).[6]

African Rhodesians were the 'man in the middle', forced to endure severe human rights abuses amid the armed struggle, perpetrated by both the Rhodesian Security Forces (RSF) and the guerrillas. At the same time, the UN Security Council was forced to take a bold step: for the first time since its creation, it passed mandatory economic sanctions to put political pressure on a government.[7] Had they worked, the sanctions could have stopped the war and the human rights violations. However, they failed, largely due to corruption. An inquiry sponsored by the British government revealed that businesses and multinational corporations deliberately colluded to burst the sanctions.[8] There were also several scientific studies of the UN's Southern Rhodesia sanctions.[9]

The war was ended with the signing of the Lancaster House Agreement, which was facilitated by Britain under international pressure to end the armed struggle. Zimbabwe was granted independence in April 1980 after Robert Mugabe's ZANU party won the elections against ZAPU and other parties. During this armed conflict and its aftermath, a number of transitional justice mechanisms and processes were

[2] Butler and Stockwell 2013.

[3] Law 2017, p. 722.

[4] Ronen 2011, p. 28.

[5] Chikwanha 2009.

[6] Dzinesa 2006, p. 1.

[7] UN Security Council Resolution 1966.

[8] Bingham 1978.

[9] See for instance Bailey 1979, pp. 128–129; Galtung 1967, pp. 378–416; Curtin and Murray 1967; Curtin 1968, pp. 100–110; Sutcliffe 1969, pp. 113–125; Strack 1978; Losman 1979.

adopted, although they almost exclusively avoided addressing the issue of corruption that underpinned the struggle. Below, we shall examine a few mechanisms that were used to deal with corruption during this period.

4.2.2 *Accountability Mechanisms*

4.2.2.1 Bingham Commission of Inquiry

The British parliament ordered a probe into the corruption surrounding the supply of oil and petroleum products to Rhodesia in contravention of the UN sanctions, which were legally supported in the UK through the Southern Rhodesia Order.[10] A renowned lawyer, Thomas Bingham, was tasked with leading the investigations. The detailed report that was released to the public alleged that international companies were involved in corrupt activities that led to the breaking of the sanctions against Rhodesia.[11]

4.2.2.2 United Kingdom Government Amnesty for Corruption

Several amnesty laws were adopted during this period, though almost all of them were for civil and political rights violations. Zinaida Miller has argued that this practice in the field of transitional justice has its drawbacks, as it may 'implicitly tell society that development and conflict may be separated in a fair fashion and that inequality itself is not to be prosecuted or amnestied'.[12] Nonetheless, the UK parliament passed the Southern Rhodesia (Sanctions) (Amnesty) Order 1980[13] 'to make provision for an amnesty, covering criminal proceedings, for offences against those measures which provided for the imposition of economic sanctions or other sanctions against Rhodesia'.[14]

The debates that ensued during its reading illustrate the misconceptions of the status of socio-economic issues within transitional justice, particularly amnesties.[15]

---

[10] Southern Rhodesia (United Nations Sanctions) Order 1968 (S.I. 1968, No. 885), dated 7 June 1968, made by Her Majesty in Council under the Southern Rhodesia Act 1965.

[11] Bingham 1978.

[12] Miller 2008, p. 268.

[13] The Southern Rhodesia (Sanctions) (Amnesty) Order 1980, SI 1980/565.

[14] Richard Luce, undersecretary of state for foreign and Commonwealth affairs. Southern Rhodesia (Sanctions and Amnesty), HC Deb 7 May 1980, vol. 984, cc 429–59, 429.

[15] Hon. Peter Shore: 'An amnesty for this class of offence is very different from the amnesties that we have previously discussed and approved. An amnesty for British sanctions breakers does not serve any process of reconciliation inside Rhodesia or between Rhodesia and the United Kingdom. It simply allows those who have defied and cheated successive British Governments to get away with it.' HC Deb 7 May 1980, vol. 984, cc 429–59, 432.

Some of the comments that were made in favour of including economic sanctions in the amnesty discourse are worthy of note. It was acknowledged by some members of the UK parliament that the corrupt practices undertaken to break the sanctions caused untold suffering to the people in Zimbabwe:

> Had there been no conspiracy to break oil sanctions and a proper oil embargo, the war in Rhodesia would have ended a great deal sooner and many more people, black and white, men women and children, would be alive today. In different parts of Zimbabwe there are people maimed, without legs or arms, in wheelchairs, badly scarred by the marks of war. Had there not been this conspiracy, which the Government now condone, these people would be running about, free, happy and healthy in wind and limb.[16]

The house voted in favour of an amnesty for those economic crimes committed in Rhodesia, including corruption, that were linked to human suffering and a violation of rights. However, regrettably this was never repeated in Zimbabwe, and so there was simply a continuation of this narrow view in relation to amnesties for civil and political rights violations, as will be shown below.

4.2.3 Subsequent Developments

In 1978, the secretary of state for foreign and Commonwealth affairs referred the Bingham report to the director of public prosecutions (DPP) to consider whether further inquiries should be undertaken with a view to possible criminal proceedings for breaches of the Southern Rhodesia sanctions order. Shortly thereafter, leading and junior counsel were instructed by the director to advise him on whether, in the circumstances disclosed by the report, criminal offences appeared to have been committed and, if so, by whom. It should be appreciated that the Bingham inquiry was neither a police investigation nor a trial, and it was not, therefore, conducted within the constraints of the rules of evidence or procedure applicable in a court of law.

Against this background, the director realised that much more factual information and research into the legal problems was required in order to particularise offences, to identify the principal persons acting on behalf of the oil companies and to collect the admissible evidence. Accordingly, a team of senior police officers was instructed to make further detailed inquiries, while counsel continued to review the material already available. Steps were taken in April 1979 under schedule 1 to the 1968 sanctions order to require the oil companies to produce all the relevant documents in their possession or under their control. By the beginning of November 1979, in an opinion running to almost fifty pages, counsel advised the DPP of the great obstacles in the way of a successful prosecution. The director therefore concluded that further investigation and public expenditure would not be justified and that the matter should proceed no further.

---

[16] Robert Hughes, HC Deb 7 May 1980, vol. 984, cc 429–59, 438.

Whilst this mechanism did not go further than an amnesty, and did not actually formulate this amnesty in the language of transitional justice, it does substantiate the need to investigate cases of corruption linked to atrocities.

4.3 Second Phase: Anti-Dissident Period (1981–1988)

4.3.1 Background

Soon after the ceasefire agreement to end the war of liberation, armed guerrilla fighters were temporarily sheltered at assembly points (APs) awaiting demobilisation and integration into the national army.[17] Frustration boiled over when the demobilisation and integration process was slow to be implemented. This resulted in conflicts along ethnic and other lines sporadic outbreaks of violence emanating from the APs took place across the country.[18] Two notable incidents occurred in February 1981, when violence broke out in Entumbane, and July 1982, when former ZIPRA guerrillas fired shots at the prime minister's residence in Harare.[19] The fledgling state was quickly plunged into crisis as some former ZIPRA combatants engaged in further instances of sabotage and banditry in parts of the Midlands and Matabeleland regions.[20]

There was no consensus on how to deal with the insecurity. Some proposed a political conciliation. However, the government chose to react to the political problem with military force.[21] Government security forces trained in North Korea, the Fifth Brigade, were deployed to quell the insurgency. However, in Zimbabwe, as in many societies troubled by guerrilla movements, it was the civilians and not the insurgents who suffered most from the regime's counterinsurgency campaign.[22] It was only after the coercive military approach, lasting from 1982 to 1985, had sufficiently subdued the political opposition in Matabeleland that a more conciliatory approach was pursued, culminating in the 1987 Unity Accord.[23] This period is colloquially known as the Gukurahundi.

In addition to the dissident challenges and the killings, which nearly sparked a civil war and genocide, the country was suffering another battle with corruption. Corruption had hijacked the transition to democratic rule, with those in power using their influential positions to loot the state coffers. A few scandals occurred during this period, such as the Fokker jet scandal and the Willowgate scandal, which at the

---

[17] Lamb 2013, p. 15.

[18] See CCJP et al. 1997.

[19] Lamb 2013, p. 15.

[20] Research Directorate, Immigration and Refugee Board, 2002.

[21] Africa Contemporary Record, 1982, 886.

[22] Weitzer 1990, p. 167.

[23] Weitzer 1990, p. 167.

time was described as the biggest scandal Africa had ever seen, making this period particularly significant. Although the Unity Accord had brought some stability, corruption triggered a number of clashes between the government and workers' and students' unions, who started to demand accountability. The following sections will discuss accountability mechanisms that were adopted to address corruption during this period.

4.3.2 Accountability Mechanisms

4.3.2.1 The Sandura Commissions of Inquiry

President Mugabe set up two commissions of inquiry (the Sandura Commissions), which were headed by former judge president Wilson Sandura.[24] The first commission focused on the Mazda Willowvale motor plant. It took over seven weeks to record statements from seventy-two witnesses, including six government ministers, two deputy ministers, three members of parliament, two senior army officers and forty directors and managers of private companies, who were allegedly involved in the scandal. The commission was set up like a court and was attended by so many members of the public that they could not be accommodated in the courtroom and had to take turns. While the commission's report was successful in pointing out wrongdoing by senior officials, it contradicted itself since it also found mitigating circumstances; this may have been a deliberate ploy to ensure the accused were not brought to justice.

A second inquiry was commissioned with terms of reference similar to the first to investigate and report on allegations of corruption at two other manufacturers, namely W. Dahmer, Leyland Manufacturing Zimbabwe and Leyland Zimbabwe. The second report, unlike the first, was not released to the public until recently. A copy of it, aptly entitled 'Report of the second commission of inquiry into the distribution of motor vehicles', is now publicly available at the University of Zimbabwe, where it has been deposited in a library. The report is now largely useless as most of those named are dead, but it gives an insight into the extent of the corruption.

4.3.3 Subsequent Developments

There were a few cases that were referred for criminal prosecution after the inquiries. One such case is *State v. Shava.*[25] Fredrick Shava, a minister of state for political affairs in the president's office, was arrested, tried and convicted for his

[24] Commissions of Inquiry Act, 1991.

[25] *S v. Shava* 1989 (2) ZLR 107 (H).

role in corruption in the Willowvale motor scandal. The president quickly intervened and pardoned him, because of the role he had played in the struggle for independence, and he was released after spending barely a day in prison. He was then appointed as an ambassador for Zimbabwe in China, a job that he retains to this day. Many others implicated in this case still hold influential positions in the government of Zimbabwe.[26]

4.4 Third Phase: The Post-One-Party-State Period (1990–1995)

4.4.1 Background

The early 90s witnessed the fall of the Iron Curtain and the Berlin Wall, and also saw 'an apparent wave of democratization [sweep] across sub-Saharan Africa, generating dramatic changes in the political map of a continent that had been dominated by one-party authoritarian regimes since the 1970s and 1980s'.[27] Zimbabwe was no exception to this, and though the country had not been a *de jure* one-party state, the merging of the dominant political parties, ZANU and ZAPU, created a *de facto* one-party state.[28] In 1990, the majority of officials in the ZANU-PF politburo voted against the idea of creating a one-party state.

Equally important, Zimbabwe replaced most of the socialist policies it had adopted upon independence with more liberalised economic policies. Derek Matyszak describes this period as 'a watershed year for the Zimbabwean polity' that witnessed the removal of the state of emergency that had been renewed since the UDI and the ratification of the ICCPR.[29] These factors precipitated a false sense of the right to compete in the political governance of the country. Ironically, when other parties tried to participate they were met with ferocious political violence.

In addition to physical violence, corruption was also on the increase. In countries around the world, from Africa to Asia to Latin America, abandoning communism did not lead to economic prosperity but to unbridled opportunism and corruption. Zimbabwe did not prove to be an exception to this pattern. The country experienced large-scale corruption in the distribution of war reparations, grain and housing, and a financial system collapse that affected more victims than political repression. Corruption became commonplace and there was little or no incentive to address large-scale corruption even when it seemingly violated human rights. The only mechanism implemented to address cases of corruption from this period is discussed below.

---

[26] Makombe 2010.

[27] Ndlovu-Gatsheni 2012, p. 1.

[28] Shaw 1986, pp. 373–394.

[29] Matyszak 2005, p. 133.

4.4.2 *Accountability Mechanisms*

4.4.2.1 The Chidyausiku Commission of Inquiry

An inquiry was commissioned to look into the administration of the War Victims Compensation Fund that was set up to assist victims and combatants of the liberation struggle. President Mugabe appointed a sitting high court judge, Godfrey Chidyausiku, to chair the commission of inquiry.[30] A summary of the report was presented by the public service, labour and social welfare minister, with the piecemeal document raising more questions than it answered. The findings of the commission were that the War Victims Compensation Fund had been defrauded of millions of dollars through a system of false, unsubstantiated and multiple claims.

4.4.3 *Subsequent Developments*

Following the Chidyausiku Commission report, a few people who were accused of corruption faced purges in the government, for instance in the case of *Sydney Michael Muchenje v. Secretary for Public Service, Labour and Social Welfare.*[31] Concurrently, prosecutions were also carried out, the most high-profile case being that of Chenjerai Hitler Hunzvi, who was responsible for issuing declarations of disability by means of which thousands of war veterans, including cabinet ministers and other high-ranking officials, claimed large payments from the government. He was, however, released early from prison and awarded a government post.

4.5 Fourth Phase: State-Sponsored Violence Post-Mugabe (1998–2017)

4.5.1 *Background*

From 1995 to 1998 there was relative peace in Zimbabwe; however, this soon came to an end when the state sponsored violence in order to contain street protests triggered by grievances and stop a full-blown political revolution. A myriad of factors contributed to this crisis, which has still not been fully addressed, with some abuses still ongoing. These factors include the food riots; protests over the war veterans' reparations and the distribution of grain and housing and the war in the Democratic Republic of Congo, where it was alleged that the Zimbabwe Defence

[30] Commissions of Inquiry Act 1991.

[31] Unreported judgment 16 of 2003, ZLR HC 153 99.

Forces were involved in looting minerals; and the human rights situation, compounded by the release of the Catholic Commission for Justice and Peace and Legal Resources Foundation's chilling report on the Gukurahundi atrocities.[32] A robust civil society and opposition parties were formed, challenging the hegemony of ZANU-PF, the violent and corrupt land reform programme and several cases of electoral fraud.

Zimbabwe was locked in a vicious circle as unaddressed socio-economic violations perpetrated in the past reappeared at the centre of the conflict.[33] Physical violence receded, and economic violence took centre stage. In 2008, ZANU-PF lost its majority in parliament and the presidential election for the first time. President Mugabe refused to accept defeat, unleashing more violence and leading to the government of national unity (GNU), comprising ZANU-PF and the opposition MDC, which lasted from 2009 to 2013. This brought about a modest economic recovery. The GNU was dissolved in 2013 when ZANU-PF regained power in another heavily disputed election.

The post-GNU opposition was heavily weakened, as was the state watchdog apparatus created in the 2013 constitution to safeguard transparency. Corruption was flourishing again. The ZANU-PF party had its own factional fights to replace the ageing Robert Mugabe. Several protests by Zimbabweans, dubbed the 'Zimbabwean Spring' after the 'Arab Spring' uprisings in the Middle East and North Africa, which were intended to address corruption in state enterprises, were met by state-sponsored violence. On 17 November 2017, the military took over government functions in order to root out corrupt elements that had captured the presidency. A new administration was installed led by Mugabe's former deputy Emerson Mnangagwa. This new administration has employed various measures to address corruption. The following sections will discuss these mechanisms and processes.

4.5.2 Accountability Mechanisms

4.5.2.1 Amnesty

Traditionally, the government has subscribed to the view that amnesties are only for civil and political rights violations. President Mnangagwa passed legislation for a three-month amnesty allowing individuals and companies to return public funds and assets corruptly acquired and illegally stashed abroad.[34] At the end of the

---

[32] Zimbabwe Human Rights NGO Forum 1998.

[33] Muvingi 2009, p. 165ff.

[34] The Presidential Powers (Temporary) Measures (Amendment of Exchange Control Act) regulations, SI 145 of 2017, gazetted on 1 December 2017, gave an amnesty in respect of the repatriation of foreign currency and assets that were externalised by commission or omission or under the liberalised Exchange Control Framework.

three-month moratorium, it was reported that around US$250 million of the expected US$1.3 billion had been repatriated in cash, equivalent to 105 out of the 1,166 reported cases. An additional thirty cases valued at US$50 million of immovable properties in various countries were reported to the RBZ, and 210 cases valued at US$287 million related to externalised funds that were used to procure imports. This gives a success rate of 45 percent by value, which is encouraging for an amnesty of this kind.

4.5.2.2 Prosecutions

The new administration has also embarked on unprecedented mass prosecutions of former senior government officials accused of various acts of corruption, such as embezzlement of resources and criminal abuse of authority. To date, more than twenty senior officials have cases pending before criminal courts, and more arrests are still being carried out. In one completed trial, the former minister of energy was convicted of corruption. However, there have been concerns that prosecution is selective, ignoring overwhelming evidence of other corrupt officials in the new administration.

4.5.2.3 Institutional Reforms

Several reforms have been made to the institutions that deal with corruption. Firstly, the revival of the ZACC, which had become almost obsolete under President Mugabe. It has been given powers to arrest in conjunction with the ZRP. Specialised courts have been put into effect to deal with corruption in all ten provinces of the country. A special presidential anti-corruption prosecution unit was created to deal with high-profile cases of corruption. International anti-corruption instruments, such as the UNCAC optional crime of illicit enrichment, have been implemented, and the government has enforced declaration of assets by senior public officials. Reforms in the form of purges have also been witnessed, with some officials being demoted or forced to resign.

4.5.2.4 Truth Inquiries

Although there has not been a truth commission as defined in Chap. 1, the new administration has given much attention to the parliamentary portfolio committees hearings. In particular, the portfolio committee on mining, a sector that has been seriously affected by corruption, has been consistently carrying out public inquiries on corruption that closely resemble anti-corruption inquiries. Its hearings are open to the public and televised, and allow experts, as well as alleged perpetrators, to give evidence under oath. The findings of the investigations are then recommended to the ZRP and ZACC for further action. So far, however, there has been little discussion about setting up a truth inquiry on all forms of corruption that are alleged to have taken place under the presidency of Robert Mugabe.

4.5.3 *Subsequent Developments*

The new government war against corruption is still ongoing. Nevertheless, it has divided opinion among citizens. Some Zimbabweans see this as the first time the government has really taken action against corruption. However, others are wary and believe that the new administration is mainly focused on reviving the economy so that members of the government can continue to enrich themselves. Questions have been raised about the suitability of President Mnangagwa to address the legacy of economic abuse under the Mugabe regime in which he served for almost four decades.

Although the mechanisms that have been adapted to fight corruption may also be used to investigate human rights abuses, contrary to expectations academics and practitioners have not seized this opportunity to lobby the new administration to investigate corruption and human rights abuses by the previous government comprehensively Due to practical constraints, the present book cannot provide a comprehensive review of the ongoing mechanisms. There is, however, plenty of scope for further progress in determining the effects of corruption on the enjoyment of socio-economic rights in Zimbabwe, and establishing how transitional justice can be adopted to address these effects.

4.6 Conclusion

Andrew Iliff, in his seminal article 'Root and Branch, Tree of Life: Sowing the Seeds of Grassroots Transitional Justice', says that 'Zimbabwe's acute need for justice and reconciliation highlights a longstanding tension in transitional justice'.[35] This tension has been highlighted by the relentless calls for justice by victims of human rights abuses and civil society. It has been claimed that the 'white heirs of the Rhodesian regime and the black leaders preferred to impose a shallow, cheap form of reconciliation without historic, restorative or economic justice'.[36] This is what has continued to happen.

There has never been official accountability for human rights violations in the history of Zimbabwe. Prosecutions at municipal level have been thwarted by legislation with political objectives under the guise of achieving peace and reconciliation. Truth inquiries have been undertaken; however, the reports have been kept

[35] Iliff 2010, p. 1.

[36] Huyse 2003, p. 39.

secret or their recommendations not implemented. Alleged perpetrators of human rights violations still hold officers responsible and are further blocking any meaningful efforts for justice for the victims of gross human rights violations, including socio-economic rights issues such as corruption.

Overall, from these 'multiple transitions' there seems to be some evidence to indicate that some mechanisms were introduced to address cases of grand corruption that may have a significant effect on society. This provides important insights into how current transitional mechanisms can be fine-tuned to address corruption that is directly related to human rights violations. The only hope lies in the civil society leaders' symposium on transitional justice, which provides not only the most comprehensive transitional justice package but also adequately outlines the framework for how socio-economic rights violations, including corruption, can be mainstreamed in the transitional justice agenda for a democratic Zimbabwe. No previous study has investigated this connection; I shall attempt to address some of the relevant issues in the next chapter.

References

Bailey M (1979) Oilgate: The Sanctions Scandal. Hodder and Stoughton, London, pp. 128–129

Bingham T (1978) Bingham Report on Evasion of Sanctions against Rhodesia by Major Oil Companies: Allegations of Continuing Breaches of Sanctions. Available at https://discovery.nationalarchives.gov.uk/details/r/C16555608 Last accessed on 23 June 2019

Butler LJ and Stockwell S (2013) The Wind of Change: Harold Macmillan and British Decolonization. Palgrave Macmillan, New York

CCJP et al. (1997) Breaking the Silent: Report on the 1980's Disturbances in Matebeleland and the Midlands. CCJP, Harare

Chikwanha A (2009) The Trajectory of Human Rights Violations in Zimbabwe. Institute for Security Studies. Available at http://www.issafrica.org/acpst/papers/the-trajectory-of-human-rights-violations-in-zimbabwe

Curtin TRC (1968) Rhodesian Economic Development under Sanctions and "the Long Haul". African Affairs 67: 100–110

Curtin TRC and Murray D (1967) Economic Sanctions and Rhodesia: An Examination of the Probable Effect of Sanctions on National and Personal Incomes in Rhodesia and of the Effectiveness of Sanctions on Rhodesian Policy. Research Monograph no. 12. Institute of Economic Affairs, London

Dzinesa GA (2006) Swords into Ploughshares: Disarmament, Demobilisation and Reintegration in Zimbabwe, Namibia and South Africa. Institute for Security Studies, Cape Town

Galtung J (1967) On the Effects of International Economic Sanctions: with Examples from the Case of Rhodesia. World Politics 19: 378–416

Huyse L (2003) Zimbabwe: Why Reconciliation Failed. In: Bloomfield D et al (eds) Reconciliation After Violent Conflict: A Handbook. International Institute for Democracy and Electoral Assistance, Stockholm, pp. 34–39

Iliff A (2010) Root and Branch, Tree of Life: Sowing the Seeds of Grassroots Transitional Justice. Oxford Transitional Justice Research. Available at http://www.csls.ox.ac.uk/documents/IliffRootandBranch_Final_OTJR.pdf

Lamb G (2013) DDR Twenty Years Later: Historical Review of the Long-term Impact of Post-independence DDR in Southern Africa. World Bank, Washington DC

Law K (2017) Pattern, Puzzle, and Peculiarity: Rhodesia's UDI and Decolonisation in Southern Africa. Journal of Imperial and Commonwealth History 45: 721–728
Losman DL (1979) International Economic Sanctions: the Cases of Cuba, Israel, and Rhodesia. University of New Mexico Press, Albuquerque
Makombe L (2010) Corrupt officials 'cleansed' by the passage of time. The Standard. Available at https://www.thestandard.co.zw/2010/09/09/corrupt-officials-cleansed-by-the-passage-of-time/ Last accessed on 23 June 2019
Matyszak D (2005) Civil Society and the Long Election. Konrad Adenauer Stiftung, Harare
Miller Z (2008) Effects of Invisibility: In Search of the Economic in Transitional Justice. International Journal of Transitional Justice 2: 253–265
Muvingi I (2009) Sitting on Powder Kegs: Socioeconomic Rights in Transitional Societies. International Journal of Transitional Justice 3: 163–182
Ndlovu-Gatsheni SJ (2012) Elections in Zimbabwe: A Recipe for Tension or a Remedy for Reconciliation? Institute for Justice and Reconciliation, Cape Town
Redress (2004) Zimbabwe from Impunity to Accountability: Are Reparations Possible for Victims of Gross and Systematic Human Rights Violations? Available at http://www.redress.org/downloads/publications/Beyond%20impunityA5.pdf
Reeler T (2009) Subliminal Terror? Human Rights Violations and Torture in Zimbabwe During 2008. Centre for the Study of Violence and Reconciliation, Cape Town
Ronen Y (2011) Transition from Illegal Regimes under International Law: Cambridge Studies in International and Comparative Law. Cambridge University Press, New York
Shaw WH (1986) Towards the One-Party State in Zimbabwe: a Study in African Political Thought. Journal of Modern African Studies 24: 373–394
Strack HR (1978) Sanctions: the Case of Rhodesia. Syracuse University Press, Syracuse
Sutcliffe RB (1969) The Political Economy of Rhodesian Sanctions. Journal of Commonwealth Political Studies 7:113–125
Weitzer RJ (1990) Transforming Settler States: Communal Conflict and Internal Security in Northern Ireland and Zimbabwe. University of California Press, Berkeley
Zimbabwe Human Rights NGO Forum (1998) A Consolidated Report on the Food Riots 19–23 January 1998. Available at http://hrforumzim.org/wp-content/uploads/1998/01/consolidatedreportonfood.pdf Last accessed on 23 June 2019

Chapter 5
Rethinking Ways of Dealing with Corruption Under Transitional Justice in Zimbabwe

Contents

P. Maguchu, *Transitional Justice and Socio-Economic Rights in Zimbabwe*,
International Criminal Justice Series 24,
https://doi.org/10.1007/978-94-6265-323-8_5

Abstract The purpose of this chapter is to shed new light on the debate about transitional justice in Zimbabwe. It defends the position that corruption is at the centre of the conflict in Zimbabwe, and makes the corruption, understood as a violation of socio-economic rights, into present or future transitional justice mechanisms.

Keywords Johannesburg Symposium · ONHRI · NPRC · NTJWG · universal jurisdiction · ILO Commission of Inquiry on Zimbabwe

5.1 Introduction

The concept of transitional justice in its modern incarnation gathered momentum in Zimbabwe in the late 1980s.[1] Today, more than three decades later, Zimbabwe is still contemplating democratisation and the implementation of transitional justice mechanisms. The end of Robert Mugabe's 37-year rule has intensified calls for transitional justice. More importantly, calls for economic justice have gained both momentum and credibility as the military intervention that eventually led to Mugabe's resignation and was carried out to get rid of corrupt elements within the party and government has proved to be a continuation of, if not even worse than, the Mugabe administration.[2]

The stages of gross human rights violations mentioned in Chap. 4 are marked by multiple state-initiated mechanisms and processes, which—although not expressed in terms of transitional justice phraseology—mirror mechanisms to redress victims, to investigate violations and to guarantee non-recurrence and to foster societal reconciliation. The task of promoting transitional justice in Zimbabwe is no longer a purview of the state alone; it is being spearheaded by a diverse range of local and international actors.

This chapter will critically review the mandate of official mechanisms to find out whether they can provide justice for victims of socio-economic rights violations, especially those perpetrated through corruption. It will also take a brief digression to explore unofficial transitional justice processes being implemented by civil

[1] The Democracy Index is an index compiled by the Economist Intelligence Unit that measures the state of democracy in 167 countries. Zimbabwe is ranked 140, as an 'Authoritarian State'.

[2] The Zimbabwean Defence Forces embarked on a coup of sorts, detaining government officials, including President Mugabe, and blocking government buildings, preventing business from going on as usual, in what was initially labelled 'Operation Restore Legacy' and later the 'National Democratic Process'.

society that have a focus on socio-economic rights violations and corruption. To that end, the chapter will also highlight and discuss currently available international mechanisms such as the option for prosecutions, based on the principle of universal jurisdiction, against those who have committed human rights crimes punishable under the ICC Statute filed before the South African constitutional court.

5.2 The Civil Society and Justice in Zimbabwe Symposium

A symposium was held in Johannesburg from 11 to 13 August 2003 on the theme 'Civil Society and Justice in Zimbabwe'. It was attended by civil society organisations from Zimbabwe and South Africa and a number of international experts on transitional justice. The main purpose of the symposium was to explore international best practices for achieving justice for the victims of past and present human rights violations in Zimbabwe.[3] The symposium ended with two important documents that constituted the primary lobby material for transitional justice in Zimbabwe: the *declaration* and the *summary*. The latter elaborated in greater detail on the mechanisms and steps that civil society and the state ought to take in order to ensure justice in Zimbabwe and on the role of socio-economic justice and corruption.

5.2.1 Background

The convening of the symposium should be understood against the backdrop of the following factors. Firstly, the paradigm shift in civil society, particularly NGOs' advocacy strategy. Zimbabwean NGOs have transformed from being passive to being more involved in policy, something Sam Moyo terms 'entryism'.[4] He defines this as a process whereby 'organisations attempt to penetrate the state machinery in order to influence policy directions and decisions from within'.[5] This resonates with Sara Dorman's findings in her thoroughly researched thesis on the inclusion and exclusion of NGOs in democratisation processes in Zimbabwe:

> In the 1990s, a new generation of organizations arose in reaction to 'new' problems, such as homeless people, Aids, and women's rights. These NGOs were interested in changing the conditions within which they operated, and focused on policy-advocacy rather than welfarist strategies.[6]

---

3 Redress 2004.

4 Moyo 1992, p. 7.

5 Moyo 1992, p. 7.

6 Dorman 2001, p. 126.

Thus, there was a change in the strategy of civil society organisations, which were becoming more proactive and policy-oriented.

Secondly, the calls for justice by civil society were, contrary to popular belief, influenced mainly not by the gross political violence but by the prevailing socio-economic situation in the country. It all began in 1995 with the World Bank's invitation to NGOs to participate in a consultation in preparation for the International Monetary Fund and World Bank meeting on the Economic Structural Adjustment Programme, colloquially known as 'A Call to Justice'.[7] The campaign was for debt forgiveness, and it was concluded with the release of a document 'which called for church people to act against an unjust government', which in turn led to a follow-up campaign dubbed 'A call for Prophetic Action'.[8] The latter campaign resulted in a report that would act as a lobby document for civil society on economic justice and governance. According to Dorman, the document centred not on violations of civil and political rights such as 'vote rigging' or the 'Matabeleland crisis',[9] but rather on socio-economic issues such as economic policies and governance, opportunities for young people AIDS, gender inequality and the environment.[10]

Thirdly, as noted by Adam Przeworski, calls for transitional justice increase when there is an alternative to the ruling elite.[11] The formation of the MDC in 1999 was undoubtedly an incredible challenge to the political hegemony of ZANU-PF. As Ruti Teitel noted it is only when NGOs are able to ally with other social forces, and when the political hegemony of the regime is starkly weakened, that NGOs are willing to confrontation violations committed in 'a not so distant past.'[12] This description fits well with the models of transitional justice that were adopted following the liberation struggle and the uprisings after independence.

It is against this background that civil society organisations in Zimbabwe decided to come up with their own approach to redressing the abuses, using both domestic and international legal and institutional mechanisms. Therefore, there is a need to situate socio-economic issues within the calls for transitional justice and accountability in Zimbabwe. A discussion of transitional justice that merely focuses on civil and political rights violations remains untenable if it excludes the corruption that led to problems such as food riots and farm invasions. As Shari Eppel notes, holding a symposium signalled 'the emergence of a vibrant civil society that struggles around economic justice, constitutionalism and human rights in Zimbabwe' and 'channelled its efforts to place transitional justice questions on the national political agenda'.[13]

---

7 Dorman 2001, p. 172.

8 Dorman 2001, p. 176.

9 Dorman 2001, p. 176.

10 Dorman 2001, p. 176.

11 Przeworski 1986, pp. 51–53.

12 Teitel 2003, pp. 84–85.

13 Eppel and Raftopoulos 2008, p. 2.

5.2.2 *Legal Basis*

At the time the symposium was held, Zimbabwe was grappling with draconian legislation and amnesties that were passed to pardon human rights violations. Therefore, the symposium was advocating for legal reform to facilitate transitional justice processes. The symposium relied on the increasingly unified international legal framework that governs approaches to transitional justice: in particular, instruments that bind Zimbabwe as a result of being a states party and, under international customary law, establish parameters for how to deal with past human rights abuses. The symposium also called for the repeal of amnesty laws passed in Zimbabwe that were in violation of international instruments on reparations and remedies.

5.2.3 *Mandate*

The *declaration* of the symposium was the first such document to recommend that 'there should be special commissions to deal with economic crimes such as corruption, asset stripping and debts incurred by previous governments in connection with human rights abuses'.[14] The symposium also recommended that these specialised commissions 'must be given an explicit mandate to recommend measures aimed at redressing socio-economic injustices of the colonial and post-colonial periods'.[15]

The symposium also brought an interesting perspective to socio-economic issues such as corruption and reparations:

> The new Government must immediately establish a reparations fund to compensate victims of human rights abuses. Concerted efforts must be made to tap all possible sources of local and international finance for this fund, including assets recovered by the Economic Crime Commission. If financially feasible, full compensation should be paid to those who suffered the greatest harm as a result of grave human rights abuses, and some more limited compensation should be paid to other victims. The fund should also be used to establish local development projects in areas particular [*sic*] badly affected by past human rights abuses.[16]

The reparations are to be partly funded using the assets recovered from the ill-gotten assets of those perpetrators involved in economic crimes and corruption, and 'should be devoted to compensating individuals and communities harmed by past human rights abuses'.[17] Asset recovery is therefore an important issue for future research.

---

[14] Morrell and Pigou 2004.

[15] Morrell and Pigou 2004.

[16] Morrell and Pigou 2004.

[17] Morrell and Pigou 2004.

5.2.4 *Findings*

The *summary* notes that the need for transitional justice in Zimbabwe is due not only to civil and political abuses but also to historical social and economic imbalances.[18] It explains these violations as follows:

> The human rights abuses, and the social and economic injustices suffered by the people, are not merely the product of colonial injustices, but also the product of misgovernance, massive corruption, and asset stripping by state officials, persons within the private business sector, and others.[19]

Although the symposium is an unofficial process, its findings on the linkage between corruption and socio-economic rights abuses play a significant role in the future of transitional justice in Zimbabwe.

5.2.5 *Special Remarks*

The civil society symposium laid out the framework and basis for future transitional justice in Zimbabwe, which resonates with the objectives of the present book. It should be mentioned that the process did not usurp the citizens' and victims' right to determine the methods for dealing with the legacy of human rights violations. The symposium detailed the different mechanisms of transitional justice that were to be included in public consultations. It was this symposium that set the precedent for what justice could take, in the event of a political transition in Zimbabwe. Consequently, today a handful of organisations are trying to further the objectives of the symposium, as discussed below in the section on the national working group.

5.3 The Organ on National Healing, Integration and Reconciliation

The Organ on National Healing, Reconciliation and Integration (ONHRI) was set up to devise a mechanism to properly advise on what measures might be necessary and practicable to achieve national healing, cohesion and unity in respect of victims of pre- and post-independence political conflicts.[20]

---

[18] Morrell and Pigou 2004.

[19] Morrell and Pigou 2004.

[20] GPA Article 7(7)(1)(c).

5.3.1 Background

Following the disputed 2008 harmonised election and the violent presidential runoff, the international community, including the regional economic organisation, the Southern African Development Community (SADC), through its Organ on Politics, Defence and Security, persuaded ZANU-PF to form a government with the MDC 'in the hope that this will facilitate an orderly transition of power'.[21] This was put into practice through the Global Political Agreement (GPA) signed by ZANU-PF and the two MDC formations (the MDC party had split into two parties in October 2005), leading to the formation of a transitional government, also known as a government of national unity (GNU) in February 2009. The GNU was a temporary solution to facilitate a new constitution and new elections. It also accommodated the demands for transitional justice.

5.3.2 Legal Basis

As discussed above, the creation of the ONHRI, as contemplated by the GPA, was a result of the unity accord between ZANU-PF and the two formations of the MDC facilitated by the SADC. The legal basis for the ONHRI is found in one of the provisions of the GPA:

> The Parties hereby agree that the new Government: a) will ensure equal treatment of all regardless of gender, race, ethnicity, place of origin and will work towards equal access to development for all; b) will ensure equal and fair development of all regions of the country and in particular to correct historical imbalances in the development of regions; c) shall give consideration to the setting up of a mechanism to properly advise on what measures might be necessary and practicable to achieve national healing, cohesion and unity in respect of victims of pre and post independence political conflicts; and d) will strive to create an environment of tolerance and respect among Zimbabweans and that all citizens are treated with dignity and decency irrespective of age, gender, race, ethnicity, place of origin or political affiliation. e) will formulate policies and put measures in place to attract the return and repatriation of all Zimbabweans in the Diaspora and in particular will work towards the return of all skilled personnel.[22]

5.3.3 Mandate

The ONHRI mandate, which was derived from the GPA, was to promote equality, national healing, cohesion and unity. The way the mandate is framed means it can

[21] Muvingi 2009.

[22] GPA Article 7(7)(1)(c).

be interpreted in various ways.[23] A critical analysis of the article setting out the mandate revealed ambiguity and vagueness when it comes to defining issues of equality, national healing, cohesion and unity. Article VII fails to articulate more complex questions of transitional justice and human rights abuses in specific terms.[24] The provisions of the GPA establishing the ONHRI are vague; this is contrary to the requirements of the Paris Principles,[25] which demand that institutions for human rights should have a clear mandate.

5.3.4 Findings

The ONHRI was faced with many operational problems, which made it impossible to carry out its mandate. The main challenge is that the population was divided about which option to choose:

> citizens were deeply divided into polarised camps, and where one set of partisans associated with state power is responsible for most abuses, mass preferences are profoundly shaped by party political allegiances. The partisans of a democratic opposition are vigorous in calling for legal redress, while loyalists of the old ruling group are strongly resistant.[26]

The question of justice was subjected to competing ideologies and interests. For instance, when determining the scope and functions of the ONHRI, the MDC parties would weigh the risks and threats of its decisions for the GNU. By and large, the MDC-T (the main MDC faction)[27] was of the view that talk of accountability would jeopardise the fragile unity.

The work of the ONHRI faced other significant problems. For instance, there were power imbalances and asymmetries, as the alleged perpetrators of human rights abuses remained in power and occupied some of the most important positions. Therefore, 'the distribution of power between incumbent and emergent elites during the transition period has a large impact on whether abusers can be held to account'.[28] In a heated debate with the minister in charge of the ONHRI, one civil society leader said:

> the dilemma is how do you do national healing with people who have created the atmosphere for national healing having been part of the violence and the perpetration? It's an unenviable task for the Organ for National Healing. And I don't think that it was designed actually to deliver the goods in the lifetime of this transitional processes, it cannot because

[23] Machakanja 2010, p. 2.

[24] Machakanja 2010, p. 3.

[25] UN Commission on Human Rights 1994.

[26] Bratton 2001, p. 354.

[27] The main faction headed by the founding leader, Morgan Tsvangirai.

[28] Bratton 2001, pp. 355–356.

> if it does, it has to dismantle the inclusive government because it has to reconcile ourselves with the fact that we have to live with this inconvenient reality of national healing being a pending agenda for the next democratically elected government [*sic*].[29]

Moreover, the ONHRI eschewed restorative justice and went for the less contentious issues by adopting traditional justice mechanisms. It then continued with this limited approach to justice. Due to the inherent limitations of traditional methods when it comes to economic crimes, the ONHRI did not make meaningful findings or address socio-economic rights violations or corruption. The ONHRI was located in the office of the president and did not have sufficient funding, and the environment was still polarised by threats of political violence, with some meetings being interrupted by rowdy youths.[30]

5.3.5 *Special Remarks*

The existence of the ONHRI has been the subject of intense debate within the human rights community. It is not clear whether the ONHRI was disbanded by the new constitution when it established the National Peace and Reconciliation Commission (NPRC). The ONHRI has continued with its mandate since 2013. Its staff continue to work alongside the NPRC, and there is sometimes conflict or duplication of ideas.

5.4 The ILO Inquiry on Truth, Reconciliation and Justice in Zimbabwe

The International Labour Organisation (ILO) has a procedure which allows a complaint to be filed against a member state by another member state to the convention, a delegate to the ILC or the governing body for non-compliance with the convention.[31] The governing body may institute a commission of inquiry, consisting of three independent members, to carry out investigations of the complaint, ascertain the facts and make recommendations on measures to address the problems raised by the complaint.[32] A commission of inquiry is the ILO's highest-level investigative procedure, and is generally set up when a member state is accused of committing persistent and serious violations and has repeatedly refused to address them. To date, twelve commissions of inquiry have been established, the latest one being on Zimbabwe in November 2008.

---

[29] Shana 2010.

[30] Research and Advocacy Unit 2012.

[31] ILO constitution, Articles 26–34.

[32] ILO constitution, Articles 26–34.

5.4.1 Background

The ILO carried out a commission of inquiry on Zimbabwe as a result of complaints from workers' delegates from Zimbabwe and a delegation of workers' representatives from thirteen countries filing a complaint under Article 26 of the constitution of the ILO against the government of Zimbabwe for non-observance of freedom of association and protection of the right to organise.[33] The complaints made serious allegations of violations of basic civil liberties, such as systematic arrests, unlawful detention, harassment and intimidation of trade union leaders and members over the exercise of legitimate trade union activities.[34] It was alleged the government was targeting workers because they were perceived to be sympathetic to the MDC, a political party that was formed by a trade union organisation and whose membership is drawn mainly from workers.

5.4.2 Legal Basis

The ILO commission of inquiry was established in terms of the ILO constitution and international labour law instruments to which Zimbabwe is party: firstly, under Article 26 of the constitution of the ILO to examine the government of Zimbabwe's observance of freedom of association; secondly, protection of the right to organise, which is guaranteed under the convention of 1948 (no. 87); and thirdly, the right to organise and collective bargaining under the convention of 1949 (no. 98).

5.4.3 Mandate

The mandate of this commission was limited to the issues surrounding freedom of expression in the form of freedom of association, the right to organise and the right to collective bargaining. To this end, the ILO commission indicated that it was competent only to examine Zimbabwe's fulfilment of the obligations it undertook upon ratifying conventions no. 87 and no. 98, and that therefore questions which did not relate to freedom of association would be outside its competence.[35] The overall objective of the ILO commission was as follows: to work in the judicial spirit that characterises ILO commissions of inquiry, and ideally to contribute to the

---

[33] Freedom of Association and Protection of the Right to Organise Convention, 1948 (no. 87), and the Right to Organise and Collective Bargaining Convention, 1949 (no. 98), ratified by Zimbabwe on 9 April 2003 and 27 August 1998 respectively.

[34] ILO 2010, p. 22.

[35] ILO 2010, p. 22.

process of reconciliation and healing in Zimbabwe on the basis of international standards on labour relations and human rights.[36]

5.4.4 *Findings*

The ILO commission undertook a fact-finding mission to Zimbabwe from 12 to 26 August 2009. It concluded that there was systematic violation of the conventions, in the form of arrests, detentions, violent treatment and torture of trade union leaders and members by security forces targeting Zimbabwe Congress of Trade Unions (ZCTU) events, indicating some form of organised violence. The ILO commission also noted a litany of human rights violations, including the use of draconian legislation such as the Public Order and Security Act (POSA), discrimination, the use of state security agents against strikes, widespread interference in ZCTU affairs and the failure to guarantee judicial independence and the rule of law, resulting in a situation of impunity for those perpetrating atrocities.[37]

5.4.5 *Special Remarks*

The ILO commission did not have a broad mandate to investigate socio-economic issues. However, it carried out an investigation into the historical and current socio-economic context and included a separate note on the 'socio-economic components of the events'.[38] The commission recommended that Zimbabwe should look at the current socio-economic context in the country and review national legislation in relation to freedom of association.[39]

It is for the above reasons that this special mechanism should be considered in the history of transitional justice in Zimbabwe. Doing so can also serve to provide some logistical, and other, examples illustrating how a truth and justice commission could be set up in Zimbabwe to deal with socio-economic rights violations of all classes, including corruption. The ILO commission of inquiry should not be viewed as a substitute for a truth commission for Zimbabwe; in fact, it recommended that the government of Zimbabwe set up a truth commission.[40]

---

[36] ILO 2010, p. 19.

[37] ILO 2010, p. 22.

[38] ILO 2010, p. 77.

[39] ILO 2010.

[40] ILO 2010.

5.5 The National Peace and Reconciliation Commission

The new constitution of Zimbabwe has introduced independent commissions to address various topical issues, ranging from gender to media rights. The NPRC is one of the independent commissions in the constitution of Zimbabwe established to redress political conflicts and human rights abuses.[41]

5.5.1 Background

The GPA created the Constitution Parliamentary Select Committee (COPAC) to lead the constitutional reform during the GNU. It collected views from Zimbabweans from across the political divide, who expressed the need for transitional justice to be constitutionalised. In spite of this, the government-sponsored constitutional draft was silent on transitional justice. Similarly, the Kariba draft constitution created clandestinely by the major political parties in 2007 (at a meeting by Lake Kariba, hence the name) did not have a clause on transitional justice. However, NGOs lobbied the government to include such a clause, which led to the creation of the NPRC in the final COPAC constitutional draft.

5.5.2 Legal Basis

The NPRC was established under Sections 251–253 of the constitution to ensure post-conflict justice, healing and reconciliation, and to develop programmes to promote national healing, unity and peaceful conflict resolution, and will run for the next ten years.[42] The NPRC is a creature of the constitution: not only did it establish the NPRC, it also sets out provisions on its goals and functions, its reporting and recommendations, the selection of its commissioners and staff, and its funding.[43]

5.5.3 Mandate

The NPRC has a very ambitious constitutional mandate. Section 252(1) of the constitution sets out the NPRC's functions at length, in both very broad and highly specific terms, as follows:

---

[41] ILO 2010.

[42] Constitution of Zimbabwe Amendment (20) Act 2013, Chapter 12, part 6.

[43] Constitution of Zimbabwe Amendment (20) Act 2013, Chapter 12, part 6.

Goals and objectives

- To ensure post-conflict justice, healing and reconciliation;
- To develop and implement programmes to promote national healing, unity and cohesion in Zimbabwe and the peaceful resolution of disputes;
- To bring about national reconciliation by encouraging people to tell the truth about the past and facilitating the making of amends and the provision of justice;
- To develop procedures and institutions at a national level to facilitate dialogue among political parties, communities, organisations and other groups, in order to prevent conflicts and disputes arising in the future;

Specific objectives to address human rights abuses

- To develop programmes to ensure that persons subjected to persecution, torture and other forms of abuse receive rehabilitative treatment and support;

Specific objectives to address conflict

- To receive and consider complaints from the public and to take such action in regard to the complaints as it considers appropriate;
- To develop mechanisms for early detection of areas of potential conflicts and disputes, and to take appropriate preventive measures;
- To do anything incidental to the prevention of conflict and the promotion of peace;
- To conciliate and mediate disputes among communities, organisations, groups and individuals;

Specific objectives to make recommendations

- To recommend legislation to ensure that assistance, including documentation, is rendered to persons affected by conflicts, pandemics or other circumstances.[44]

In addition to its constitutional mandate, the NPRC has other functions that are added to it by the enabling legislation, the National Peace and Reconciliation Commission Act:[45]

> to conduct investigations into any dispute or conflict within the mandate of the Commission as set out in Section 252 of the Constitution or as provided by any other law;[46]
>
> to conduct research on the— nature, scope, extent and causes of disputes and conflict subject to the constitutional mandate of the Commission; or intervening strategies of disputes and conflict;[47]

---

[44] Constitution of Zimbabwe Amendment (20) Act 2013, Chapter 12, part 6, s252 (1)(a)–(j). Headings in italics inserted by me.

[45] General Notice 2 of 2018 in the Government Gazette published in terms of Section 131(6) of the Constitution of Zimbabwe—National Peace and Reconciliation Commission Act, Chapter 10:32 (no. 11 of 2017).

[46] NPRC Act, s. 3(2)(a).

[47] NPRC Act, s. 3(2)(b)(i)(ii).

to perform any other function that the Commission may be required or permitted to do by or under this Act or any other enactment.[48]

It is clearly an ambitious task for the NPRC to carry out all those functions; it will have to decide which of them to prioritise. Moreover, transitional justice mainly focuses on addressing past gross human rights abuses, while the NPRC has a mandate to look at both future and past conflicts.

5.5.4 *Findings*

The NPRC has not been able to carry out its work properly in the whole time since the constitution, which established the commission, came into effect. It recently started its first outreach meetings. According to the NPRC Act, it should issue annual reports that are available to the public; however, at the time of writing there has not yet been a single report.

5.5.5 *Special Remarks*

The NPRC does not seem to have an explicit mandate to investigate corruption and the violation of socio-economic rights. Section 252(1)(e) states that the NPRC has 'to develop programmes to ensure that persons subjected to persecution, torture and other forms of abuse receive rehabilitative treatment and support'.[49] This specific reference to a group of rights violations, namely civil and political rights abuses related to the physical security of a person, means the NPRC does not have a mandate over socio-economic rights violations.

This is in accordance with the principle of *ejusdem generis*, a rule of statutory interpretation: where general words follow an enumeration of things of a particular and specific meaning, such general words are not to be interpreted in their widest extent, but are to be held as applying only to things of the same general kind or class as those specifically mentioned. For instance, if a law refers to cows, goats, sheep and other animals then the term animals would not include lions, since the list referred to domestic livestock. Thus, the specific mention of persecution and torture means the NPRC is restricted to dealing with similar civil and political rights violations, such as murders and abductions.

[48] NPRC Act, s. 3(2)(c).

[49] Constitution of Zimbabwe Amendment (20) Act 2013.

5.6 The National Transitional Justice Working Group of Zimbabwe

The use of transitional justice working groups as interim organs prior to the creation of formal transitional justice processes is becoming widespread. At the international level, there is the UN Transitional Justice Working Group. At the regional level, there are groups such as the Arab Working Group on Transitional Justice.[50] Some national transitional justice working groups have been formed prior to formal transitional justice processes. For instance, a working group on transitional justice for Iraq was established to 'do practical preliminary planning on a variety of issues for the inevitable "day after" the fall of the Saddam Hussein regime'.[51] Similarly, in Seoul, South Korea, a working group was established in 2014 with the mission of creating advanced frameworks to address human rights violations and advocating for justice and victims' rights in North Korea.[52]

Other transitional justice working groups have been established to inform ongoing processes. They vary in size, from smaller ones such as the group in Liberia, which is composed of twenty civil society organisations,[53] to the Uganda working group, which is composed of 130 organisations. In Zimbabwe, civil society organisations have made a coalition to form the National Transitional Justice Working Group (NTJWG) to bridge the gap between formal and informal processes and push the envelope for people-driven transitional justice processes.

5.6.1 Background

The NTJWG is a loose coalition of various stakeholders interested in transitional justice in Zimbabwe that has been set up primarily to engage with the official transitional justice processes. It is linked to the justice symposium discussed in detail above.

5.6.2 Legal Basis

The NTJWG is the brainchild of forty-six civil society organisations (CSOs) that have independent legal standing. Although it is not registered to operate as a

[50] The Arab Working Group on Transitional Justice (AWGTJ) convened for the first time in Manama, Bahrain, on 28 March 2009.

[51] Iraq Watch 2002.

[52] TJWG 2019.

[53] Moore 2009.

separate entity, it facilitates unofficial process that derives its legal basis from the CSOs' role in engaging with the formal processes.

5.6.3 *Mandate*

The NTJWG is a direct product of the civil society symposium. Its primary objective is to further the goals of the latter, namely to

> set up institutions to deal with past and present human rights violations and that such institutions be empowered not only to investigate and seek truth but also to recommend criminal prosecution, provide redress and reparations for victims, and lead to the healing of the nation.[54]

It aims to inform and feed into the current official institution, the NPRC. Therefore, the creation of the NPRC accelerated the move to establish the NTJWG, so as to create 'an opportunity for transitional justice stakeholders to contribute to any national process aimed at achieving post-conflict justice, healing and reconciliation'.[55]

5.6.4 *Findings*

In its first press release, the NTJWG pointed out that 'the current transitional justice discourse is top–down and there is a need to activate the bottom so as to create a bottom-up approach'.[56] Notably, the NTJWG also bemoaned the fact that 'violations of human rights are still ongoing and the *economic aspects* of transitional justice have been largely ignored'.[57] Based on this finding, the NTJWG seeks to ensure that transitional justice in Zimbabwe is all-encompassing. The NTJWG will set the tone for transitional justice in Zimbabwe by influencing official and unofficial justice and reconciliation discourse and enhancing the role of local non-state actors and institutions.

In contrast to the NPRC, the NTJWG's work is structured around six 'thematic areas': the Promotion of Truth; Justice and Accountability; Reparations and Guarantees of Non-Recurrence; Memorialisation; Gender; and Institutional Reform.[58] Each of these thematic areas is overseen by a representative appointed in accordance with best practices for the staffing of transitional justice commissions.

---

[54] Zimbabwe Human Rights NGO Forum 2014, p. 1.

[55] Zimbabwe Human Rights NGO Forum 2014, p. 1.

[56] Zimbabwe Human Rights NGO Forum 2014, p. 2.

[57] Zimbabwe Human Rights NGO Forum 2014, p. 4.

[58] Zimbabwe Human Rights NGO Forum 2014, p. 3.

Additionally, the NTJWG has independent experts who assist on other areas that may not fit in perfectly with the existing thematic areas.

5.6.5 *Special Remarks*

The NTJWG tracks, analyses and publicises all the activities of the NPRC in its publication *NPRC Watch*. Among other activities, it has established a transitional justice information centre to monitor majority views and opinions on the course of transitional justice in Zimbabwe. To that end, it is currently lobbying the government to fulfil its obligations as enshrined in the new constitution, to select the commissioners transparently and to pass relevant enabling legislation.

5.7 Universal Jurisdiction

There is no general consensus on the definition of universal jurisdiction in conventional or customary international law, as with many other international terms. Generally, the concept is an assertion of jurisdiction by any state over crimes that are exceptionally heinous, regardless of any nexus the State may have with the offence, the offender, or the victim even if its nationals have not been injured by the acts. Universal jurisdiction offenses are injuries to 'the international community as a whole'.[59] Recent debates about the application of universal jurisdiction have led to the proliferation of principles that provide guidance in this important area of law; a few notable principles of universal jurisdiction are discussed briefly below.

The Princeton Project on Universal Jurisdiction brought together eminent scholars and jurists to develop universal standards on the exercise and legitimacy of universal jurisdiction. According to the Princeton Project on Universal Jurisdiction's draft principles, universal jurisdiction can be applied under international law to a non-exhaustive list of serious crimes, which includes piracy, slavery, war crimes, crimes against peace, crimes against humanity, genocide and torture.[60]

Another set of principles was developed by a regional NGO, Africa Legal Aid (AFLA), with the aid of local and international legal experts who convened to discuss and draft principles on universal jurisdiction from an African perspective. They met in Cairo from 30 to 31 July 2001 and in Arusha from 18 to 21 October

[59] Joyner 1996, p. 165.

[60] Bass et al. 2001, Principle 2, 1–2.

2002, hence the name the Cairo–Arusha Principles on Universal Jurisdiction in Respect of Gross Human Rights Offences: An African Perspective.[61]

The Cairo–Arusha Principles on Universal Jurisdiction take into consideration the specific context of Africa as well as certain additional considerations and needs, including cultural, economic and social aspects. Corruption is a classic problem in Africa, and so the Cairo–Arusha Principles identify crimes such as plunder and gross misappropriation of public funds as subject to universal jurisdiction.[62]

In the same vein, a new set of principles, the Madrid–Buenos Aires Principles of Universal Jurisdiction, was developed by international legal experts in order to strengthen the function of the ICC.[63] The drafters of the Madrid–Buenos Aires Principles of Universal Jurisdiction sought to respond to the changes and developments that the application of universal jurisdiction has undergone since the Princeton and Cairo–Arusha principles on universal jurisdiction came into being.

More importantly, the Madrid–Buenos Aires Principles attempted to close gaps that needed to be bridged and to update and broaden the existing principles. This set of principles seeks to extend the crimes to include 'serious crimes against nature and the environment, and economic crimes that seriously and widely affect the fundamental rights of persons and the community'.[64] Collectively, the last two principles indicate that corruption is fast becoming a central issue in the debate on what constitutes an international crime.

5.7.1 Background

The application of universal jurisdiction in Zimbabwe should be understood against this background. In March 2007, the Zimbabwean police, allegedly acting on instructions from ZANU-PF officials, raided the headquarters of the MDC.[65] During the raid more than a hundred people were taken into custody, including workers in nearby shops and offices.[66] These individuals were detained for several days and allegedly tortured by the Zimbabwean police.[67] The detention and torture was allegedly part of a widespread and systematic attack on MDC officials and supporters in the run-up to the national elections. Domestic prosecutions were not

---

[61] The Cairo–Arusha Principles on Universal Jurisdiction in Respect of Gross Human Rights Offences: An African Perspective, Africa Legal Aid, Accra – The Hague – Pretoria. Meetings in Cairo, 30–31 July 2001, and Arusha, 18–21 October 2002.

[62] Cairo–Arusha Principles on Universal Jurisdiction, Principle 4.

[63] The Madrid–Buenos Aires Principles on Universal Jurisdiction, FIBGAR, Madrid, 2015. Meetings in Madrid, 20–23 May 2014, and Buenos Aires, 9–10 September 2015.

[64] Madrid–Buenos Aires Principles of Universal Jurisdiction, Principle 3.

[65] BBC News 2008.

[66] BBC News 2008.

[67] *National Commissioner of the South African Police Service v. Southern African Human Rights Litigation Centre and Another*, 2014, ZACC 30.

possible because of amnesty legislation, and attempts to sue Mugabe for the violations using extra-territorial legislation such as the US Alien Tort Claims Statute were rendered a nullity when the US government successfully claimed that the former president is protected by diplomatic immunity.[68]

A South African NGO, the Southern Africa Litigation Centre (SALC), compiled detailed evidence of the alleged torture and made a court application arguing that South African law enforcement agencies are legally obliged to investigate international crimes (including torture) and to hold the perpetrators of these crimes accountable in South African courts,[69] since, under the ICC Statute, states parties should not grant criminal immunity on the basis of international law to government officials, including a head of state or government, a member of a government or parliament, an elected representative or a government official.[70] In a landmark decision, the South African constitutional court opened the door for future international criminal prosecutions; however, this door has since been locked again after several unsuccessful attempts by victims and civil society to lobby for prosecutions of perpetrators of serious human rights abuses.

5.7.2 Legal Basis

The decision is based on a complex interpretation of the South African legal obligation to investigate and prosecute international crimes, based on its national constitution, national legislation, international law commitments and international customary law obligations. South Africa incorporated the ICC Statute into its legal system through the Rome Statute of the International Criminal Court Act (South African ICC Act).[71] The provisions of the South African ICC Act extend the jurisdiction of South African courts in respect to international crimes where 'that person, after the commission of the crime, is present in the territory of the Republic'.[72]

The South African constitution stipulates that 'national legislation must establish the powers and functions of the police service and must enable the police service to discharge its responsibilities effectively, taking into account the requirements of the provinces'.[73] The national legislation enacted in terms of the SAPS Act,[74] in particular Section 17C(1), establishes the Directorate for Priority Crime Investigation

---

[68] See *Chiminya Tachiona v. Mugabe*, 216 F. Supp. 2d 262 (S.D.N.Y. 2002).

[69] *National Commissioner of the South African Police Service v. Southern African Human Rights Litigation Centre and Another*, 2014, ZACC 30.

[70] ICC Statute, 17 July 1998, entry into force on 1 July 2002, Article 27(1).

[71] South African ICC Act 27, 2002.

[72] South African ICC Act 27, 2002, subs 4(3)(e).

[73] South African ICC Act 27, 2002, s205(2).

[74] South African ICC Act 27, 2002, s205(2).

(DPCI, colloquially known as the Hawks) within the SAPS. Meanwhile, Section 17D(1)(a) of the act sets out that the functions of the Hawks 'are to prevent, combat and investigate national priority offences, which in the opinion of the National Head of the Directorate need to be addressed by the Directorate'. The Hawks, in turn, are mandated to investigate crimes against humanity, including torture, under the aforementioned South African ICC Act.[75]

5.7.3 *Mandate*

As a result of this intricate legal web, the constitutional court of South Africa ruled that, on the basis of the doctrine of universal jurisdiction, South Africa has the mandate to 'assert prescriptive and, to some degree, adjudicative jurisdiction by investigating the allegations of torture as a precursor to taking a possible next step against the alleged perpetrators such as a prosecution or an extradition request'.[76]

5.7.4 *Findings*

The court ruled in the case of *National Commissioner of the South African Police Service v. Southern African Human Rights Litigation Centre and Another*[77] that the South African police have an obligation to investigate torture cases and violations of other crimes against humanity punishable under the ICC Statute that are committed in Zimbabwe against Zimbabweans by Zimbabweans.

5.7.5 *Special Remarks*

5.7.5.1 African Union Anti-ICC Stance

The African Union has adopted a resolution instructing its member states not to cooperate with the ICC.[78] The AU's argues that the ICC has been used as an instrument to target African leaders by the powerful nations, as virtually all the

---

[75] Act 27 2002.

[76] *National Commissioner of the South African Police Service v. Southern African Human Rights Litigation Centre and Another*, 2014, ZACC 29.

[77] *National Commissioner of the South African Police Service v. Southern African Human Rights Litigation Centre and Another*, 2014, ZACC 30.

[78] Decision on Africa's Relationship with the International Criminal Court (ICC), Ext/Assembly/AU/Dec.1 (October 2013).

instances of its use have been on the African continent.[79] The arrest and indictment of the Kenyan president and his deputy further complicated the ICC–AU relationship.[80] The African Union believes that the requirement to arrest a sitting head of state violates the law on diplomatic immunity and that this conflict in international law gives the African Union discretion not to implement the arrest warrant in respect of a sitting head of state, such as Omar Al Bashir.[81]

Moreover, the inability or unwillingness of the ICC to address other problematic situations, such as Syria, Iraq and Palestine, is given as an example of the ICC's double standards.[82] The referral of cases to the ICC by the UN Security Council is also a contentious issue, as it is seen as giving political power to an entity that is constituted by states who are not party to the ICC Statute, such as the US, China, Russia and the UK.[83]

South Africa is now reconsidering its obligations under the ICC Statute. For instance, South Africa did not implement the decision of the ICC issued on 13 June 2015 by the Pre-Trial Chamber, an urgent order reminding it that it had an obligation to immediately arrest and surrender Omar Al Bashir as soon as he entered its territory.[84] Al Bashir has two outstanding warrants of arrest issued by the ICC in 2009 and 2010 for crimes against humanity and genocide.[85] South Africa also failed to respect the order that was granted by its own supreme court to arrest Al Bashir, who was in the country attending the AU summit.[86] This order was made after local rights groups applied to the courts for an order to compel the South African authorities to abide by the decision of the ICC and its obligations under international and domestic law.[87] The court ordered that Al Bashir not be allowed to leave the country pending the decision in the main case. However, he was able to do so without obstruction before the matter was finalised in the courts.[88]

Following South Africa's failure to arrest Al Bashir despite obligations under both international and domestic law, new doubts arose about the commitment of the South African government to ending impunity for grave violations of international criminal law. Critics say South Africa failed the ultimate test of its commitment to

---

[79] Du Plessis 2013, p. 2.

[80] Du Plessis 2013, p. 4.

[81] Du Plessis 2013, p. 4.

[82] Du Plessis 2013, p. 6.

[83] The Security Council may take such decisions where it determines 'the existence of any threat to the peace, breach of the peace, or act of aggression' in accordance with Article 39 of the ICC Statute.

[84] *The Prosecutor v. Omar Hassan Ahmad Al Bashir* (ICC-02/05-07/09-241).

[85] Decision on the Prosecution's Application for a Warrant of Arrest against Omar Hassan Ahmad Al Bashir, 4 March 2009, ICC-02/05-01/09, Pre-Trial Chamber I.

[86] *Southern Africa Litigation Centre* v. *Minister of Justice and Constitutional Development & 9 Others,* (unreported) case no. 27740/15, North Gauteng HC, Pretoria.

[87] ICC Statute, Articles 86 and 89.

[88] *Southern Africa Litigation Centre v. Minister of Justice and Constitutional Development & 9 Others,* (unreported) case no. 27740/15, North Gauteng HC, Pretoria.

ensuring international justice.[89] This has poured cold water on the hopes that Zimbabwean perpetrators will one day find themselves accountable before foreign jurisdictions. According to commentators, 'what remains to be seen is whether the SAPS will indeed follow through with an investigation; whether evidence will be gathered speedily and expertly; and whether arrest warrants will be issued for and executed against alleged perpetrators'.[90]

5.7.5.2 Prosecuting Corruption Under the ICC Statute

Can the ICC prosecute corruption under the ICC Statute? A Nigerian NGO, the Socio-Economic Rights and Accountability Project (SERAP),[91] called on the ICC prosecutor to use

> his position and powers to examine and investigate whether the systemic/grand corruption in Nigeria amounts to a crime against humanity within the jurisdiction of the ICC, and to prevail on the Nigerian government to fulfil its obligations to effectively and fairly investigate and prosecute all allegations of grand corruption since 1985.[92]

Despite the fact that the request is outside the subject matter and also the temporal jurisdiction of the ICC, the request was received by the ICC prosecutor and widely covered by the media, but it has not yet received a response from the prosecutor.

Similarly, Kenyan legislator Kiraitu Murungi was the first to declare that grand corruption is a crime against humanity at the anti-corruption seminar in Seoul, South Korea, in 2003.[93] This assertion has become a topic of academic debate. Dustin Sharp argues that the comment was made 'as a non specific placeholder for "terrible crime"' and should therefore not be taken literally.[94] However, the call to treat corruption as a crime against humanity has already been heeded by NGOs: for instance, the Global Organization of Parliamentarians Against Corruption (GOPAC) adopted a declaration that corruption is a crime against humanity.[95]

A number of scholars have made similar calls to upgrade corruption to the level of a crime against humanity. Examples include Ndiva Kofele-Kale, who argues that customary law is emerging that treats corruption as a crime against humanity,[96] Ilias Bantekas, who also suggests that corruption can be classified as a crime of extermination under Article 7(2)(b) of the ICC Statute,[97] Sonja Starr, Gerald

---

89 Du Plessis 2014.

90 Du Plessis 2014.

91 SERAP website.

92 SERAP website.

93 Muvingi 2009.

94 Murungi 2003 (citation omitted).

95 Declaration for the Fifth Forum of Parliamentarians, 27 November 2013.

96 Kofele-Kale 2000, p. 172.

97 Bantekas 2006, p. 474.

Acquaah-Gaisie and a host of other authors who argue that corruption can fit into the requirements of 'any other act' under Article 7(2)(k) of the ICC Statute[98] and Martine Boersma, has carried out an exhaustive study of corruption as an international crime and crime against humanity.[99]

Taking a historical perspective, Boersma examined the proposal by a group of Caribbean and Latin American states led by Trinidad and Tobago at the General Assembly special session on drug trafficking in 1989.[100] During the debate a few countries, such as Libya, discussed the inclusion of corruption.[101] However, there was no intention to include non-violent crimes such as corruption in the ICC Statute because of the two following realities of international law: firstly, it deals mainly with atrocities committed in periods of crisis, such as war; secondly, it focuses on severe and massive physical violence and has a bias towards civil and political rights.[102]

Moreover, Boersma observes that regarding corruption as extermination under Article 7(1)(b) as suggested above is invalid, as there is a lack of *mens rea* in the acts of corruption that are supposed to fit the criteria of a crime against humanity; the provision requires *dolus directus* in the first and second degree. Concerning Article 7(2)(k), she also finds the arguments problematic on the basis of *mens rea*, arguing that 'in cases of grand corruption, the degree of intent required by *dolus directus* will not be present in most cases, since corrupt high-level officials will not primarily intend to harm the persons, but rather aim to enrich themselves'.[103] Boersma concludes that 'under the Rome Statute, corruption cannot be conceptualized as extermination or as any other inhumane act',[104] though she also adds: 'However, there might be possibilities to view corruption as such an offence in customary international law, which might allow for a broader *mens rea*, which does not include *dolus eventualis*.'[105]

According to Boersma, the solution could lie in providing a separate provision in the ICC Statute to curb corruption. There are two options to achieve this end. The first option would be to add a fifth crime of corruption to the statute, in addition to the crimes of aggression, genocide, war crimes and crimes against humanity. Secondly, Article 7 on crimes against humanity could be amended to include grand corruption, with corresponding amendments to the *mens rea* requirements.[106]

Having said that, a practical and currently available option is to refer the sorts of corruption cases under discussion here to the ICC. Boersma remarks:

---

98 Starr 2007, p. 1297; Acquaah-Gaisie 2005, p. 1.

99 Boersma 2012.

100 Boersma 2012, p. 290.

101 Boersma 2012, p. 102, para 82.

102 Boersma 2012, p. 294.

103 Boersma 2012, p. 338.

104 Boersma 2012, p. 338.

105 Boersma 2012, p. 338.

106 Boersma 2012, pp. 340–344.

> While it is at the moment not possible to bring high-level officials before the ICC because of corruption charges, the current cases before the Court may allow the Court to deal with corruption in relation to other crimes. While the charge itself cannot mention corruption, the trial may show the links between the commission of the crimes against humanity or war crimes, and corrupt practices. For instance, ICC cases can offer insights into the ways in which violent conflict is financed.[107]

Therefore, the possibility of having Zimbabwean cases dealt with before the ICC in the event of the prosecutor taking the Zimbabwean docket still remains.

5.8 Conclusion

The pursuit of transitional justice in Zimbabwe has played directly into perceptions that transitional justice only seeks to address civil and political rights abuses. Civil and political rights violations, for a myriad of reasons discussed in the previous chapter, have become the dominant normative lens through which to view transitional justice in Zimbabwe. It is already foreseeable that the NPRC will face the same legal and political challenges as its predecessor, the ONHRI. These include a strict mandate to only address civil and political rights abuses.

This is because one of its main functions is explicitly described as 'to develop programmes to ensure that persons subjected to persecution, torture and other forms of abuse receive rehabilitative treatment and support'.[108] If the legal interpretation of this provision presented in this chapter is accurate, it means that the NPRC authority to develop programmes is limited to focusing only on civil and political rights violations that are linked to the physical integrity and freedom of a person. The constitution does not take into account the question of impunity for socio-economic rights violations.

Therefore, the current transitional justice model envisioned in the new constitution is short-sighted, as it continues to ignore calls to investigate cases of corruption that have contributed to human rights violations. This may be deeply problematic, as it will not satisfy the victims and the community at large. Corruption is at the centre of human rights violations in Zimbabwe and therefore should be part of the transitional justice project. The NPRC's exclusive focus on civil and political rights violations will drastically diminish its capacity to provide the comprehensive post-conflict justice that is needed in Zimbabwe.

Moreover, the above discussion of the official mechanism to address past human rights violations shows that the state is not in any position to accept accountability for human rights violations. Measures are pursued in a top-down manner without including the victims and the general public. Moreover, in Zimbabwe hopes of a democratic transition have always been pinned on the constitution and its

---

[107] Boersma 2012, p. 346.

[108] Constitution of Zimbabwe Amendment (20) Act 2013, s252(e).

amendments. The topic of transitional justice has had a profound influence on the legitimacy of Zimbabwean constitutional reform; it is therefore not far-fetched to imagine that transitional justice provisions such as the creation of the NPRC were simply included to appease the citizenry as a whole rather than to curb impunity and restore democracy and respect for the law.

The only glimmer of hope lies with local non-state-actor initiatives working collectively under the umbrella of the NTJWG. They will continue to mobilise and harness the discourse and practices of transitional justice and extend them to the previously uncharted territory of socio-economic issues such as corruption. As can be seen, political transition and democratisation of the institutions of authority are required before transitional justice processes can be introduced. It is currently impossible to establish transitional justice mechanisms, in particular a truth commission to deal with socio-economic issues, given that the alleged perpetrators and beneficiaries of the systematic violations are still in power and are immensely rich. They can successfully challenge any accountability processes. Ismael Muvingi's critical analysis of Zimbabwean transitional justice prospects in 'Transitional Justice Will Have to Wait'[109] may sound pessimistic, but it still remains relevant. Be that as it may, at this juncture practitioners and academics still shoulder the burden of formulating strategies that will be implemented in the wake of a democratic government.

References

Acquaah-Gaisie GA (2005) Grand Corruption: A Crime Against Humanity. In: Delener N and Chao C (eds) Global Markets in Dynamic Environments: Making Positive Connections through Strategy, Technology and Knowledge: Proceedings of the International Conference USA: The Global Business and Technology Association pp. 1–8

Bantekas I (2006) Corruption as an International Crime and a Crime against Humanity: An Outline of Supplementary Criminal Justice Policies. Journal of International Criminal Justice 4: 466–484

Bass GJ et al (2001) The Princeton Principles on Universal Jurisdiction, Program in Law and Public Affairs and Woodrow Wilson School of Public and International Affairs, Princeton University, International Commission of Jurists, American Association for the International Commission of Jurists, Netherlands Institute of Human Rights, Urban Morgan Institute for Human Rights, published by the Program in Law and Public Affairs, Princeton University

Boersma M (2012) Corruption: A Violation of human Rights and a Crime Under International Law. Intersentia, Cambridge

Bratton M (2001) Violence, Partisanship and Transitional Justice in Zimbabwe. Journal of Modern African Studies 49: 353–380

Dorman S (2001) Inclusion and Exclusion: NGOs and Politics in Zimbabwe. Unpublished DPhil Thesis, University of Oxford

du Plessis M (2014) South Africa's Police Must Investigate Zimbabwe Torture Allegations. Institute for Security Studies. Available at http://www.issafrica.org/iss-today/south-africas-police-must-investigate-zimbabwe-torture-allegations

[109] Muvingi 2009.

du Plessis M et al (2013) Africa and the International Criminal Court. Chatham House. Available at https://www.chathamhouse.org/publications/papers/view/193415

Eppel S and Raftopoulos B (2008) Political Crisis, Mediation and the Prospects for Transitional Justice in Zimbabwe. Oxford Transitional Justice Working Paper Series. Available at http://otjr.crim.ox.ac.uk/materials/papers/42/EppelandRaftopolous_Zim_Final.pdf

ILO (2010) Truth, reconciliation and justice in Zimbabwe: Report of the Commission of Inquiry established to examine the complaints concerning the observance by the Government of Zimbabwe of the Freedom of Association and Protection of the Right to Organise Convention, 1948 (No. 87), and the Right to Organise and Collective Bargaining Convention, 1949 (No. 98) Available at https://www.ilo.org/gb/GBSessions/WCMS_123293/lang–en/index.htm Last accessed on 23 June 2019

Joyner CC (1996) Arresting Impunity: The Case for Universal Jurisdiction in Bringing War Criminals to Accountability. Law and Contemporary Problems 59: 153–172

Kofele-Kale N (2000) The Right to a Corrupt-Free Society as an Individual and Collective Human Right: Elevating Official Corruption to a Crime under International Law. International Lawyer 34: 149–178

Machakanja P (2010) National healing and reconciliation in Zimbabwe: Challenges and Opportunities. Institute for Justice and Reconciliation, Cape Town

Moore JL (2009) Transitional Justice Working Group in Liberia, Strengthening Coexistence and Transitional Justice in Liberia' International Center for Transitional Justice. Available at http://heller.brandeis.edu/coexistence/pdfs/transitional-justice/transjustliberia09.pdf

Morrell P and Pigou P (eds) (2004) Civil Society and Justice in Zimbabwe, Proceedings of a Symposium held in Johannesburg, 11–13 August 2003. Themba Lesizwe on behalf of the Southern African Trauma Coalition, Johannesburg

Moyo S (1992) NGO Advocacy in Zimbabwe: Systematizing an old Function or Inventing a New Role? Zero, Harare

Muvingi I (2009) Transitional Justice Will Have to Wait. Oxford Transitional Justice Research Series. Available at https://www.law.ox.ac.uk/sites/files/oxlaw/muvingi_final1.pdf

Przeworski A (1986) Some Problems in the Study of Transition to Democracy. In: O'Donnell et al (eds) Transitions From Authoritarian Rule: Comparative Perspectives. John Hopkins University Press, Baltimore and London, pp. 51–53

Redress (2004) Zimbabwe from Impunity to Accountability: Are Reparations Possible for Victims of Gross and Systematic Human Rights Violations? Available at https://www.univie.ac.at/bimtor/dateien/zimbabwe_redress_2004_from_impunity_to_accountability.pdf

Research and Advocacy Unit (2012) The Organ of National Healing: Is Zimbabwe a Genetically Violent Nation? Available at https://researchandadvocacyunit.wordpress.com/tag/the-organ-of-national-healing/

Shana G (quoted in Gonda V) (2010) Heated debate on national healing programme (Part 2) The Zimbabwean. Available at https://www.thezimbabwean.co/2010/05/heated-debate-on-national-healing-programme-part-2/ Last accessed on 23 June 2019

Starr S (2007) Extraordinary Crimes at Ordinary Times: International Justice Beyond Crises Situations. Northwestern University Law Review 3: 1257–1313

Teitel RG (2003) Transitional Justice Genealogy. Harvard Human Rights Journal 16: 69–94

TJWG (2019) Website Homepage. Available at https://en.tjwg.org Last accessed on 23 June 2019

Chapter 6
Zimbabwe in a Comparative Perspective

Contents

Abstract In light of the fact that transitional justice has become a global project, this chapter critically examines the law and practice of countries that have investigated corruption as a violation of socio-economic rights in their transitional justice initiatives. Using two criteria, physical geographic location and type of accountability mechanisms, the chapter will select countries that lend themselves to comparative analysis with Zimbabwe.

Keywords Arab Spring and transitional justice · decolonisation · lustration · amnesties · truth and reconciliation commissions

P. Maguchu, *Transitional Justice and Socio-Economic Rights in Zimbabwe*, International Criminal Justice Series 24,
https://doi.org/10.1007/978-94-6265-323-8_6

6.1 Introduction

In recent years, there has been an increasing amount of literature on general trends and patterns in the adoption of the five transitional justice accountability mechanisms across different times and places.[1] According to Tricia Olsen et al., for instance, post-authoritarian states in Europe have led the implementation of lustration policies and reparations, whereas truth commissions (adopted following civil wars) are spread evenly across Latin America, Africa and Asia, alongside the use of amnesties.[2]

This chapter will undertake a regional analysis of the countries, looking first at the third wave of democratisation, which spans around sixty countries across various continents and gave birth to transitional justice as a field. It also examines what other commentators call the fourth wave of democratisation that recently occurred in the Middle East and North Africa (MENA) and how it has sparked renewed interest in corruption and transitional justice.

There is no model that can be transplanted from one situation to another, particularly in view of the historical, cultural, political and other differences that different transitions are confronted with. This chapter, however, will pay special attention to those states where economic crimes by a prior regime have been as prominent—and in the public's mind as egregious—as the civil and political rights violations, and where citizens have agreed to broaden transitional justice processes such as truth commissions, amnesties, prosecutions, institutional reforms and reparations to include corruption and other economic crimes, and to investigate violations of social and economic rights.[3]

Finally, it is important to note that although a cross-regional comparison provides significant insights that enrich the current study, this book does not treat regions as homogeneous or disregard important differences within regions, but instead points out significant interregional differences where they help to illustrate the transitional justice anti-corruption nexus. Therefore, this chapter does not impose a trend on the findings; rather, it presents the case studies in a manner that allows a trend to emerge.

6.2 Sub-Saharan Africa

6.2.1 *Background*

In Sub-Saharan Africa, more than any other region of the world, the implementation of transitional justice processes has taken on a wide array of forms, including

---

1 Olsen et al. 2010; Teitel 2003.

2 Olsen et al. 2010.

3 OHCHR 2006, p. 9.

international tribunals, the use of national courts and truth commissions, and other traditional justice mechanisms and amnesties.[4] Since decolonisation, Africa has been riven by renewed inter- and intra-state conflicts based on myriad factors, including ethnicity, religion, race, natural resources and colonial legacies. Consequently, the continent has witnessed a diverse range of transitional justice mechanisms, which are intended to address the aftermath of these perennial conflicts and human rights atrocities.

Transitional justice was initially conceptualised as a national affair, primarily as a way for an individual state to deal with its mass abuses a state response to dealing with its mass abuses—in many cases without the context of a transition from dictatorship to democracy.[5] In many African countries, transitional justice was put as a clause in peace treaties, which were sometimes brokered by regional economic blocs such as the SADC and ECOWAS.[6] The direct involvement of the AU organs and regional economic communities has led to the formidable African Transitional Justice Framework (ATJF), which is discussed below.

6.2.2 *Law*

The ATJF does not create new obligations on member states; rather, it forges links between transitional justice, governance, human rights, peace and security, and development.[7] Thus, the principal regional legislation on transitional justice in Sub-Saharan Africa remains the key regional human rights instruments such as the AChtPHR, the African Charter on Democracy, Elections and Governance (ACDEG) and the Constitutive Act of the African Union (CAAU). These legal instruments have common approaches to consolidating peace, reconciliation and justice, and preventing impunity.

The socio-economic rights perspective in the African region is more pronounced in the landmark decision of *SERAC v. Nigeria* before the ACmPHR:

> Until the SERAC communication, individual communications rarely dealt with socio-economic rights and in considering the Commission's jurisprudence, it becomes evident that the Commission showed a reluctance to elaborate on socio-economic rights. Not only was the African human rights system the first regional system to recognise the right to a satisfactory environment but it was also the first system to pronounce on the meaning and content of the right.

This case has not only served to promote jurisprudence on reparations, which is a key aspect of transitional justice, but it has also enhanced the inclusion of socio-economic issues in the African transitional justice debate.

---

4 CSVR 2019.

5 Brankovic and van de Merwe 2014.

6 Brankovic and van de Merwe 2014.

7 ATJF, p. 5.

6.2.3 Practice

Sub-Saharan African countries have been slowly leading the move away from the traditional practice of solely focusing on violations of bodily integrity such as rape, murder and torture.[8] Sub-Saharan Africa has the highest and growing number of countries incorporating socio-economic rights and corruption into transitional justice.[9] This is not surprising given that Sub-Saharan Africa is perceived to be the most corrupt region in the world and one of the worst human rights violators. Below is an analysis of a few of the pioneering countries whose transitional justice commissions have included corruption and economic crimes in their mandate or as part of their main findings.

6.2.3.1 Chad

Chad established the elaborately titled Commission of Inquiry into the Crimes and Misappropriations Committed by ex-President Hissène Habré, His Accomplices and/or Accessories.[10] The commission had a mandate to investigate violations of the physical and mental integrity of persons, such as unlawful detentions, deaths and torture, and all violations of human rights, including socio-economic issues such as illicit narcotics trafficking and embezzlement of state funds.[11] The Chad commission final report included a list of officials involved in plundering national resources and recommended asset recovery and the vetting of these people before they can assume public positions.[12]

6.2.3.2 Sierra Leone

Just as with the Zimbabwean NPRC, the Sierra Leone Truth and Reconciliation Commission (SL-TRC) did not have an explicit mandate to redress the issue of corruption. Its explicit mandate was only to produce a report on human rights violations, provide a forum for both victims and perpetrators, and recommend policies to facilitate reconciliation and prevent future violations.[13] However, in its

---

[8] Cavallaro and Albuja 2008; Sharp 2012.

[9] Carranza 2008.

[10] Decree Creating the Commission of Inquiry into the Crimes and Misappropriations Committed by ex-President Habré, His Accomplices and/or Accessories, Decree No. 014/P.CE/CJ/90.

[11] Decree Creating the Commission of Inquiry into the Crimes and Misappropriations Committed by ex-President Habré, His Accomplices and/or Accessories, Decree No. 014/P.CE/CJ/90, Article 2.

[12] Tchad Ministère de la Justice 1993, pp. 27–28.

[13] Truth and Reconciliation Commission Act 2000 (Sierra Leone), Part III(6)(2)(a).

findings the SL-TRC indicated that the main cause of the war in Sierra Leone was corruption.[14]

Further, another important transitional justice mechanism was implemented when an agreement was reached between the UN and the government of Sierra Leone to establish a hybrid court, the Special Court of Sierra Leone (SCSL), which had a mandate to prosecute crimes against humanity and municipal crimes.[15] In the main trial against former Liberian president Charles Taylor, the SCSL included economic crimes in the charges as part of the five counts of war crimes, including widespread looting of civilian property throughout Sierra Leone.[16]

6.2.3.3 Liberia

After signing a comprehensive peace agreement with the government and the main rebel groups, a transitional government was established in Liberia. It set up the Truth and Reconciliation Commission (TRC) with an extensive mandate to

> investigat[e] gross human rights violations and violations of international humanitarian law as well as abuses that occurred, including massacres, sexual violations, murder, extra-judicial killings and *economic crimes*, such as the exploitation of natural or public resources to perpetuate armed conflicts, during the period January 1979 to October 14, 2003.[17]

Fulfilling this mandate was a very complex task; the TRC had to determine whether abuses were isolated incidents or part of a systematic pattern, establish the antecedents, circumstances, factors and context of such violations and abuses, and determine those responsible for the commission of the violations, their motives and the impact of the abuses on victims.[18]

After completing its mandate, the TRC produced a specialised report on economic crimes. The TRC cited a lack of accountability, particularly in relation to transparency and misappropriation of resources, as one of the main causes of the conflict. Part of the report reads as follows:

---

[14] Consolidated Final Report, vol. II, p. 16.

[15] Security Council Resolution 1315, 2000, Articles 2–5.

[16] *Prosecutor v. Charles Ghankay Taylor*, SCSL-03-1-T, Violations of Article 3 Common to the Geneva Conventions and of Additional Protocol II, punishable under Article 3 of the Statute, count 11.

[17] Truth and Reconciliation Commission (TRC) Act (Liberia), Article 4(4)(a). The Liberian TRC had a mandate to investigate gross human rights violations and violations of international humanitarian law as well as abuses including massacres, sexual violations, murder, extra-judicial killings and economic crimes, such as the exploitation of natural or public resources to perpetuate armed conflicts, that occurred during the period January 1979 to 14 October 2003.

[18] Government of Kenya, p. 216.

> The commission of and the opportunity for the commission of economic crimes contribute immensely to the exacerbation and prolongation of the Liberian conflict
>
> All warring factions, participated in, encouraged and benefited with impunity from the commission of economic crimes through the illicit trading in Liberian natural resources, looting and illegal sale of public properties and assets[19]

6.2.3.4 Kenya

The Kenyan experience is relevant to Zimbabwe because of the intriguing parallels between the two countries. In both states, colonisation by Britain brought massive socio-economic rights violations. Restrictive post-colonial constitutions only granted political freedoms and further perpetuated the violation of socio-economic rights that began during the colonial era. In addition, post-colonial governments continued to use the repressive laws, policies and practices of the erstwhile colonial governments to perpetuate a litany of socio-economic rights abuses. Both states have sponsored violence to suppress opposition. In 2007 and 2008, in Kenya and Zimbabwe respectively, elections were followed by violence, which led to internationally sponsored mediation processes and the creation of transitional governments. Both states set up truth inquiry mechanisms and transitional justice without a political transition.

The mandate of the Kenyan Truth, Justice and Reconciliation Commission (TJRC) was largely informed by the debates that took place in 2003 surrounding the recommendations made by the Makau Mutua Task Force (Task Force on the Establishment of a Peace Commission), which was set up earlier to address transitional justice issues.[20] When the task force made its recommendations, there were other commentators who were of the view that a truth commission should not address issues such as corruption or economic crimes, as this would overburden its mandate and distract it from concentrating on human rights violations.[21]

The task force remained adamant that 'the investigation of past economic crimes should be included [because otherwise it would] represent such a yawning gap in the record of truth of Kenya'.[22] The task force is believed to have proposed a method of truth seeking very similar to the Philippines's, which had earlier managed to address its legacies of corruption and human rights abuses simultaneously.[23] The task force proposed that the truth commission be 'organized into two

[19] Government of Kenya, p. 216.

[20] On 17 April 2003, by a special issue of the Kenya Gazette, the government of the Republic of Kenya, through the minister for justice and constitutional affairs, appointed the Task Force on the Establishment of a Truth, Justice, and Reconciliation Commission.

[21] Hayner and Bosire 2003.

[22] Hayner and Bosire 2003 (citation omitted).

[23] Carranza 2008, p. 322.

chambers, one to look into past gross violations of human rights abuses and another to deal with past grave economic crimes'.[24]

The task force further recommended that a Kenyan truth commission should focus on the following six violations and/or issues: political assassinations and killings; massacres and possible genocides; political violence and killings of democracy advocates; torture, detention, exile, disappearances, rape and persecution of opponents; politically instigated ethnic clashes; and violations of social, economic and cultural rights.[25]

The task force argued that 'it is a well-established fact in human rights law that all human rights including economic, social and cultural rights are indivisible, inter-dependent, and inter-related'.[26] According to the task force, human rights law is not only restricted to civil and political rights, due to Kenya's international obligations under the ICCPR and the ICESCR to protect all human rights, that is, both civil and political rights and economic, social and cultural rights.[27] Consequently, the task force recommended that the TJRC 'should investigate the violations of civil and political rights as well as those of economic, social and cultural rights'.[28]

No truth commission was set up in the wake of the report, since further political developments in Kenya made it impossible to carry out transitional justice. However, following the post-election mayhem in 2007, the recommendation to set up a truth commission was repeated at the Kenya National Dialogue and Reconciliation (KNDR) negotiations. This process gave birth to the TJRC, which in turn considered the mandate to address socio-economic rights violations so that corruption and economic crimes could be investigated.[29]

The KNDR concurred with the Makau Mutua Task Force report that 'economic crimes lead to the violations of the entire gamut of human rights and in particular of economic, social and cultural rights'.[30] However, it went further than the task force and expanded the list to include a plethora of other issues, including what it called historical injustices. In this regard, the TJRC Agreement states:

> The Commission will inquire into human rights violations, including those committed by the state, groups, or individuals. This includes but is not limited to politically motivated violence, assassinations, community displacements, settlements and evictions. The Commission will also inquire into major economic crimes, in particular grand corruption, historical land injustices, and the illegal and irregular acquisition of land, especially as these relate to conflict or violence. Other historical injustices shall be investigated.[31]

[24] Hayner and Bosire 2003.

[25] Government of Kenya 2003, pp. 30–33.

[26] Government of Kenya 2003, p. 33.

[27] Government of Kenya 2003, p. 33.

[28] Government of Kenya 2003, p. 33.

[29] TJRC 2013, vol. 1, p. 68, para 101.

[30] TJRC 2013, vol. 1, p. 67, quoting Makau Mutua Task Force Report 33.

[31] TJRC 2013, vol. 1.

The subject matter mandate of the TJRC was drawn from the recommendations of both the task force and the TJRC Agreement.

In particular, Section 5 of the Truth, Justice and Reconciliation Commission Act (TJRC Act), which outlines the objectives of the commission, provides for investigation of economic crimes, including grand corruption and the exploitation of natural or public resources, under Subsection 6(n).[32] The TJRC made an important contribution to the field of transitional justice as this highlighted the importance of socio-economic rights by confirming the dynamics of including economic crimes and corruption in transitional justice programmes.

> loss or destruction of public property or revenue, especially in the area of public procurement, public contracts, public land and general management of public funds. These crimes inevitably involve very senior powerful public servants awarding large public contracts running into billions of shillings, with the assurance of getting a certain amount as a commission. This ultimately constitutes what is referred to as grand corruption. Grand corruption is therefore a direct product of economic crimes. In other words, economic crimes result in grand corruption. The two are inextricably linked to each other, and for our purposes, we use the terms interchangeably.[33]

It is noteworthy that there were other proposals to deal with corruption through an amnesty law.[34] The proposals were to pass a law that would grant amnesty for the full disclosure and return of looted assets. The draft Anti-Corruption and Economic Crimes Bill was due to be published for debate in the Kenyan legislature but never saw the light of day after facing constitutional challenges.[35] Outside parliament other eminent anti-corruption activists, like the former Kenyan ethics and governance chief John Githongo, were also arguing that people accused of corruption should be offered amnesty if they confess in full and voluntarily surrender stolen wealth.[36] However, this proposal was rejected and singled out for attacks by citizens and civil society.[37]

In order to fulfil its mandate to address corruption and economic crimes, the TJRC took the approach of building cases from the already-existing anti-corruption commission and reports from previous commissions of inquiry into large-scale corruption scandals.[38] The TJRC's main role was to expose 'the profound cost the nation is paying through corruption'.[39] It made clear that its role was 'not to provide "the" solution to the problem of corruption'.[40] Accordingly, it identified the Ethics

32 TJRC 2013, vol. 2b, p. 343, para 3.
33 TJRC 2013, vol. 2b, p. 350, para 31.
34 TJRC 2013, vol. 1, p. 71, para 115.
35 Kenya National Assembly Official Record (Hansard), 7 May 2002, 848.
36 Kisiangani 2009.
37 Kisiangani 2009.
38 TJRC 2013, vol. 2b, p. 32.
39 Robinson 2014, p. 8.
40 Robinson 2014, p. 8.

and Anti-Corruption Commission (EACC) as the appropriate forum in which to tackle accountability and long-term prevention initiatives.[41]

Thus, although the TJRC was mandated to 'investigate economic crimes, including grand corruption', it relied primarily on investigations already carried out by the EACC, as well as previous independent commissions of inquiry. As a result, the TJRC was not hampered by its lack of the necessary skills or expertise to investigate complex cases of high-level corruption. Moreover, the TJRC did not simply duplicate what had already been done by anti-corruption bodies. Rather, it appears to have contributed an additional perspective lacking from anti-corruption processes in Kenya by exposing the human cost of corruption.[42] Isabel Robinson has observed that 'the primary contribution of the TJRC was to emphasize the impact of corruption on human rights'.[43]

In furthering its objectives as a truth commission, the TJRC collected statements from members of the public. The TJRC gave the people an opportunity to present cases that were frustrated by civil courts and ignored by the anti-corruption commission. A staggering figure of 5,646 of those who were interviewed by the TJRC attributed corruption to human rights violations in Kenya.[44] The TJRC also received testimonies from informants about acts of grand corruption including in relation to elections and in the procurement of essential goods.[45] In spite of the explicit mandate of the TJRC to address only grand corruption, it also investigated cases of petty corruption.[46]

6.3 Latin America

6.3.1 Background

The loss of US hegemony on the continent after the Cuban Revolution was followed by military dictatorships that adopted the doctrine of national security on the pretext of developing a common strategy to fight against communism. This period is also marked by state brutality, massive human rights violations and large-scale looting of national resources. Following the fall of military regimes, the region of Latin America, in particular the southern cone, became the first region to undergo concentrated transitional justice experiences in modern history.[47]

---

41 Robinson 2014, p. 8.
42 Robinson 2014, p. 9.
43 Robinson 2014, p. 9.
44 TJRC 2013, vol. 2b, p. 416, para 269.
45 TJRC 2013, vol. 2b, p. 416, para 269.
46 TJRC 2013, vol. 2b, p. 416, para 269.
47 Skaar, Garcia-Godos and Collins 2019.

Consequently, the South American continent has a special understanding of some of the mechanisms of transitional justice.[48] This is mainly because in Latin America transitional justice practices have been dominated by truth commissions and amnesties relating to the violation of civil and political rights.[49] However, Latin America's transitional justice experiences have influenced the practice and discourse of the field around the world, and countries continue to learn from them. For this reason, it still remains an indispensable reference point regarding the engagement of transitional justice mechanisms with the question of corruption.[50]

6.3.2 Law

In Latin America, as in Sub-Saharan Africa, policymakers used the underlying principles of human rights treaties such as the American Convention on Human Rights (ACHR)[51] and the American Declaration of the Rights and Duties of Man (ADRDM)[52] to provide the impetus for transitional justice mechanisms. What is more, the development of transitional justice law in Latin America is quite intriguing, in particular the careful and innovative development of regional and national legal strategies to abrogate amnesty laws or the use of lacunae to bypass them in order to prevent continuing impunity.[53]

This process is exemplified by the watershed case of *Velásquez Rodríguez v. Honduras*, in which the Inter-American Commission (IAC) took the position that amnesty laws inconsistent with its jurisprudence were unlawful on the grounds that they violated a victim's right to a remedy and a fair trial.[54] This position was further bolstered in 2001 by the Inter-American Court of Human Rights (IACtHR) in *Barrios Altos v. Peru*,[55] where the court made clear that it would take a consistent stance on any amnesty case brought before it, and by *Almonacid Arellano et al. v. Chile,* which confirmed the idea that self-amnesty laws were incompatible with the ACHR.[56]

Following these decisions by the IACtHR, many Latin American states increasingly resorted to pre-hearing settlements in the form of reparations to avoid stiff reparations orders from the court.[57] However, rather than being motivated by

[48] De Campos Mello 2009, p. 84.

[49] Cavallaro and Albuja 2008.

[50] Carranza 2008.

[51] Organization of American States (OAS), American Convention on Human Rights, adopted on 21 November 1969, entry into force on 18 July 1978, 1144 UNTS 123.

[52] (1949) 43 AJIL Supp 133.

[53] Roht-Arriaza 2014, p. 2.

[54] 29 July 1988, IACtHr (Ser. C) No. 4 (1988).

[55] *Barrios Altos v. Peru,* judgment of 14 March 2001 (Merits), IACtHr, para 39

[56] *Almonacid Arellano et al. v. Chile*, judgment of 26 September 2006, IACtHr, paras 123–124.

[57] Roht-Arriaza 2014, p. 2.

financial compensation, victims and human rights advocates gradually began using the IACtHR's rulings to demand investigations, prosecutions, further reparations and truth-telling, only returning to the court when states failed to implement rulings, thereby building the norms of transitional justice in Latin America as we know them today.[58]

6.3.3 Practice

In the beginning, most transitional justice mechanisms in Latin America were narrowly focused on the extremely violent physical human rights abuses committed by former military dictatorships, such as enforced disappearances, torture and murder.[59] Although a few countries, such as Peru and Chile, had included economic crimes in their transitional justice mechanisms, they were an exception rather than the norm.[60] However, recent developments are bringing transitional justice back to the region that has long dominated the field, this time with a deeper and wider application encompassing economic crimes. This section will look at some pre-transitional justice mechanisms in Brazil, which is one of the countries to have included corruption in its transitional justice approach, in order to add to the discussion and draw a comparative analysis.

6.3.3.1 Brazil

Like Zimbabwe, Brazil has implemented some piecemeal transitional justice measures, mainly based on impunity rather than accountability. Consequently, accountability for the gross violations of human rights committed during the years of military dictatorship between 1964 and 1985 has in most cases been extremely limited.[61] This is attributed to the country's top-down transitional justice policies. For instance, in 1974 the country experienced some slow transition when moderate elements within the military took control of the government. This resulted in the passage of the 1979 Amnesty Law to shield perpetrators of violence from prosecution, truth-telling or other forms of accountability. In particular, the amnesty law ensured immunity from prosecution for security forces and dissidents who had engaged in political violence.[62]

Events in December 2007 reignited a national campaign for truth and justice for the unaddressed abuses of Brazil's past. Just as in the Zimbabwean amnesty case

---

58 Roht-Arriaza 2014, p. 2.

59 Cavallaro and Albuja 2008.

60 Carranza 2008.

61 O'Donnell 1998, p. 281.

62 O'Donnell 1998, p. 281.

before the ACmHPR,[63] the IACtHR ruled that provisions of the Amnesty Law of 1979 that prevented investigations of and sanctions for grave rights violations are incompatible with the IACtHR and thus are of no effect.[64]

Brazil formed the National Truth Commission (NTC) as a diplomatic gesture to appease the international community after the IACtHR ruling.[65] It has contributed to the process of truth-telling by including narratives on financial complicity, and by investigating and exposing links between the dictatorship period and economic crimes.[66] The NTC has also has helped to develop historical education programmes for schools that include this financial dimension of the dictatorship period. It can use its authority to recommend reforms to financial institutions. Unlike most of the truth commissions that have dominated the narratives of transitional justice in Latin America, the Brazilian NTC has adopted a broad, holistic approach that goes beyond the traditional, narrower goals of transitional justice.[67]

6.4 Asia

6.4.1 Background

Like Africa and Latin America, Asia is another region in the global south that has had unique experiences with transitional justice. Firstly, it is important to note that conditions in Asia are significantly less conducive to transitional justice than in Africa and Latin America, as Park Won Soon has observed:

> (1) relatively low levels of public awareness, especially in countries like South Korea where a Confucian mentality prevents many from demanding the punishment of past rulers; (2) Buddhist populations that object to ideas of revenge; (3) populations concerned more with the capability of the new government to improve the quality of life by revitalizing the devastated economy than rectifying the past; (4) weak civil societies and an unmet need for new leadership; (5) the lack of historical examples in the region; and (6) the absence of regional human rights mechanisms and regional cohesion.[68]

Therefore, Asia is not an immediately intuitive place to look for guidance on transitional justice in general and on engagement with economic crimes and corruption in particular. However, it does provide some significant lessons on what to avoid when attempting to engage with corruption using transitional justice mechanisms.

---

63 *Zimbabwe Human Rights NGO Forum v. the Republic of Zimbabwe* (Communication No. 245/2002) [2006] ACHPR 73; (25 May 2006).

64 *Julia Gomes Lund and Others v. Brazil* IACHR, Report No. 71/15, Case 12.879, (28 Oct 2015).

65 Schneider and Iecker de Almeida 2018, p. 639.

66 Schneider and Iecker de Almeida 2018, p. 639.

67 Sharp 2012, p. 235.

68 Cited in Cook 1997.

6.4.2 Law

As hinted at above, unlike Africa and the Americas, Asia-Pacific does not have a region-wide intergovernmental system—such as treaties, courts, commissions or other institutions—to protect and promote human rights, and which could be used to help formulate and implement transitional justice policies. On the whole, Asia has relied on international legal norms and standards, such as those of the UN, which set a minimum accountability threshold for transitional justice processes, and has ensured compliance with these international norms and standards when designing and implementing transitional justice measures to redress its violent past.

6.4.3 Practice

It is not easy to generalise about a region; Asia as a region has pursued a variety of transitional justice approaches, especially in relation to corruption. Some Asian countries have seen transitional justice at the same time with development and economic growth focused on development rather than the past.[69] South Korea is an example where corrupt dictators were allowed to keep their ill-gotten gains. On the other hand, we have countries like the Philippines, Cambodia and East Timor, which have successfully incorporated or addressed corruption in their transitional justice models.[70] The way corruption and transitional justice policies are formulated, implemented and later rejected in Asia offers many important insights into transitional justice practice that are of relevance beyond the region.

6.4.3.1 Philippines

The case of the Philippines shows how economic crimes and human rights violations have mutually reinforced impunity in the region. For instance, Ferdinand Marcos and his associates, including his widow, Imelda Marcos, have not been imprisoned for human rights violations or for the corruption they perpetrated. Surprisingly, the post-Marcos governments have failed to hold the former dictator criminally accountable for either corruption or human rights violations.[71] The Marcos clan and military conspirators remain unaccountable and their families continue to enjoy the ill-gotten gains of their economic crimes, preventing any efforts to come to a reckoning with the past.[72]

---

69 Soon 1997.
70 Carranza 2008.
71 Carranza 2008.
72 Carranza 2008.

Recently, a truth commission to look into corruption was ruled illegal by the constitutional court. On 30 July 2010, President Benigno Simeon C. Aquino III issued Executive Order (E.O.) No. 1 creating the Philippine Truth Commission of 2010 (PTC), which was

> primarily tasked to conduct a thorough fact-finding investigation of reported cases of graft and corruption involving third level public officers and higher, their co-principals, accomplices and accessories from the private sector, if any, during the previous administration and thereafter submit its findings and recommendations to the President, Congress and the Ombudsman.[73]

The Supreme Court of the Philippines held that E.O. 1 should be struck down as a violation of the equal protection clause in the Philippines constitution:

> Not to include past administrations similarly situated constitutes arbitrariness which the equal protection clause cannot sanction. Such discriminating differentiation gave the majority an impression that the PTC is just being used 'as a vehicle for vindictiveness and selective retribution' and that E.O. 1 is only an 'adventure in partisan hostility'.[74]

6.4.3.2 Bangladesh

Bangladesh is considered to be one of the most corrupt nations in the world according to various international corruption rankings. Successive governments have tried to tackle this problem by introducing new laws and establishing anti-corruption commissions. It is important to note that any truth inquiry into corruption as part of the transitional justice processes should still serve the purposes of transitional justice, such as reconciliation and the ultimate establishment of the rule of law. Thus, the 2008 Truth and Accountability Commission (TAC), which was established to offer partial amnesties in return for information about corruption,[75] was ruled illegal and unconstitutional by the High Court.[76] The stated rationale of TAC Bangladesh was ostensibly to clear a massive backlog of corruption cases and not to address human rights related issues.

Together, these two case studies provide important insights into the adoption of anti-corruption mechanisms in transitional justice. However, there exists little systematic research into engagement with corruption and transitional justice in Asia. Further work is required to establish this missing link.

---

[73] Executive Order No. 1. Creating the Philippine Truth Commission of 2010.

[74] *Louis Biraogo v. Philippine Truth Commission,* judgment of 7 December 2010, G.R. No. 192935, and *Rep. Edcel Lagman et al. v. Executive Secretary Paquito Ochoa et al.*, judgment of 2010, G.R. No. 192936.

[75] Truth and Accountability Commission Ordinance 2008.

[76] *Adilur Rahman Khan v. Bangladesh*, 16 BLC 100.

6.5 Central and Eastern Europe and the Former Soviet Union

6.5.1 Background

Before analysing this region, it is important to mention that there is a difference between the Central and East European (CEE) and Former Soviet Union (FSU) countries, although for present purposes they have been grouped under one region.[77] The regime transitions in both the CEE and FSU countries occurred around the same time as the fall of communism and the collapse of authoritarian regimes in Latin America, Africa and South-East Asia. Despite the availability of lessons from other regions on what mechanisms to use, post-communist states constructed a distinct form of transitional justice: lustration. The unique use of lustration in its various incarnations in post-communist countries makes comparison with other regions difficult.

Nevertheless, lustrations still serve the same purpose whether they are pursued to achieve truth and reconciliation, or as in Latin America, Sub-Saharan Africa and CEE and FSU countries, to identify past wrongs, punish those who benefited and then draw a line between the past and the present so as to rebuild political and social institutions.[78] More importantly, as Yuliya Zabyelina has noted with reference to Ukraine's experience, lustrations reconciled transitional justice with socio-economic imperatives, such as the fight against corruption, not only as a discursive practice but as a legal matter.[79]

6.5.2 Law

There is no specific reference to transitional justice in the corpus of treaties establishing the EU. In contrast to other regions, the ECtHR case law relating to transitional justice includes hundreds of judgments and decisions dealing with a wide range of issues, namely compensation and restitution, prosecutions, lustration, memorialisation and truth inquiries.[80] The lack of a coherent legal framework for transitional justice in the EU is due to the fact that many CEE and FSU countries joined the EU after the transition. The ECtHR has frequently ruled that the ways in which some states have dealt with their authoritarian past have violated human rights norms. The ECtHR has developed criteria intended to ensure that transitional justice measures conform to human rights standards.

---

[77] Horne and Stan 2018.

[78] Brown 2013.

[79] Zabyelina 2017, p. 55.

[80] Brems 2011, pp. 282–303.

6.5.3 Practice

Until recently, there have been no reliable studies to prove the linkages between lustrations and corruption. Some insightful lessons can be salvaged from preliminary work undertaken recently by Peter Rožič and Yuliy Nisnevich. The pioneering research examines the role of transitional justice in addressing corruption by analysing original panel data from thirty post-communist states from 1996 to 2011. It is interesting to note that in all the cases examined, it was found that lustration is effective in lowering corruption.

The observed correlation between lustration as a means of transitional justice and a reduction in corruption might be explained as follows: lustration disrupts the political, economic and administrative malpractice of the preceding regimes by limiting opportunities for corruption by former communist elites. Rožič and Nisnevich's study breaks new ground with a novel system-level explanation and an integrative approach to causation for the entire post-communist world.[81] The case of Poland discussed below is illustrative of the general practice.

6.5.3.1 Poland

Poland is one of the CEE countries that adopted lustration policies to signal a break with the past. In 1989, the first parliamentary motion on lustration was passed, and in 1992 the first lustration exercises were carried out. However, it was not until 1996 that the *Sejm* (lower house of parliament) began work on a comprehensive draft law, and in August 1997 a screening law finally entered into force. The law created a lustration court to verify the declarations of senior officials, and to punish them in the event of false statements. The Institute of National Remembrance (IPN) was created in 1998 and charged with archiving and custodial functions, as well as responsibilities to assist with reviewing collaboration claims and running background checks on those seeking public office.

In November 2006, a new lustration plan was ratified, which went into effect on 15 March 2007. The new programme substantially expanded the scope and transparency of previous lustration efforts. By linking lustration with anti-corruption measures, the expanded justice programme aimed to redress continued economic and political *nomenklatura* networks.[82] The economic inequalities and continued aggrandising tendencies of the Polish elites were two important reasons given by the then Polish government for enacting the 2007 lustration law.[83]

---

[81] Rožič and Nisnevich 2016.

[82] Horne 2009.

[83] Horne 2009.

6.6 Middle East and North Africa

6.6.1 Background

The recent wave of protests in the MENA region, which came to be collectively known as the Arab Spring, has fast become an important area of study in the field of transitional justice. Much of the literature pays attention to the similarities between the Arab Spring and the '1989 moment',[84] and there also appear to be parallels between the conditions in this region and those that typified the third wave of democratisation which gave birth to transitional justice as a discipline in other regions discussed above.

Although the transitional justice in the wake of the Arab Spring is comparable to the third wave of democratisation, there are significant differences. For instance, while the third wave of democratisation was restrictive, the Arab Spring transitional justice involves a broad range of human rights claims, relating to both civil and political rights and socio-economic rights.

Above all, the Arab Spring not only put transitional justice on the political agenda in a region of the world where it was seldom discussed, but also put forward a broader view of transitional justice than that which has traditionally been implemented.[85] Most importantly, it highlighted the need for economic elements to be incorporated into transitional justice in a way that has not been seen in other regional transitions.[86]

6.6.2 Law

The MENA is a predominantly Islamic region where Sharia law is very influential. However, transitional justice in this region has largely remained distant from Islamic principles. The transitional justice template is generally framed in secular terms and usually in the legal language of international law. The current developments and arrangements for transitional justice in the MENA region have adopted an approach that is being spearheaded by the UN Under-Secretary-General, supported jointly by UNDP and OHCHR.[87]

---

[84] Teti et al. 2018, p. 1.

[85] See Sriram 2017.

[86] Fisher and Stewart 2014, p. 7.

[87] Yusuf 2017, p. 154.

6.6.3 *Practice*

There is a common trend in the MENA countries undergoing transitional justice that claims against corruption have been raised to a par with claims for the redress of violations of civil and political rights.[88] Corruption appeared as one of the main grievances in Yemen, Libya, Egypt, Tunisia, Bahrain and Syria, on par with violations of civil and political rights.[89] However, most of the cases are rather controversial, and there is no general agreement among scholars and practitioners about whether transitional justice has been properly applied or was only abused to replace one tyranny with another, the case of Tunisia discussed below is highly illustrative.

By focusing on one state that has pursued economic crimes in its post-uprising transitional justice mechanisms and processes, this section will investigate the anti-corruption transitional justice trajectories between the Arab countries and Zimbabwe.

6.6.3.1 Tunisia

The Arab Spring started in Tunisia when a young vendor set himself on fire in protest at police corruption, triggering protests across the country and in several other Arab states, with people calling for an end to impunity for human rights abuses and corruption. Tunisia offers interesting parallels with Zimbabwe. In both states, public corruption came to be part of daily life and to pose a great threat to survival, creating serious tensions and widespread discontent that culminated in a general uprising.[90]

Although in Zimbabwe the November 2017 military-assisted transition led to the end of the Mugabe regime, it is yet to bring democracy. In Tunisia, by contrast, the transition process culminated in the appointment of a new parliament and president through an election that was declared to be in accordance with the new constitution. This election consolidated the foundations of the political transition.[91] After the implementation of transitional justice measures, Tunisia formally qualified as a democracy in 2017. Below is a discussion of how corruption was handled in these mechanisms.[92]

Truth Commissions

The governments following the Ben Ali dictatorship have created truth commissions with a direct mandate to address corruption. The provisional technocratic government set up in the aftermath of the crisis immediately established a

[88] Kora 2012.

[89] Kora 2012.

[90] Yerkes and Muasher 2010, p. 14.

[91] Boughzala and Romdhane 2016, pp. 107–132.

[92] Boughzala and Romdhane 2016, pp. 107–132.

commission of inquiry,[93] the Amor Commission (named after its head, Abdelfattah Amor), to address cases of corruption and embezzlement committed by Ben Ali and his associates. The new government formally created the National Commission to Investigate Corruption and Embezzlement (NCICE).[94] The Truth and Dignity Commission Organic Law[95] replaced the NCICE with the Truth and Dignity Commission of Tunisia (TDCT), a truth commission with an explicit mandate to investigate economic crimes and human rights violations committed between 1955 and 2013.

Specialised Chambers

The new government also created specialised chambers, the Financial Judiciary Pole, to deal with transitional justice.[96] This specialised judicial unit was entrusted to adjudicate cases referred to it by the TDCT. The specialised criminal chambers have received cases relating to election fraud, financial corruption, misuse of public funds and individuals forced to migrate for political reasons.[97]

Institutional Reforms

Tunisia has adopted institutional reforms aimed at dismantling and rectifying the system of corruption, oppression and tyranny that was created and allowed to flourish under the presidency of Ben Ali, so as to guarantee non-repetition of the violations, respect for human rights and the establishment of rule of law. Institutional reform measures that were adopted include legislative reforms, reforms to state institutions which were used to perpetrate corruption and human rights violations, and vetting and rehabilitating public sector employees in accordance with the new law.[98]

Amnesties

Concurrently with the TDCT and the special criminal chambers, the Tunisian government also passed (controversial) amnesty laws in the form of the Economic Reconciliation Law and the Law on Administrative Reconciliation (a revised version of the former economic reconciliation bill) to offer amnesties in exchange for asset recovery from perpetrators of corruption under the Ben Ali regime.[99]

Reparations

In its effort to provide justice for victims of corruption during the pre-revolutionary period, as part of its transitional justice efforts the Tunisian government has adopted

---

[93] Decree not publicly available.

[94] Decree Law 2011-7.

[95] Decree Law 2013-53.

[96] Basic Law 57 of 2016.

[97] Organic Law on Transitional Justice (Tunisia), Article 8.

[98] Organic Law on Transitional Justice (Tunisia), Article 14.

[99] Organic Law on Transitional Justice (Tunisia), Article 43.

reparations programmes. These programmes are unique in the field of transitional justice in that they are the first to have formally ‘recognize[d] socio-economic harms as violations warranting justice and material reparation’.[100]

6.7 Conclusion

There is no internationally agreed framework for transitional justice and corruption, but there are signs that corruption is gradually coming to be seen as a human rights issue and a cause for concern for transitional justice. The countries discussed in this chapter offer prime examples. The fact that transitional justice mechanisms are mainstreaming corruption is very encouraging, and helps to set a precedent. Despite the growing literature on the topic, there is still no concise framework for engaging with corruption using transitional justice mechanisms and processes. However, as Dustin Sharp remarks regarding the emerging trends: ‘while these efforts have varied in terms of quality, rigor, and the amount of attention paid to economic violence, they nevertheless represent an important step in moving economic violence into the foreground of the transitional justice agenda.’[101] Thus, the engagement with corruption is slowly moving from being a moot academic point to a practical reality.

References

Boughzala M and Romdhane SB (2016) Tunisia: The Prospects for Democratic Consolidation. In: Elbadawi I and Makdisi S (eds) Democratic Transitions in the Arab World. Cambridge University Press, Cambridge, pp. 107–132

Brankovic J and van der Merwe H (2014) Transitional Justice in Post-Conflict Societies: Conceptual Foundations and Debates. Centre for the Study of Violence and Reconciliation. Available at https://www.csvr.org.za/publications/2604-tj-in-post-conflict-societies-conceptual-foundations-and-debates Last accessed on 23 June 2019

Brems E (2011) Transitional Justice in the Case Law of the European Court of Human Rights. International Journal of Transitional Justice 5: 282–303

Brown S (2013) The National Accord, Impunity and the Fragile Peace in Kenya. In: Sriram CL et al (eds) Transitional Justice and Peacebuilding on the Ground: Victims and Ex Combatants. Routledge, London

Carranza R (2008) Plunder and Pain: Should Transitional Justice Engage with Corruption and Economic Crimes? International Journal of Transitional Justice 2: 310–330

Cavallaro JL and Albuja S (2008) The Lost Agenda: Economic Crimes and Truth Commissions in Latin America and Beyond. In: McEvoy K and McGregor L (eds) Transitional Justice from Below: Grassroots Activism and the Struggle for Change (Human Rights Law in Perspective). Hart, Oxford, pp. 121–141

---

[100] Yerkes and Muasher 2010, p. 14.

[101] Sharp 2012, p. 80.

Cook T (1997) Introduction: Transitional Justice in East Asia and its Impact on Human Rights. Carnegie Council for Ethics in International Affairs. Available at https://www.carnegiecouncil.org/publications/archive/dialogue/1_08/articles/550 Last accessed on 23 June 2019

De Campos Mello C (2009) Transitional Justice in South America: The Role of the Inter-American Court of Human Rights. Debates Sobre Derechos Humanos y el Sistema Interamericano. Available at http://www.corteidh.or.cr/tablas/r24268.pdf Last accessed on 23 June 2019

Fisher KJ and Stewart R (2014) After the Arab Spring: A New Wave of Transitional Justice. In: Fisher KJ and Stewart R (eds) Transitional Justice and the Arab Spring. Routledge Taylor and Francis, London, pp. 1–14

Government of Kenya (2003) Report of the Task Force on the Establishment of a Truth, Justice and Reconciliation Commission

Hayner PB and Bosire L (2003) Should Truth Commissions Address Economic Crimes? Considering the Case of Kenya. International Center for Transitional Justice. Available at http://www.tikenya.org/documents/TruthComm.doc

Horne C (2009) Late Lustration Programmes in Romania and Poland: Supporting or Undermining Democratic Transitions? Democratization 16: 344–376

Horne C and Stan L (eds) (2018) Transitional Justice and the Former Soviet Union: Reviewing the Past, Looking toward the Future. Cambridge University Press, Cambridge

Kisiangani E (2009) Kenya's Economic Crimes: Can a conditional Amnesty be meaningful? Oxford Transitional Justice Series. Available at https://www.law.ox.ac.uk/sites/files/oxlaw/justice_in_africa1.pdf

Kora A (2012) Dealing With a 'New' Grievance: Should Anticorruption Be Part of the Transitional Justice Agenda? Journal of Human Rights 11: 537–557

O'Donnell G et al (eds) (1998) Transitions From Authoritarian Rule: Comparative Perspectives. John Hopkins University Press, Baltimore and London, pp. 51–53

OHCHR (2006) Rule of Law Tools: Truth Commissions. United Nations, New York and Geneva

Olsen TD et al (2010) The Justice Balance: When Transitional Justice Improves Human Rights and Democracy. Human Rights Quarterly, 32: 980–1007

Report of the Truth Justice and Reconciliation Commission (Vol 1 Truth, Justice and Reconciliation Commission, Kenya 2013)

Report of the Truth Justice and Reconciliation Commission (Vol 2b Truth, Justice and Reconciliation Commission, Kenya 2013)

Robinson I (2014) Truth Commissions and Anti-Corruption: Towards a Complementary Framework? International Journal of Transitional Justice 9: 33–50

Roht-Arriaza N (2014) Reparations and Economic, Social, and Cultural Rights. In: Sharp D (ed) Justice and Economic Violence in Transition. Springer, New York, pp. 109–138

Rožič P and Nisnevich Y (2016) Lustration Matters: A Radical Approach to the Problem of Corruption. Studies in Comparative International Development, 51: 257–285

Schneider N and Iecker de Almeida G (2018) The Brazilian National Truth Commission (2012–2014) as a State-Commissioned History Project. In: Bevernage B and Wouters N (eds) The Handbook of State-Sponsored History After 1945. Palgrave Macmillan, London, pp. 637–652

Sharp DN (2012) Addressing Economic Violence in Times of Transition: Toward a Positive-Peace Paradigm for Transitional Justice, 35 Fordham Int'l L.J. 780 Available at https://ir.lawnet.fordham.edu/ilj/vol35/iss3/3 Last accessed on 23 June 2019

Skaar E, Garcia-Godos J and Collins C (2019) Transitional Justice in Latin America. The Uneven Road from Impunity towards Accountability, 1st edn. Routledge, London

Soon W (1997) Transitional Justice in East Asia. Carnegie Council for Ethics in International Affairs. Available at https://www.carnegiecouncil.org/publications/archive/dialogue/1_08/articles/550 Last accessed on 23 June 2019

Sriram CL (ed) (2017) Transitional Justice in the Middle East and North Africa. Oxford University Press, Canada

Tchad Ministère de la Justice (1993) Les crimes et détournements de l'ex-Président Habré et de ses complices: rapport de la Commission d'enquête nationale

Teitel RG (2003) Transitional Justice Genealogy. Harvard Human Rights Journal 16: 69–94
Teti A et al (2018) Introduction and Background. In: Teti A et al (eds) The Arab Uprisings in Egypt, Jordan and Tunisia. Palgrave Macmillan, New York, pp. 1–25
Yerkes S and Muasher M (2010) Tunisia's Corruption Contagion A Transition at Risk. Carnegie Endowment for International Peace
Yusuf H (2017) Transitional Justice in the Middle East and North Africa: Taking Account of Islam. Muslim World Journal of Human Rights 14: 145–170
Zabyelina Y (2017) Lustration Beyond Decommunization: Responding to the Crimes of the Powerful in Post-Euromaidan Ukraine. State Crime Journal 6: 55–78.

Chapter 7
Conclusion

In the same way, the UN estimates that seven hundred thousand people were directly affected through loss of shelter and livelihoods during what the government of Zimbabwe called the 'clean up operation' of its cities. Were a truth commission to be set up at some point in Zimbabwe, it is hard to imagine that we could argue that it would be capable of investigating summary executions and disappearances, ill treatment or arbitrary detention, but that it would not be capable of investigating such massive violations of the right to housing, or the deliberate targeting of food aid to exclude opponents of the regime.
Louise Arbour (Arbour 2007, p. 15)

Zimbabwe did not start decaying today. As a matter of fact, the decay of emerging economies that were once well run happens over many years, and mainly happens gradually, well under the threshold of the average person's consciousness. The decay tends to happen in small doses over time. Zimbabwe's decay and collapse of its moral fibre started way back in the 80's and was allowed to slowly eat away the society's fabric over decades. Many signs of this decay require careful piecing together, and if you are engrossed in them, you can hardly notice. It took me a long period of study of official documents and several visits to Zimbabwe to arrive at this empirical conclusion.
Ken Yamamoto (Yamamoto 2016)

Contents

P. Maguchu, *Transitional Justice and Socio-Economic Rights in Zimbabwe*,
International Criminal Justice Series 24,
https://doi.org/10.1007/978-94-6265-323-8_7

Abstract The main aim of this study has been to investigate ways of addressing corruption within the transitional justice framework. This chapter presents some findings, notes some challenges and suggests recommendations for how the discourse and practice of transitional justice in Zimbabwe can be improved and become more satisfactory by including corruption as a violation of socio-economic rights. The final section summarises the conclusions drawn from the discussions in the preceding chapters.

Keywords Inclusivity · consultative · comprehensive · synergies · economic crimes commission of Zimbabwe

7.1 Introduction

The main aim of this study has been to explore the engagement of transitional justice with the issue of corruption. To achieve this, it was necessary to show whether corruption could be a violation of human rights, particularly socio-economic rights. I have argued that dealing with massive corruption as part of transitional justice will lead to a deeper sense of justice.

Even so, within the field of transitional justice there are dissenting views. Some research seems to suggest that transitional justice is already overburdened with many issues and so it is unwise to continue overstretching the mandate of the field.[1] What is more, other scholars who are sceptical of the linkages argue that trying to incorporate corruption into the field of human rights is like trying to fit a square peg into a round hole.[2] This would entail that transitional justice, which is based on human rights, should not include corruption.

---

[1] Albin-Lackey 2014, p. 147.

[2] Albin-Lackey 2014, p. 147.

It is against this background that the present book has, from the outset, sought to answer general questions such as: how can transitional justice mechanisms address corruption as a violation of socio-economic rights? Which in turn begs the question: is corruption a human rights violation? It has also sought to answer more specific questions such as: are there any acts of corruption that have been perpetrated in Zimbabwe that can be classified as socio-economic rights violations? Should official approaches to transitional justice in Zimbabwe treat corruption as a violation of socio-economic rights? What are the challenges of pursuing accountability for corruption as a violation of socio-economic rights?

This final chapter will discuss the practical and legal implications of the findings, briefly analysing each research question in turn before giving recommendations. This will be followed by the final conclusion, which highlights areas that would benefit from further research.

7.2 Findings

The findings of this study are chapter-specific. Each chapter addressed one of the main questions guiding the research. This final chapter draws upon the entire book, tying up the various theoretical and empirical strands in order to have a clear understanding of how transitional justice accountability mechanisms can address corruption.

7.2.1 Can Transitional Justice Mechanisms Address Corruption?

As noted in Chap. 1, 'The Linkages between Corruption and Transitional Justice', the main accountability mechanisms for transitional justice, namely truth commissions, prosecutions, amnesties, reparations and institutional reforms, can all address corruption that is linked to, or a violation of, fundamental rights.[3]

For instance, institutional reforms to address corruption in transitional justice settings were commonplace in former communist countries. Truth commissions were created in the aftermath of conflicts to deal with corruption that led to massive human rights abuses in Chad, Sierra Leone, Timor-Leste and other states.[4] In the case of Alberto Fujimori in Peru, corruption prosecutions opened the way for human rights investigations.[5] Reparations in the Philippines were fully funded by

[3] Carranza 2008; Kora 2012; Robinson 2014.

[4] Kora 2012.

[5] *In re Fujimori*, judgment of 11 July 2007, Supreme Court of Chile, first instance, no. 5646-05.

funds recovered from the estate of the former dictator Ferdinand Marcos.[6] Meanwhile, amnesties have been used to incentivise truth-telling and the return of ill-gotten gains in the aftermath of the 'Arab Spring' revolutions.[7]

In general, therefore, the question of whether transitional justice mechanisms can address corruption has been thoroughly answered. The study has not only shown that it has been done before, but also that there is a growing demand for transitional justice to expand its domain to include a wide range of economic crimes.

7.2.2 *Is Corruption a Human Rights Violation?*

The second question, regarding whether corruption is a human rights violation, is answered in Chap. 2, 'Understanding Linkages between Corruption and Transitional Justice'. Chapter 2 begins by meticulously addressing the question of whether freedom from corruption is a human right in its own right, what links corruption to transitional justice and the distinction between socio-economic rights and issues.

The unsurprising finding of this analysis was that there is no stand-alone right of freedom from corruption and that this might not be necessary for the argument that transitional justice should address corruption issues. A more interesting finding was that the relationship between corruption and human rights violations is multi-faceted. In this vein, human rights need to be considered in the fight against corruption, since some methods of fighting corruption can lead to violation of human rights. However, the present book is only concerned with the violation of human rights as a result of corruption.

To that end, the most important finding was that corruption generally has a negative impact on human rights, and acts of corruption can in exceptional cases be a violation of human rights in and of themselves. In order to determine how corruption can be a human rights violation, Chap. 3 critically analyses the normative content of socio-economic rights and states' obligations under national and international law. It then explores how corruption can violate these obligations, resulting in violations of the respective rights.[8]

Taken together, these findings can be used to develop a framework allowing transitional justice to address the question of corruption. Transitional justice is a response to systematic or widespread violations of human rights. Widespread corruption also leads to systemic human rights violations. *A fortiori*, the field of transitional justice should engage with cases of corruption that have violated fundamental rights.

---

[6] Republic Act 10368, also known as the Human Rights Victims' Reparation and Recognition Act 2013 (Philippines). See also Carranza 2008, p. 310; Robinson 2014.

[7] Organic Law on Establishing and Organizing Transitional Justice (Organic Law No. 53/2013); Kora 2012, p. 539.

[8] International Council on Human Rights Policy and Transparency International 2009, p. 27.

7.2.3 *Did Zimbabwe Violate Socio-economic Rights Through Corruption?*

The third question this study sought to answer was whether there are any acts of corruption that have been perpetrated in Zimbabwe which can be classified as socio-economic rights violations under international law. This question is primarily addressed in Chap. 3, aptly entitled 'The Phenomenon of Corruption and Socio-economic Rights in Zimbabwe'. The chapter explored a few selected hypotheses from the literature concerning the role of corruption and the violation of the rights to health and water in the cholera outbreak in Zimbabwe in 2008.

The conclusion was that certain acts of corruption in essential services led to the violation of socio-economic rights in Zimbabwe. The cholera outbreak example illustrates this point clearly. This case is comparable to many other cases relating to the rights to housing and food, which may have been violated as a result of major corruption scandals.

7.2.4 *Should Transitional Justice in Zimbabwe Address Corruption?*

Another key question the study sought to answer was whether transitional justice in Zimbabwe should address corruption as a violation of socio-economic rights. This question is best answered by examining the former and current transitional justice processes in Zimbabwe, as was done in Chaps. 4 and 5 of this book.

Chapter 4, 'Addressing Past Corruption and Human Rights Violations in Zimbabwe', analyses different mechanisms that were employed to address various periods of violence in Zimbabwe, from the UDI of 1965 to the latest dispute, which culminated in the military intervention and the resignation of the former president in 2017. Interestingly, the results show that there have been several instances where mechanisms were used to address corruption, albeit without using the language of transitional justice.

The findings of Chap. 4 coincide with findings in the literature that in its 'first phase'[9] transitional justice was preoccupied with short-term measures such as truth commissions and amnesties that had a narrow mandate to address the violation of civil and political rights, in particular those limited to people's physical integrity.[10] There are strong indications that the field of transitional justice became caught up in the debate of whether socio-economic rights are justiciable and whether these rights should be addressed in post-conflict situations.[11]

---

[9] Teitel 2000, p. 5.

[10] Teitel 2000, p. 5.

[11] Cavallaro and Albuja 2008.

Chapter 5, 'Ways of Dealing with Corruption under Transitional Justice in Zimbabwe', discusses various transitional mechanisms that have been implemented or proposed in order to help bring about a democratic Zimbabwe. It examines official transitional justice mechanisms, which are still centred on civil and political rights violations, and the mechanisms sponsored by civil society in collaboration with the international community, which are trying to bridge the gap between the formal and informal processes by encompassing issues such as socio-economic rights and corruption.

These findings suggest several possible courses of action, discussed later in the recommendations section, for how transitional justice in Zimbabwe should address corruption. However, at the time of writing, the transition is incomplete; the party that stands accused of perpetrating most of the human rights violations and corruption that the process is intended to address is still in control. These results therefore need to be interpreted with caution.

7.3 Challenges

Addressing corruption using the transitional justice framework is a noble idea, fraught with many practical and legal challenges. So the final question this study sought to answer was whether there are any impediments to the pursuit of accountability for socio-economic violations, which was investigated by looking at corruption in Zimbabwe. This question is answered in Chap. 6, 'Zimbabwe in a Comparative Perspective'. This section provides a summary of the findings of my investigations into the challenges of engaging with corruption under the mandate of transitional justice processes.

7.3.1 *Broad Mandate*

Transitional justice is often faced with a serious problem of managing victims' expectations. Survivors and victims usually have high expectations that the mechanisms will be broad and cover a wide array of violations. However, this poses a dilemma, as there is a danger the mandate will become too broad and impracticable, to the extent of making it difficult for transitional justice to achieve its objectives.

Thus, there is often an argument that extending the mandate of transitional justice to socio-economic rights and issues might open the floodgates. In this regard, the UNHCR has warned that

> a broad focus on 'violations of economic and social rights' might suggest the need to look into poverty, homelessness, education policy failures and other social ills. Although these are critically important subjects, this could risk expanding the mandate of the commission so broadly that it may be impossible to reasonably complete its task.[12]

Moreover, a broad mandate may lead to time management challenges: for instance, although it was a welcome development for truth commissions to include corruption as a violation of socio-economic rights, it proved an ambitious task given they have a period of normally two years to meet their objectives. A passage from a leading international human rights organisation underscores the dilemma of the Kenyan TJRC:

> The draft bill gives the commission only two years to address all forms of historical injustices, including corruption, land issues, and reparations for victims. This array of injustices is very wide. It would be better if the commission was given a much longer life, or perhaps the scope of its investigations was reduced, for example with land and compensation issues being dealt with separately.[13]

When the Kenyan TJRC finally handed over a finished report after a very long delay, it 'undermined one of the main rationales of the commission and denied the people of Kenya information to which they were entitled as they went to the polls'.[14]

7.3.2 *Pursuing Transitional Justice Without 'Transition'*

As mentioned in Chap. 1, although at its inception transitional justice addressed past abuses of deposed authoritarian regimes or of states emerging from civil strife or conflict that were transitioning into democracy, transitional justice processes are now increasingly being carried out in countries where there has been no transition and autocratic rule or conflict are still ongoing.[15] The reason is that 'in recent years, this traditional transitional justice narrative has become increasingly intertwined with a view of transitional justice as a component of postconflict peacebuilding more generally, including in societies not undergoing a paradigmatic liberal transition'.[16]

In modern times, transitional justice is being carried out without a clean break from the past. Recently, in many countries the processes of transitional justice have consistently been implemented in a spirit of *quid pro quo*, with priority given to achieving peace and stability. The challenges of this approach have been described

---

[12] UNHCR 2006, p. 9.

[13] Human Rights Watch 2008.

[14] ICTJ 2013.

[15] Sharp 2014, p. 7.

[16] Sharp 2014, pp. 1–2.

as follows in the context of the Colombian transitional justice policy, which was carried out despite an ongoing conflict with the armed guerrillas:

> It is possible to identify at least two uses of the transitional justice discourse, which depend on the different interests it may serve: the manipulative use and the democratic use of transitional justice.[17]

The same can be said with regard to transitional justice processes in Zimbabwe, which eschew accountability but mainly focus on measures, which in some cases will not be implemented.

Accordingly, Pondai Bamu has boldly claimed that 'until Mugabe and ZANU-PF leave power, there will be no real transition and no real transitional justice in Zimbabwe'.[18] Ismael Muvingi has also taken this view, warning that 'talk of transitional justice before political transition in Zimbabwe is premature and possibly pointless. The focus of discussion therefore needs to shift toward the more immediate and pressing imperative of political change'.[19] He adds that 'repressive regimes rarely engage seriously in accountability processes that focus on their own actions'.[20]

7.3.3 Polarised Environment

A closely related point is that the transitional justice process can be very difficult if carried out in a highly polarised climate. This is exemplified by Kenya's transitional justice experience, which was 'crudely politicized to protect the interests of the powerful'.[21] The Kenyan TJRC was faced with great difficulties in meeting its obligations to collect an accurate record of past human rights atrocities and foster reconciliation amid a highly charged political environment: 'the initial planning of transitional justice measures was thwarted by the fluid and erratic domestic politics which resulted in haphazard timing, sequencing and coordination of difficult activities.'[22]

Factors found to cause or exacerbate the political tension in transitional settings have been explored in several studies. For instance, it has been reported that truth commissions may be pressured to release their reports before elections, which may cause politicisation and even instigate further violence.[23] Furthermore, the mandate of a truth commission may coincide with the drafting of a new constitution, and

---

[17] Uprimny and Saffon 2007, p. 15.

[18] Bamu 2008, p. 4.

[19] Muvingi 2009, p. 1.

[20] Muvingi 2009, p. 1.

[21] Magara 2014.

[22] Magara 2014.

[23] Brown 2013, p. 5.

constitutional debates and disagreements on some of the issues could affect the work of the truth commission as a result.

Parallel accountability mechanisms may also impact negatively on transitional justice, especially external processes. For example, in some countries the question of having local or international criminal justice mechanisms may be a potential source of tension. Additionally, power struggles within interim unity or transitional governments may derail transitional justice processes.

7.3.4 Methodology

Designing a methodology that can accommodate the investigation of corruption as a violation of human rights within the framework of transitional justice remains a challenge. Although the issue has received attention from various scholars, there seems to be no agreement on the exact framework. As Dustin Sharp laments, while African truth commissions have made great strides in moving economic violence into the foreground, they have rarely chosen to frame the issues in question as human rights issues, even where claims of violations of economic and social rights would be strong.[24]

Similarly, research conducted by Isabel Robinson has shown that, when dealing with the more problematic socio-economic rights, the majority of truth commissions make a serious omission:[25] they identify corruption as a violation of many socio-economic rights but fail to explain how certain acts of corruption violate socio-economic rights by linking the corrupt act to the various obligations of the state towards socio-economic rights, such as the 'obligation of non-discrimination'; this amounts to 'deliberately retrogressive steps without a valid justification based on limited resources or […] a direct violation of a state's minimum core obligations'.[26]

This could be the reason why in some cases the practice and discourse of transitional justice still sideline corruption.

7.3.5 Framing Reparations

Another major theoretical and practical obstacle to transitional justice engaging with broader economic issues such as corruption is how to frame reparation programmes in such cases.

[24] Sharp 2013, p. 81.

[25] Robinson 2014, p. 10.

[26] Robinson 2014, p. 10.

A key aspect of human rights law is that for every violation of a human right, socio-economic or otherwise, there follows a duty for reparations.[27] When dealing with grand corruption, there are legal and practical challenges to awarding reparations to the victims, due to the lack of a clear causal relationship between an act of grand corruption and a specific victim.[28] As a result, many truth commissions do not cite specific victims of grand corruption for the purposes of reparations. One example is the Kenyan TJRC's recommendations, which do not mention the victims of corruption, but only call for the recovery of stolen assets through the courts and redistribution thereof to the Ethics and Anti-Corruption Commission for the purposes of reparations.[29]

According to Robinson, a solution would be for transitional justice to address grand corruption and petty corruption separately, for the simple reason that there are 'distinct causal connections between the perpetrator and the victim(s)'.[30] When awarding reparations for petty corruption, there are fewer hurdles to clear, as there is a clear connection between the act of corruption and a victim, which is not the case with grand corruption. Given that the victims of petty corruption will be in large numbers in a country like Zimbabwe where corruption is systemic, this still renders the issue of reparations a Herculean task.[31]

7.4 Recommendations

7.4.1 Recommendation One: Inclusivity

Transitional justice processes should be more inclusive. That is to say, they should include corruption and socio-economic rights within their framework. In the case of Zimbabwe, there are four legal routes by which this can be achieved. First, an amendment to Section 252 of the constitution to increase the mandate of the NPRC to address all human rights violations and not only civil and political rights violations. The second option is to enact enabling legislation on transitional justice that includes economic violence, in particular corruption. The third option is to legislate a mandate for the NPRC to draft its own working regulations using its broad constitutional mandate and include in its mandate socio-economic rights and corruption. The fourth option is to use the existing legislation to establish a commission of inquiry on public corruption linked to human rights abuses.

---

[27] See Human Rights Committee 2004. See also UNGA Resolution 2005.

[28] Robinson 2014, p. 11.

[29] Robinson 2014, p. 11.

[30] Robinson 2014, p. 11.

[31] Robinson 2014, p. 11.

7.4.2 Recommendation Two: Consultation

Transitional justice should also involve many actors, and not only the state. The state should actively engage civil society, citizens and international actors, such as the UN, specialised transitional justice organisations and development partners, as well as neighbouring countries and countries where Zimbabweans who left the country as economic migrants during periods of crisis are now living.

Most significantly, the official and non-official transitional justice processes should be merged. The official process is a top-down approach developed by politicians without adequate consultation (if any at all). It can benefit from more explicitly people-driven, bottom-up, unofficial processes. Once the legal basis is established, Zimbabwe should enforce the civil society declaration on transitional justice, which recommended thorough investigation of corruption cases.

7.4.3 Recommendation Three: Comprehensive Approach

The mandate of the NPRC should follow the 'corruption-human rights nexus', i.e. it should recognise that not all acts of corruption are rights violations. Similarly, the work of the NPRC should go beyond the violation of civil and political rights and include in its focus the violation of socio-economic rights, such as the rights to health, housing and water.

7.4.4 Recommendation Four: Synergies

Synergies among transitional justice mechanisms should be enhanced in order to address corruption. This can be achieved by, for instance, linking the work of the NPRC to other transitional justice mechanisms, such as establishing a special chamber trial for corruption and economic crimes; linking reparation programmes to proceeds recovered from corrupt officials; various institutional reforms to remove corrupt elements from the system; and using amnesties as measures to ensure collaboration.

7.4.5 Recommendation Five: Strengthen Anti-Corruption Mechanisms

Transitional justice mechanisms should not only focus on human rights mechanisms but also strengthen anti-corruption mechanisms. The ZACC should be given greater powers to address corruption and work with the ZHRC, and vice versa. The office of public protector or ombudsman could be reintroduced. The ombudsman is uniquely tasked to investigate both human rights abuses and corruption in a wider sense. This strategically put the office at the centre of the fight against corruption during the transitional and post-transitional era in Zimbabwe.

There is a need to harmonise different legal frameworks and fully implement international instruments such as the UNCAC, AUCPCC and SADC Protocol against Corruption.

7.5 Final Conclusion

This study has shown that Zimbabwe has experienced socio-economic rights violations and corruption simultaneously. This finding has important implications supporting the theory that the violation of socio-economic rights and corruption are intertwined and that, under certain conditions, corruption can be a violation of human rights, as illustrated by the cholera outbreak of 2008. This combination of findings provides strong support for the view that transitional justice processes should address corruption in some cases.

Another significant conclusion that can be drawn from this study is that official transitional justice efforts in Zimbabwe should not continue to ignore the violation of socio-economic rights. Although the constitution of Zimbabwe provides for transitional justice mechanisms, there is no clear mention of or reference to socio-economic rights and issues, which have also precipitated conflict in Zimbabwe at various points. If this remains unchallenged, the constitutional mandate to bring peace and reconciliation will fail to meet its intended objectives.

This is because many Zimbabweans have suffered as a result of the violation of socio-economic rights rather than the violation of civil and political rights. The narrow approach of including only torture, murders and enforced disappearances does not meet the expectations of the victims and many citizens. Therefore, Zimbabweans deserve an inclusive transitional justice package that covers all categories of human rights violations.

In this regard, reference can be made to the civil society initiatives that have explored the intersection between corruption and socio-economic rights violations in Zimbabwe. They have explicitly recommended setting up a truth inquiry into corruption, implementing transitional justice measures and using asset recovery to fund reparations for victims of all human rights violations. Furthermore, the lessons from other states that were briefly discussed above particularly those countries that have successfully implemented anti-corruption measures in their transitional justice programmes can be illustrative.

In view of all that has been said so far, the final conclusion that can be drawn from this study is that the investigation of corruption is central to the investigation of socio-economic rights violations. Added to this is the fact that since corruption is linked to, and in some exceptional cases the cause of, these violations, tackling it must be regarded as a strategic goal of any transitional justice efforts in the country.

In the course of this study, many significant questions have not been treated in detail, such as whether transitional justice can cope with the increased mandate, how to address issues of asset recovery and how to measure the success of addressing corruption using transitional justice principles. It could be that more research on this topic needs to be undertaken before the association between corruption and transitional justice can be more clearly understood.

References

Albin-Lackey C (2014) Corruption, Human Rights and Activism: Useful Connections and their Limits. In: Sharp D (ed) Justice and Economic Violence in Transition. Springer, New York, pp. 139–163

Arbour L (2007) Economic and Social Justice for Societies in Transition. International Law and Politics 40: 1–26

Bamu P (2008) Zimbabwe: Transitional Justice without Transition. Oxford Transitional Justice Research Series. Available at https://www.law.ox.ac.uk/sites/files/oxlaw/bamu_zim_final1.pdf

Brown S (2013) The National Accord, Impunity and the Fragile Peace in Kenya. In: Sriram CL et al. (eds) Transitional Justice and Peacebuilding on the Ground: Victims and Ex Combatants. Routledge, London

Carranza R (2008) Plunder and Pain: Should Transitional Justice Engage with Corruption and Economic Crimes? International Journal of Transitional Justice 2: 310–330

Cavallaro JL and Albuja S (2008) The Lost Agenda: Economic Crimes and Truth Commissions in Latin America and Beyond. In: McEvoy K and McGregor L (eds) Transitional Justice from Below: Grassroots Activism and the Struggle for Change (Human Rights Law in Perspective). Hart Publishing, Oxford, pp. 121–141

ICTJ (2013) ICTJ Welcomes Kenya's TJRC Report. Available at https://www.ictj.org/news/ictj-welcomes-kenyas-tjrc-report Last accessed on 23 June 2019

International Council on Human Rights Policy and Transparency International (2009) Corruption and Human Rights: Making the Connection. International Council on Human Rights Policy, Geneva

Kora A (2012) Dealing With a 'New' Grievance: Should Anticorruption be Part of the Transitional Justice Agenda? Journal of Human Rights 11: 537–557

Magara IS (2014) Transitional Justice Process in Kenya: Unfinished Business? Pambazuka New. Available at https://www.pambazuka.org/governance/transitional-justice-process-kenya-unfinished-business Last accessed on 23 June 2019

Muvingi I (2009) Transitional Justice Will Have to Wait. Oxford Transitional Justice Research Series. Available at https://www.law.ox.ac.uk/sites/files/oxlaw/muvingi_final1.pdf

Report of the Truth, Justice and Reconciliation Commission (Vol 2b Truth, Justice and Reconciliation Commission, Kenya 2013)

Report of the Truth, Justice and Reconciliation Commission (Vol Truth, Justice and Reconciliation Commission, Kenya 2013)

Robinson I (2014) Truth Commissions and Anti-Corruption: Towards a Complementary Framework? International Journal of Transitional Justice 9: 33–50

Sharp D (2013) Economic Violence in the Practice of African Truth Commissions and Beyond. In: Sharp D (ed), Justice and Economic Violence in Transition. Springer, New York, pp. 79–107

Sharp D (2014) Emancipating Transitional Justice from the Bonds of Paradigmatic Transition. International Journal of Transitional Justice 9: 150–169

Teitel RG (2000) Transitional Justice. Oxford University Press, New York

Uprimny R and Saffon MP (2007) Uses and Abuses of Transitional Justice Discourse in Colombia. PRIO Policy Brief, 6. PRIO, Oslo

Yamamoto K (2016) Robert Mugabe's Corruption 1980–2014, 22 May 2016, Zimbabwean Situation. Available at https://www.zimbabwesituation.com/news/zimsit-m-robert-mugabes-corruption-1980-2014-the-zimbabwean/ Last accessed on 23 June 2019

Table of Cases

African Commission on Human and Peoples Rights

Democratic Republic of Congo v. Burundi, Rwanda, Uganda, Comm. No. 227/99
Free Legal Assistance Group and Others v. Zaire, Comm. No. 25/89, 47/90, 56/91, 100/93
Zimbabwe Human Rights NGO Forum v. the Republic of Zimbabwe Comm. No. 245/2002

Bangladesh

Adilur Rahman Khan v. Bangladesh, 16 BLC 100

Chile

In re Fujimori, judgment of 11 July 2007, Supreme Court of Chile, first instance, No. 5646-05

ECOWAS

Socio-Economic Rights and Accountability Project v. Federal Republic of Nigeria and Universal Basic Education Commission, judgment of 30 November 2010, ECW/CCJ/JUD/07/10 ECOWAS

Inter-American Court of Human Rights (IACtHR)

Almonacid Arellano et al. v. Chile, judgment of 26 September 2006, IACtHr
Barrios Altos v. Peru, judgment of 14 March 2001, IACtHr
Julia Gomes Lund and Others v. Brazil, judgment of 28 October 2015, IACtHr
Velásquez Rodríguez v. Honduras, judgment of July 29 1988, IACtHr

International Criminal Court

The Prosecutor v. Omar Hassan Ahmad Al Bashir (ICC-02/05-07/09-241)

P. Maguchu, *Transitional Justice and Socio-Economic Rights in Zimbabwe*,
International Criminal Justice Series 24,
https://doi.org/10.1007/978-94-6265-323-8

Philippines

Louis Biraogo v. Philippine Truth Commission, judgment of 7 December 2010, G.R. No. 192935

Rep. Edcel Lagman et al. v. Executive Secretary Paquito Ochoa et al., judgment of 2010, G.R. No. 192936

South Africa

Hugh Glenister v. President of the Republic of South Africa and Others, judgment of 17 March, CCT 48/10 ZACC

National Commissioner of the South African Police Service v. Southern African Human Rights Litigation Centre and Another, 2014, ZACC 30

Southern Africa Litigation Centre v. *Minister of Justice and Constitutional Development & 9 Others*, (unreported) case no. 27740/15, North Gauteng HC, Pretoria

Special Court of Sierra Leone

Prosecutor v. Charles Ghankay Taylor, SCSL-03-1-T

USA

Chiminya Tachiona v. Mugabe, 216 F. Supp. 2d 262 (S.D.N.Y. 2002)

Zimbabwe

Kereke v. Zimbabwe Anti-Corruption Commission and Others, citation not available

S v. Gumbo, citation not available

S v. Shava 1989 (2) ZLR 107 (H)

State v. Grace Pfumbidzayi and Another HH-726-15 (Unreported)

Sydney Michael Muchenje v. Secretary for Public Service, Labour and Social Welfare, ZLR HC 153 99 (Unreported)

Telecel Zimbabwe (Private) Limited v. Postal and Telecommunications Regulatory Authority of Zimbabwe and Others, HH/446/15 (Unreported)

Table of Legislation

Table of International Instruments

Hague Convention respecting the Laws and Customs of War on Land, entry into force 26 January 1910

International Convention against Torture and other Cruel, Inhuman or Degrading Treatment or Punishment, adopted and opened for signature, ratification and accession by General Assembly Resolution 39/46 of 10 December 1984, entry into force 26 June 1987

International Convention on the Elimination of All Forms of Discrimination against Women, adopted and opened for signature, ratification and accession by General Assembly Resolution 34/180 of 18 December 1979, entry into force 3 September 1981

International Convention on the Elimination of All Forms of Racial Discrimination, adopted and opened for signature and ratification by General Assembly Resolution 2106 (XX) of 21 December 1965, entry into force 4 January 1969

International Convention on the Rights of Persons with Disabilities, adopted 24 January 2007, A/RES/61/106

International Convention on the Rights of the Child, adopted and opened for signature, ratification and accession by General Assembly Resolution 44/25 of 20 November 1989

International Covenant on Civil and Political Rights adopted by the United Nations General Assembly Resolution 2200A (XXI) of 16 December 1966, entry into force 23 March 1976

International Covenant on Economic, Social and Cultural Rights, adopted and opened for signature, ratification and accession on 16 December 1966, entry into force 3 January 1976, United Nations Treaty Series, vol. 993

Protocol Additional to the Geneva Conventions relating to the Protection of Victims of International Armed Conflicts, entry into force 7 December 1978

P. Maguchu, *Transitional Justice and Socio-Economic Rights in Zimbabwe*,
International Criminal Justice Series 24,
https://doi.org/10.1007/978-94-6265-323-8

Rome Statute of the International Criminal Court; the Statute entered into force on 1 July 2002

Universal Declaration of Human Rights, adopted by General Assembly Resolution 217 A(III) of 10 December 1948

Table of Regional Instruments

African Charter on the Rights and Welfare of the Child, entry into force 29 November 1999

African Convention on Human and Peoples' Rights ('Banjul Charter'), entry into force 21 October 1986

African Union Convention on Preventing and Combating Corruption, adopted by the 2nd Ordinary Session of the Assembly of the Union, Maputo, 11 July 2003, entry into force 5 August 2006

American Convention on Human Rights, adopted on 22 November 1969, entry into force 18 July 1978

Inter-American Convention against Corruption, adopted on 29 March 1996, entry into force 6 March 1997

Protocol to the African Charter on Human and Peoples' Rights on the Rights of Women in Africa as adopted at the second summit of the African Union in Maputo, Mozambique on 21 July 2003

Southern Africa Development Community Protocol against Corruption, entry into force 14 August 2001

Statute of the Inter-American Commission on Human Rights, 1 October 1979, entered into force 30 days after its approval, O.A.S. Off. Rec. OEA/Ser. P/IX.0.2/80

Table of National Legislation

Bangladesh

Truth and Accountability Commission Ordinance XXVII of 2008

Chad

Commission of Inquiry into the Crimes and Misappropriations Committed by ex-President Habré, His Accomplices and/or Accessories, Decree No. 014/P. CE/CJ/90

Liberia

Truth and Reconciliation Commission Act of 2005

Philippines

Republic Act 10368, also known as the Human Rights Victims' Reparation and Recognition Act of 2013

Philippine Truth Commission Executive Order No. 1 of 2010

Sierra Leone

Truth and Reconciliation Commission Act of 2000

South Africa

South African ICC Act 27 of 2002

Tunisia

Economic and Financial Reconciliation Law (Draft Organic Law No. 49/2015

Organic Law on Establishing and Organizing Transitional Justice (No. 53/2013)

UK

The Southern Rhodesia (Sanctions) (Amnesty) Order 1980, SI 1980/565

USA

Corporate and Auditing Accountability and Responsibility Act 2002 (The Sarbanes-Oxley Act of 2002)

Zimbabwe

Audit Office Act 12 of 2009

Commissions of Inquiry Act of 4 of 1991

Constitution of Zimbabwe Act Amendment No. 20 of 2013

Criminal Codification and Reform Act Criminal Law (Codification and Reform) Act 23 of 2004

National Peace and Reconciliation Commission Act 11 of 2017

Presidential Powers (Temporary) Measures (Amendment of Exchange Control Act) regulations, SI 145 of 2017

Zimbabwe Anti-Corruption Commission Act 13 of 2004

Bibliography

Abushouk AI (2016) The Arab Spring: A Fourth Wave of Democratization? Digest of Middle East Studies 25: 52–69

Acquaah-Gaisie GA (2005) Grand Corruption: A Crime Against Humanity. In: Delener N and Chao C (eds) Global Markets in Dynamic Environments: Making Positive Connections through Strategy, Technology and Knowledge: Proceedings of the International Conference USA: The Global Business and Technology Association, pp. 1–8

Adžanela A (2012) Petty Corruption and Human Rights Implications—The Case of Bosnia and Herzegovina. Available at http://www.humiliationstudies.org/documents/AdzanelaPettyCorruptionBosniaandHerzegovina.pdf

Ahmed S et al (2011) The 2008 cholera epidemic in Zimbabwe: Experience of the ICDDR, B Team in the Field. Journal of Health Population, and Nutrition 29: 541–546

Albin-Lackey C (2014) Corruption, Human Rights and Activism: Useful Connections and their Limits. In: Sharp D (ed) Justice and Economic Violence in Transition. Springer, New York, pp. 139–163

Amundsen I (1999) Political Corruption: An Introduction to the Issues. Chr. Michelsen Institute Development Studies and Human Rights Working Paper 19991. Available at https://www.cmi.no/publications/file/1040-political-corruption.pdf

Anders G and Nuijten M (eds) (2009) Corruption and the Secret of Law: A Legal Anthropological Perspective. Ashgate, Aldershot

Antwi-Boateng O (2015) No Spring in Africa: How Sub-Saharan Africa has Avoided the Arab Spring Phenomenon. Politics and Policy 43: 754–784

Arbour L (2007) Economic and Social Justice for Societies in Transition. International Law and Politics 40: 1–27

Arbour L (2016) Economic and Social Justice for Societies in Transition Second Annual Transitional Justice Lecture hosted by the Center for Human Rights and Global Justice at New York University School of Law and by the ICTJ

Arthur P (2009) How "Transitions" Reshaped Human Rights: A Conceptual History of Transitional Justice. Human Rights Quarterly 31: 321–367

Bacio-Terracino J (2008) Corruption as a Violation of Human Rights. International Council on Human Rights Policy. Available at http://ssrn.com/abstract=1107918

Bailey M (1979) Oilgate: The Sanctions Scandal. Hodder and Stoughton, London, pp. 128–129

Bamu P (2008) Zimbabwe: Transitional Justice without Transition. Oxford Transitional Justice Research Series. Available at https://www.law.ox.ac.uk/sites/files/oxlaw/bamu_zim_final1.pdf

P. Maguchu, *Transitional Justice and Socio-Economic Rights in Zimbabwe*,
International Criminal Justice Series 24,
https://doi.org/10.1007/978-94-6265-323-8

Bantekas I (2006) Corruption as an International Crime and a Crime against Humanity: An Outline of Supplementary Criminal Justice Policies. Journal of International Criminal Justice 4: 466–484

Bantekas I and Oette L (2013) International Human Rights Law and Practice. Cambridge University Press, New York

Bass GJ et al (2001) The Princeton Principles on Universal Jurisdiction, Program in Law and Public Affairs and Woodrow Wilson School of Public and International Affairs, Princeton University, International Commission of Jurists, American Association for the International Commission of Jurists, Netherlands Institute of Human Rights, Urban Morgan Institute for Human Rights, published by the Program in Law and Public Affairs, Princeton University

Benjamin J (2012) Corruption: Violation of Human Rights. In: Vishwanathan VN (ed) Corruption and Human Rights. Allied Publisher, New Delhi, pp. 23–32

Bevernage B (2012) History, Memory, and State-Sponsored Violence: Time and Justice. Routledge, Abingdon

Beyrer C (2002) Zimbabwe Cholera Outbreak Has Roots in Corruption. Yale Medical Journal. Available at http://ymm.yale.edu/spring2009/dialogue/oncampus/52597#

Boersma M (2012) Corruption: A Violation of Human Rights and a Crime under International Law? Intersentia, Cambridge

Boughzala M and Romdhane SB (2016) Tunisia: The Prospects for Democratic Consolidation. In: Elbadawi I and Makdisi S (eds) Democratic Transitions in the Arab World. Cambridge University Press, Cambridge, pp. 107–132

Brahm E (2009) What is a Truth Commission and Why Does it Matter? Peace and Conflict Review 3: 1–14

Bratton M (2001) Violence, Partisanship and Transitional Justice in Zimbabwe. Journal of Modern African Studies 49: 353–380

Brems E (2011) Transitional Justice in the Case Law of the European Court of Human Rights. International Journal of Transitional Justice 5: 282–303

Brown S (2013) The National Accord, Impunity and the Fragile Peace in Kenya. In: Sriram CL et al (eds) Transitional Justice and Peacebuilding on the Ground: Victims and Ex Combatants. Routledge, London

Butler LJ and Stockwell S (2013) The Wind of Change: Harold Macmillan and British Decolonization. Palgrave Macmillan, New York

Carmona MS and Bacio-Terracino J (2010) Corruption and Human Rights: Making the Connection. In Boersma M and Nelen H (eds) Corruption and Human Rights: Interdisciplinary Perspectives. Intersentia, Antwerp, pp. 25–50

Carranza R (2008) Plunder and Pain: Should Transitional Justice Engage with Corruption and Economic Crimes. International Journal of Transitional Justice 2: 310–330

Cavallaro JL and Albuja S (2008) The Lost Agenda: Economic Crimes and Truth Commissions in Latin America and Beyond. In: McEvoy K and McGregor L (eds) Transitional Justice from Below: Grassroots Activism and the Struggle for Change (Human Rights Law in Perspective). Hart, Oxford, pp. 121–141

CCJP et al. (1997) Breaking the Silent: Report on the 1980's Disturbances in Matebeleland and the Midlands. CCJP, Harare

Chiduza L (2015) The Zimbabwe Human Rights Commission: Prospects and Challenges for the Protection of Human Rights. Law Democracy and Development. Available at http://www.scielo.org.za/scielo.php?script=sci_arttext&pid=S2077-49072015000100008

Chigara B (2002) Amnesty in International Law: The Legality under International Law of National Amnesty Laws. Longman, London

Chikwanha A (2009) The Trajectory of Human Rights Violations in Zimbabwe. Institute for Security Studies. Available at http://www.issafrica.org/acpst/papers/the-trajectory-of-human-rights-violations-in-zimbabwe

Cuneo CN et al (2017) The Cholera Epidemic in Zimbabwe, 2008–2009: A Review and Critique of the Evidence. Health and Human Rights Journal 19: 249–263

Curtin TRC (1968) Rhodesian Economic Development under Sanctions and "the Long Haul". African Affairs 67: 100–110

Curtin TRC and Murray D (1967) Economic Sanctions and Rhodesia: An Examination of the Probable Effect of Sanctions on National and Personal Incomes in Rhodesia and of the Effectiveness of Sanctions on Rhodesian Policy. Research Monograph no. 12. Institute of Economic Affairs, London

David R (2010) Transitions to Clean Government: Amnesty as an Anticorruption Measure. Australian Journal of Political Science 45: 391–406

De Beco G (2011) Monitoring Corruption from a Human Rights Perspective. International Journal of Human Rights 15: 1107–1124

de Greiff P (2012) Report of the Special Rapporteur on the Promotion of Truth, Justice, Reparation and Guarantees of Non-Recurrence. Accessed at http://www.ohchr.org/Documents/HRBodies/HRCouncil/RegularSession/Session21/A-HRC-21-46_en.pdf

de Maria W (2008) Measurements and Markets: Deconstructing the Corruption Perception Index. International Journal of Public Sector Management 21: 777–797

De Schutter O (2013) Economic, Social and Cultural Rights as Human Rights: An Introduction. CRIDHO Working Paper 2013/2. Available at https://cridho.uclouvain.be/documents/Working.Papers/CRIDHO-WP2013-2-ODeSchutterESCRights.pdf

Doig A (2006) Dirty Hands and the Donors: Dealing with Corruption in a Post Mugabe Zimbabwe. Political Quarterly 77: 71–78

Dorman S (2001) Inclusion and Exclusion: NGOs and Politics in Zimbabwe. Unpublished DPhil Thesis, University of Oxford

du Plessis M (2014) South Africa's Police Must Investigate Zimbabwe Torture Allegations. Institute for Security Studies. Available at http://www.issafrica.org/iss-today/south-africas-police-must-investigate-zimbabwe-torture-allegations

du Plessis M et al (2013) Africa and the International Criminal Court. Chatham House. Available at https://www.chathamhouse.org/publications/papers/view/193415

Dzinesa GA (2006) Swords into Ploughshares: Disarmament, Demobilisation and Reintegration in Zimbabwe, Namibia and South Africa. Institute for Security Studies, Cape Town

Epp CR (1998) The Rights Revolution Lawyers, Activists and Supreme Courts in Comparative Perspective. Chicago University Press, Chicago

Eppel S and Raftopoulos B (2008) Political Crisis, Mediation and the Prospects for Transitional Justice in Zimbabwe. Oxford Transitional Justice Working Paper Series. Available at http://otjr.crim.ox.ac.uk/materials/papers/42/EppelandRaftopolous_Zim_Final.pdf

Feltoe G (2012) A Guide to Administrative Law and Local Government Law in Zimbabwe. Legal Resources Foundation, Harare

Fisher KJ and Stewart R (2014) After the Arab Spring: A New Wave of Transitional Justice. In: Fisher KJ and Stewart R (eds) Transitional Justice and the Arab Spring. Routledge Taylor and Francis, London, pp. 1–14

Fisk M (1989) The State and Justice: An Essay in Political Theory. Cambridge University Press, New York

Fuller LL (1969) The Morality of Law Yale. University Press, New Haven

Galtung J (1967) On the Effects of International Economic Sanctions: with Examples from the Case of Rhodesia. World Politics 19: 378–416

Gathii JT (2009) Defining the Relationship Between Human Rights and Corruption. University of Pennsylvania Journal of International Law 31: 125–202

Gee J and Button M (2014) European Healthcare Fraud & Corruption Network. Financial Cost of Healthcare Fraud Report. University of Portsmouth-Centre for Counter Fraud Studies. Available at http://www2.port.ac.uk/media/contacts-and-departments/icjs/ccfs/The-Financial-Cost-of-Healthcare-Fraud-Report-2015.pdf

Ghione L (1969) Justice in Transition and Corruption–Changing the Agenda. Available at http://www.righttononviolence.org/rn-seminar-constitutionalism-justice-in-transition/

Gildenhuys JSH (2004) Ethics and Professionalism: The Battle Against Corruption. Stellenbosch University Press, Stellenbosch

Government of Kenya (2003) Report of the Task Force on the Establishment of a Truth, Justice and Reconciliation Commission

Gready P and Robin S (2014) From Transitional Justice to Transformative Justice: A New Agenda for Practice. International Journal of Transitional Justice 8: 339–361

Gready P et al (2010) Transformative Justice: A Concept Note. Transformative Justice Workshop. Centre for Applied Human Rights, University of York

Gubbay AR (1997) The Protection and Enforcement of Fundamental Human Rights: The Zimbabwean Experience. Human Rights Quarterly 19: 227–254

Guellali A (2015) Tunisia: Transitional Justice in the Crosshairs. Open Democracy. Available at https://www.opendemocracy.net/arab-awakening/amna-guellali/tunisia-transitional-justice-in-crosshairs

Hallo de Wolf A and Toebes B (2016) Assessing Private Sector Involvement in Health Care and Universal Health Coverage in Light of the Right to Health. Health and Human Rights 18: 79–92

Hatchard J (1986) The Institution of the Ombudsman in Africa with Special Reference to Zimbabwe. International and Comparative Law Quarterly 35: 255–270

Hayner PB (2010) Unspeakable Truths: Transitional Justice and the Challenge of Truth Commissions, 2nd edn. Routledge, New York

Hayner PB and Bosire L (2003) Should Truth Commissions Address Economic Crimes? Considering the Case of Kenya. ICTJ. Available at http://www.tikenya.org/documents/TruthComm.doc

Hecht L and Michalowski S (2012) The Economic and Social Dimensions of Transitional Justice. Essex Transitional Justice Network Concept Paper. Available at https://www.essex.ac.uk/tjn/documents/TheeconomicandsocialdimensionsofTJ.pdf

Hellman J and Kaufmann D (2001) Confronting the Challenge of State Capture in Transition Economies. Finance and Development 38: 31–35

Horne C (2009) Late Lustration Programmes in Romania and Poland: Supporting or Undermining Democratic Transitions? Democratization 16: 344–376

Horne C and Stan L (eds) (2018) Transitional Justice and the Former Soviet Union: Reviewing the Past, Looking toward the Future. Cambridge University Press, Cambridge

Howard AED (1991) The Essence of Constitutionalism. In: Thompson KW and Ludwikowski RT (eds) Constitutionalism and Human Rights in America, Poland, and France. Lanham, New York, pp.3–41

HRW (2002) Troubled Water: Burst Pipes, Contaminated Wells, and Open Defecation in Zimbabwe's Capital. HRW, Washington DC

http://www.essex.ac.uk/tjn/documents/TheeconomicandsocialdimensionsofTJ.pdf

Huyse L (2003) Zimbabwe: Why Reconciliation Failed. In: Bloomfield D et al (eds) Reconciliation After Violent Conflict: A Handbook. International Institute for Democracy and Electoral Assistance, Stockholm, pp. 34–39

ICTJ (2009) What is Transitional Justice? ICTJ Fact Sheet. Available at https://www.ictj.org/sites/default/files/ICTJ-Global-Transitional-Justice-2009-English.pdf

Iliff A (2010) Root and Branch, Tree of Life: Sowing the Seeds of Grassroots Transitional Justice. Oxford Transitional Justice Research. Available at http://www.csls.ox.ac.uk/documents/IliffRootandBranch_Final_OTJR.pdf

International Council on Human Rights Policy and Transparency International (2009) Corruption and Human Rights: Making the Connection. International Council on Human Rights Policy, Geneva

Johnston M (1998) Fighting Systematic Corruption: Social Foundations for Institutional Reform. European Journal of Development Research 10: 85–104

Joyner CC (1996) Arresting Impunity: The Case for Universal Jurisdiction in Bringing War Criminals to Accountability. Law and Contemporary Problems 59: 153–172

Kälin W and Künzli J (2009) The Law of International Human Rights Protection. Oxford University Press, Oxford

Keith LC (2010) Human Rights Instruments. In: Cane P and Kritzer H (eds) The Oxford Handbook of Empirical Legal Research. Oxford University Press, New York, pp. 353–375

Kelsen H (1957) What is Justice? Justice Law and Politics in the Mirror of Science. University of California Press, Berkeley

Kirya T (2011) Performing "Good Governance": Commissions of Inquiry and the Fight against Corruption in Uganda. (Unpublished PhD Thesis) University of Warwick

Kisiangani E (2009) Kenya's Economic Crimes: Can a conditional Amnesty be meaningful? Oxford Transitional Justice Series. Available at https://www.law.ox.ac.uk/sites/files/oxlaw/justice_in_africa1.pdf

Koch IE (2005) Dichotomies, Trichotomies or Waves of Duties? Human Rights Law Review 5: 81–103

Koechlin L and Carmona M (2009) Corruption and Human Rights: Exploring the Connection. In: Rotberg RI (ed) Corruption, Global Security, and World Order. Brookings Institution, Washington DC, pp. 310–340

Kofele-Kale N (2000) The Right to a Corrupt-Free Society as an Individual and Collective Human Right: Elevating Official Corruption to a Crime under International Law. International Lawyer 34: 149–178

Kora A (2012) Dealing With a 'New' Grievance: Should Anticorruption be Part of the Transitional Justice Agenda? Journal of Human Rights 11: 537–557

Kritz NJ (1995) Transitional Justice: How Emerging Democracies Reckon with Former Regimes Vol 2. US Institute of Peace Press, Washington DC

Lamb G (2013) DDR Twenty Years Later: Historical Review of the Long-term Impact of Post-independence DDR in Southern Africa. World Bank, Washington DC

Laplante L (2008) Transitional Justice and Peace Building: Diagnosing and Addressing the Socioeconomic Roots of Violence through a Human Rights Framework. International Journal of Transitional Justice 2: 331–355

Law K (2017) Pattern, Puzzle, and Peculiarity: Rhodesia's UDI and Decolonisation in Southern Africa. Journal of Imperial and Commonwealth History 45: 721–728

Losman DL (1979) International Economic Sanctions: the Cases of Cuba, Israel, and Rhodesia. University of New Mexico Press, Albuquerque

Ludwikowski RR (1996) Constitution Making in the Region of Former Soviet Dominance. Duke University Press, Durham, NC

Ludwin King EB (2012) Does Justice Always Require Prosecution? The International Criminal Court and Transitional Justice Measures. George Washington International Law Review 45: 85–120

Machakanja P (2010) National healing and reconciliation in Zimbabwe: Challenges and Opportunities. Institute for Justice and Reconciliation, Cape Town

Maguchu PS (2018) The law is Just the Law: Analysing the Definition of Corruption in Zimbabwe. Journal of Financial Crime 25: 354–361

Mallinder L and Hadden T (2013) Belfast Guidelines on Amnesty and Accountability: With Explanatory Guidance. Transitional Justice Institute, Belfast

Mani R (2008) Editorial Dilemmas of Expanding Transitional Justice, or Forging the Nexus between Transitional Justice and Development. International Journal of Transitional Justice 2: 253–264

Marauhn T (2004) Social Rights Beyond the Traditional Welfare State: International Instruments and the Concept of Individual Entitlements. In: Benvenisti E and Nolte G (eds) The Welfare State Globalization and International Law. Springer Verlag, Berlin, Heidelberg, pp. 275–319

Matyszak D (2005) Civil Society and the Long Election. Konrad Adenauer Stiftung, Harare

McGill D (2017) Different Violence, Different Justice? Taking Structural Violence Seriously in Post-Conflict and Transitional Justice Processes. State Crime Journal 6: 79–101

Miller Z (2008) Effects of Invisibility: In Search of the 'Economic' in Transitional Justice. International Journal of Transitional Justice 2: 266–291

Moore JL (2009) Transitional Justice Working Group in Liberia, Strengthening Coexistence and Transitional Justice in Liberia' International Center for Transitional Justice. Available at http://heller.brandeis.edu/coexistence/pdfs/transitional-justice/transjustliberia09.pdf

Morrell P and Pigou P (eds) (2004) Civil Society and Justice in Zimbabwe, Proceedings of a symposium held in Johannesburg, 11–13 August 2003. Themba Lesizwe on behalf of the Southern African Trauma Coalition, Johannesburg

Moyo S (1992) NGO Advocacy in Zimbabwe: Systematizing an old Function or Inventing a New Role? Zero, Harare

Moyo S (2014) Corruption in Zimbabwe: An Examination of the Roles of the State and Civil Society in Combating Corruption. (Unpublished PhD Thesis) University of Central Lancashire

Murray M and Spalding A (2015) Freedom from Official Corruption as a Human Right. Governance Studies at Brookings, Washington DC

Muvingi I (2009) Sitting on Powder Kegs: Socioeconomic Rights in Transitional Societies. International Journal of Transitional Justice 3: 163–182

Muvingi I (2009) Transitional Justice Will Have to Wait. Oxford Transitional Justice Research Series. Available at https://www.law.ox.ac.uk/sites/files/oxlaw/muvingi_final1.pdf

Muzila L et al (2002) On the Take: Criminalizing Illicit Enrichment to Fight Corruption. Washington, DC: World Bank. Available at https://openknowledge.worldbank.org/handle/10986/13090

Nawaz F and Chêne M (2009 Gender, Corruption and Health. U4 Helpdesk, Transparency International. Available at http://www.u4.no/publications/gender-corruption-and-health/

Ncayiyana DJ (2009) The Zimbabwe Mayhem—How Many People Must Die for the Neighbours to Act? South African Medical Journal 99: 7

Ndlovu-Gatsheni SJ (2012) Elections in Zimbabwe: A Recipe for Tension or a Remedy for Reconciliation? Institute for Justice and Reconciliation, Cape Town

Ntoubandi FZ (2007) Amnesty for Crimes Against Humanity Under International Law. Martinus Nijhoff Publishers, Leiden

O'Donnell G et al (eds) Transitions From Authoritarian Rule: Comparative Perspectives. John Hopkins University Press, Baltimore and London, pp. 51–53

OHCHR (2006) Rule of Law Tools for Post-Conflict States: Truth Commissions, United Nations, New York and Geneva

OHCHR (2008) Rule-of-Law Tools for Post-Conflict States: Reparations Programmes. United Nations, New York and Geneva

OHCHR (2012) Human Rights Indicators: A Guide to Measurement and Implementation. United Nations, New York and Geneva

Olsen TD et al (2010) The Justice Balance: When Transitional Justice Improves Human Rights and Democracy. Human Rights Quarterly, 32: 980–1007

Olsen TD et al (2012) Transitional Justice in Balance: Comparing Processes, Weighing Efficacy. United States Institute of Peace Press: Washington DC

Pesek S (2014) Combating Impunity: Transitional Justice and Anti Corruption. Freedom House, Washington DC

Pesic V (2007) State Capture and Widespread Corruption in Serbia. CEPS Working Document no. 262. Available at https://www.ceps.eu/publications/state-capture-and-widespread-corruption-serbia

Peters A (2015) Corruption and Human Rights. Basel Institute on Governance, Working Paper Series 20. Available at http://www.mpil.de/files/pdf4/Peters_Corruption_and_Human_Rights20151.pdf

Petkov M (2016) Diagnosing Corruption in Healthcare. Transparency International, London

Pienaar G (2000) The Role of the Public Protector in Fighting Corruption. African Security Review 9: 52–66

Price-Smith A (2009) Cholera and the Collapse of Governance in Zimbabwe. Harvard International Review. Available at http://hir.harvard.edu/article/?a=1819

Przeworski A (1986) Some Problems in the Study of Transition to Democracy. In: O'Donnell et al (eds) Transitions From Authoritarian Rule: Comparative Perspectives. John Hopkins University Press, Baltimore and London, pp. 51–53

Rainey B et al (2014) White and Ovey: The European Convention on Human Rights, 6th edn. Oxford University Press, Oxford

Rajagopal B (1999) Corruption, Legitimacy and Human Rights: The Dialectic of the Relationship. Connecticut Journal of International Law 14: 1–19

Redress (2004) Zimbabwe from Impunity to Accountability: Are Reparations Possible for Victims of Gross and Systematic Human Rights Violations? Available at http://www.redress.org/downloads/publications/Beyond%20impunityA5.pdf

Reeler T (2009) Subliminal Terror? Human Rights Violations and Torture in Zimbabwe During 2008. Centre for the Study of Violence and Reconciliation, Cape Town

Reeler T, Tarisayi E, and Maguchu P (2017) Transitional Justice in Pre-Transitional Times: Are there any Lessons for Zimbabwe? Sable Press, Harare

Report of the Truth Justice and Reconciliation Commission (Vol 1 Truth, Justice and Reconciliation Commission, Kenya 2013)

Report of the Truth Justice and Reconciliation Commission (Vol 2b Truth, Justice and Reconciliation Commission, Kenya 2013)

Report of the Truth Justice and Reconciliation Commission (Vol Truth, Justice and Reconciliation Commission, Kenya 2013)

Research and Advocacy Unit (2012) The Organ of National Healing: Is Zimbabwe a Genetically Violent Nation? Available at https://researchandadvocacyunit.wordpress.com/tag/the-organ-of-national-healing/

Robinson I (2014) Truth Commissions and Anti-Corruption: Towards a Complementary Framework? International Journal of Transitional Justice 9: 33–50

Roht-Arriaza N (2014) Reparations and Economic, Social, and Cultural Rights. In: Sharp D (ed) Justice and Economic Violence in Transition. Springer, New York, pp. 109–138

Ronen Y (2011) Transition from Illegal Regimes under International Law: Cambridge Studies in International and Comparative Law. Cambridge University Press, New York

Rose-Ackerman S (2002) Grand Corruption and the Ethics of Global Business. Journal of Banking and Finance 26: 1889–1918

Rose-Sender K and Godwin M (2010) Linking Anticorruption and Human Rights: A Dangerous Addition to the Development Discourse. In: Boersma M and Nelen H (eds) Corruption and Human Rights: Interdisciplinary Perspectives. Intersentia, Antwerp, pp. 221–239

Rosga A and Satterthwaie ML (2009) The Trust in Indicators: Measuring Human Rights. Berkeley Journal of International Law 27: 253–315

Rothstein B and Varraich A (2017) Making Sense of Corruption. Cambridge University Press, New York

Rožič P and Nisnevich Y (2016) Lustration Matters: A Radical Approach to the Problem of Corruption. Studies in Comparative International Development, 51: 257–285

Sandura W (1989) Report of the Second Commission of Inquiry into the Distribution of Motor Vehicles. Government Printers, Harare

Saul B et al (2014) The International Covenant on Economic, Social and Cultural Rights: Commentary, Cases, and Materials. Oxford University Press, Oxford

Savedoff W and Hussmann K (2006) Why are Health Systems so Prone to Corruption? In: Transparency International (ed) Global Corruption Report, Special Focus – Corruption and Health. Pluto Press, London, pp. 4–16

Schabas W (2012) Unimaginable Atrocities: Justice, Politics, and Rights at the War Crimes Tribunals. Oxford University Press, Oxford

Schmid E and Nolan A (2014) Do No Harm? Exploring the Scope of Economic and Social Rights in Transitional Justice. International Journal of Transitional Justice 8: 362–382

Schneider N and Iecker de Almeida G (2018) The Brazilian National Truth Commission (2012–2014) As a State-Commissioned History Project. In: Bevernage B and Wouters N (eds) The Handbook of State-Sponsored History After 1945. Palgrave Macmillan, London, pp. 637–652

Seligson MA (2002) The Impact of Corruption on Regime Legitimacy: A Comparative Study of Four Latin American Countries. Journal of Politics 64: 408–433

Shana G (2006) The State of Corruption in Zimbabwe. Mass Public Opinion Institute Seminar, Harare

Sharp D (2012) Addressing Economic Violence in Times of Transition: Toward a Positive-Peace Paradigm for Transitional Justice. Fordham International Law Journal 35: 780–814

Sharp D (2013) Economic Violence in the Practice of African Truth Commissions and Beyond. In: Sharp D (ed), Justice and Economic Violence in Transition. Springer, New York, pp. 79–107

Sharp D (2014) The Significance of Human Rights for the Debt of Countries in Transition. In: Bohoslavsky JP and Cernic JL (eds) Making Sovereign Financing and Human Rights Work. Hart, Oxford, pp. 47–60

Shaw WH (1986) Towards the One-Party State in Zimbabwe: a Study in African Political Thought. Journal of Modern African Studies 24: 373–394

Shue H (1996) Basic Rights: Subsistence, Affluence and US Foreign Policy, 2nd edn. Princeton University Press, Princeton

Sithole J (2008) Corruption a Way of Life in Zimbabwe, Institute for War and Peace Reporting. Available at https://iwpr.net/global-voices/corruption-way-life-zimbabwe

SOAS (1997) Expanding the Role of the Ombudsman in Zimbabwe. Journal of African Law 41: 247–247

Spalding A (2014) Corruption, Corporations, and the New Human Right. Washington University Law Review 91: 1365–1428

Sriram CL (ed) (2017) Transitional Justice in the Middle East and North Africa. Oxford University Press, Canada

Stan L and Nedelsky N (eds) (2013) Encyclopedia of Transitional Justice Vol. 1. Cambridge University Press, New York

Starr S (2007) Extraordinary Crimes at Ordinary Times: International Justice Beyond Crises Situations. Northwestern University Law Review 3: 1257–1313

Strack HR (1978) Sanctions: the Case of Rhodesia. Syracuse University Press, Syracuse

Sutcliffe RB (1969) The Political Economy of Rhodesian Sanctions. Journal of Commonwealth Political Studies 7: 113–125

Tchad Ministère de la Justice (1993) Les crimes et détournements de l'ex-Président Habré et de ses complices: rapport de la Commission d'enquête nationale

Teitel RG (2000) Transitional Justice. Oxford University Press, New York

Teitel RG (2003) Transitional Justice Genealogy. Harvard Human Rights Journal 16: 69–94

Teti A et al (2018) Introduction and Background. In: Teti A et al (eds) The Arab Uprisings in Egypt, Jordan and Tunisia. Palgrave Macmillan, New York, pp. 1–25

Türk D (1990) The New International Economic Order and the Promotion of Human Rights, Realization of Economic, Social and Cultural Rights, Progress Report, U.N. Doc. E/CN.4/Sub.2/1990/19

Uberti LJ (2016) Can Institutional Reforms Reduce Corruption? Economic Theory and Patron–Client Politics in Developing Countries. Development and Change 47: 317–345

UNODC (2006) United Nations Handbook on Practical-Anticorruption Measures for Prosecutors and Investigators. UNODC, Vienna

Uprimny R 'Transitional Justice Without Transition? Lessons from transitional justice discourse in Colombia' Expert Paper Workshop 5 Lessons from Negotiated Options in South Africa and Colombia. Available at http://www.peace-justice-conference.info/download/WS%205%20-%20expert%20paper%20-%20Uprimny.pdf

Uprimny R and Saffon MP (2007) Uses and Abuses of Transitional Justice Discourse in Colombia. PRIO Policy Brief, 6. Oslo: PRIO.

Van Boven et al (eds) (2008) The Maastricht Guidelines on Violations of Economic, Social and Cultural Rights, SIM Special No. 20. Netherlands Institute of Human Rights

Vargas-Hernández J G (2009) The Multiple Faces of Corruption: Typology, Forms and levels. Available at https://papers.ssrn.com/sol3/papers.cfm?abstract_id=1413976

Vasak K (1977) Human Rights: A Thirty-Year Struggle: the Sustained Efforts to give Force of Law to the Universal Declaration of Human Rights UNESCO Courier 30:11, United Nations Educational, Scientific, and Cultural Organization, Paris

Villalba CS (2011) Transitional Justice: Key Concepts, Processes and Challenges. Institute for Democracy & Conflict Resolution. Briefing Paper. Available at www.idcr.org.uk/wp-content/uploads/2010/09/07_11.pdf

Walker MU (2013) The Expressive Burden of Reparations: Putting Meaning into Money, Words and Things. In: MacLachlan A and Speight A (eds) Justice, Responsibility and Reconciliation in the Wake of Conflict. Springer, Dordrecht, pp. 205–226

Warren ME (2004) What Does Corruption Mean in a Democracy? American Journal of Political Science 48: 328–343

Weitzer RJ (1990) Transforming Settler States: Communal Conflict and Internal Security in Northern Ireland and Zimbabwe. University of California Press, Berkeley

Winter S (2013) Towards a Unified Theory of Transitional Justice. International Journal of Transitional Justice 7: 224–244

World Bank (1997) Helping Countries Combat Corruption: The Role of the World Bank. World Bank, Washington DC

Yerkes S and Muasher M (2010) Tunisia's Corruption Contagion A Transition at Risk. Carnegie Endowment for International Peace

Youde J (2010) Don't Drink the Water: Politics and Cholera in Zimbabwe. International Journal 65: 687–704

Yusuf H (2017) Transitional Justice in the Middle East and North Africa: Taking Account of Islam. Muslim World Journal of Human Rights 14: 145–170

Zabyelina Y (2017) Lustration Beyond Decommunization: Responding to the Crimes of the Powerful in Post-Euromaidan Ukraine. State Crime Journal 6: 55–78.

Zinyama T (2013) Efficiency and Effectiveness in Public Sector Auditing: An Evaluation of the Comptroller and Auditor General's Performance in Zimbabwe from 1999 to 2012. International Journal of Humanities and Social Science 3: 267–282

Index

P. Maguchu, *Transitional Justice and Socio-Economic Rights in Zimbabwe*, International Criminal Justice Series 24,
https://doi.org/10.1007/978-94-6265-323-8

MIX
Papier aus verantwortungsvollen Quellen
Paper from responsible sources
FSC® C105338

If you have any concerns about our products,
you can contact us on
ProductSafety@springernature.com

In case Publisher is established outside the EU,
the EU authorized representative is:
Springer Nature Customer Service Center GmbH
Europaplatz 3, 69115 Heidelberg, Germany

Printed by Libri Plureos GmbH
in Hamburg, Germany